The philosophy of rhetoric. By George Campbell, ... In two volumes. ... Volume 1 of 2

George Campbell

The philosophy of rhetoric. By George Campbell, ... In two volumes. ... Volume 1 of 2
Campbell, George
ESTCID: T145750
Reproduction from British Library

London : printed for W. Strahan; and T. Cadell; and W. Creech at Edinburgh, 1776.
2v. ; 8°

Eighteenth Century
Collections Online
Print Editions

Gale ECCO Print Editions

Relive history with *Eighteenth Century Collections Online*, now available in print for the independent historian and collector. This series includes the most significant English-language and foreign-language works printed in Great Britain during the eighteenth century, and is organized in seven different subject areas including literature and language; medicine, science, and technology; and religion and philosophy. The collection also includes thousands of important works from the Americas.

The eighteenth century has been called "The Age of Enlightenment." It was a period of rapid advance in print culture and publishing, in world exploration, and in the rapid growth of science and technology – all of which had a profound impact on the political and cultural landscape. At the end of the century the American Revolution, French Revolution and Industrial Revolution, perhaps three of the most significant events in modern history, set in motion developments that eventually dominated world political, economic, and social life.

In a groundbreaking effort, Gale initiated a revolution of its own: digitization of epic proportions to preserve these invaluable works in the largest online archive of its kind. Contributions from major world libraries constitute over 175,000 original printed works. Scanned images of the actual pages, rather than transcriptions, recreate the works *as they first appeared.*

Now for the first time, these high-quality digital scans of original works are available via print-on-demand, making them readily accessible to libraries, students, independent scholars, and readers of all ages.

For our initial release we have created seven robust collections to form one the world's most comprehensive catalogs of 18th century works.

Initial Gale ECCO Print Editions collections include:

History and Geography
Rich in titles on English life and social history, this collection spans the world as it was known to eighteenth-century historians and explorers. Titles include a wealth of travel accounts and diaries, histories of nations from throughout the world, and maps and charts of a world that was still being discovered. Students of the War of American Independence will find fascinating accounts from the British side of conflict.

Social Science
Delve into what it was like to live during the eighteenth century by reading the first-hand accounts of everyday people, including city dwellers and farmers, businessmen and bankers, artisans and merchants, artists and their patrons, politicians and their constituents. Original texts make the American, French, and Industrial revolutions vividly contemporary.

Medicine, Science and Technology
Medical theory and practice of the 1700s developed rapidly, as is evidenced by the extensive collection, which includes descriptions of diseases, their conditions, and treatments. Books on science and technology, agriculture, military technology, natural philosophy, even cookbooks, are all contained here.

Literature and Language
Western literary study flows out of eighteenth-century works by Alexander Pope, Daniel Defoe, Henry Fielding, Frances Burney, Denis Diderot, Johann Gottfried Herder, Johann Wolfgang von Goethe, and others. Experience the birth of the modern novel, or compare the development of language using dictionaries and grammar discourses.

Religion and Philosophy
The Age of Enlightenment profoundly enriched religious and philosophical understanding and continues to influence present-day thinking. Works collected here include masterpieces by David Hume, Immanuel Kant, and Jean-Jacques Rousseau, as well as religious sermons and moral debates on the issues of the day, such as the slave trade. The Age of Reason saw conflict between Protestantism and Catholicism transformed into one between faith and logic -- a debate that continues in the twenty-first century.

Law and Reference
This collection reveals the history of English common law and Empire law in a vastly changing world of British expansion. Dominating the legal field is the *Commentaries of the Law of England* by Sir William Blackstone, which first appeared in 1765. Reference works such as almanacs and catalogues continue to educate us by revealing the day-to-day workings of society.

Fine Arts
The eighteenth-century fascination with Greek and Roman antiquity followed the systematic excavation of the ruins at Pompeii and Herculaneum in southern Italy; and after 1750 a neoclassical style dominated all artistic fields. The titles here trace developments in mostly English-language works on painting, sculpture, architecture, music, theater, and other disciplines. Instructional works on musical instruments, catalogs of art objects, comic operas, and more are also included.

The BiblioLife Network

This project was made possible in part by the BiblioLife Network (BLN), a project aimed at addressing some of the huge challenges facing book preservationists around the world. The BLN includes libraries, library networks, archives, subject matter experts, online communities and library service providers. We believe every book ever published should be available as a high-quality print reproduction; printed on-demand anywhere in the world. This insures the ongoing accessibility of the content and helps generate sustainable revenue for the libraries and organizations that work to preserve these important materials.

The following book is in the "public domain" and represents an authentic reproduction of the text as printed by the original publisher. While we have attempted to accurately maintain the integrity of the original work, there are sometimes problems with the original work or the micro-film from which the books were digitized. This can result in minor errors in reproduction. Possible imperfections include missing and blurred pages, poor pictures, markings and other reproduction issues beyond our control. Because this work is culturally important, we have made it available as part of our commitment to protecting, preserving, and promoting the world's literature.

GUIDE TO FOLD-OUTS MAPS and OVERSIZED IMAGES

The book you are reading was digitized from microfilm captured over the past thirty to forty years. Years after the creation of the original microfilm, the book was converted to digital files and made available in an online database.

In an online database, page images do not need to conform to the size restrictions found in a printed book. When converting these images back into a printed bound book, the page sizes are standardized in ways that maintain the detail of the original. For large images, such as fold-out maps, the original page image is split into two or more pages

Guidelines used to determine how to split the page image follows:

- Some images are split vertically; large images require vertical and horizontal splits.
- For horizontal splits, the content is split left to right.
- For vertical splits, the content is split from top to bottom.
- For both vertical and horizontal splits, the image is processed from top left to bottom right.

THE
PHILOSOPHY
OF
RHETORIC.

BY

GEORGE CAMPBELL, D.D.
PRINCIPAL OF THE MARISCHAL COLLEGE,
ABERDEEN.

Certo sciant homines, ARTES INVENIENDI SOLIDAS ET VERAS
ADOLESCERE ET INCREMENTA SUMERE CUM IPSIS INVENTIS.
Bac. De Augm. Scient. l. v. c. 3.

IN TWO VOLUMES.

VOL. I.

LONDON:
Printed for W. STRAHAN; and T. CADELL, in the Strand;
and W. CREECH at Edinburgh.
MDCCLXXVI.

PREFACE.

THERE are several reasons which have induced the Author of the following sheets, to give the Public some account of their origin and progress, previously to their coming under its examination. They are a series of Essays closely connected with one another, and written on a subject, in the examination of which, he has at intervals employed himself for a considerable part of his life. Considered separately, each may justly be termed a whole, and complete in itself; taken together, they are constituent parts of one Work. The Author entered on this inquiry as early as the year 1750; and it was then that the two first Chapters of the first Book were composed. These he intended as a sort of groundwork to the whole. And the judicious Reader will perceive, that, in raising the superstructure, he has entirely conformed to the plan there delineated. That first outline he showed soon after to several of his acquaintance, some of whom are still living. In the year 1757, it was read to a private literary society, of which the Author had the honour to be a member. It was a difference in his situation at that time, and his connection with the gentlemen of that society, some of whom have since honourably distinguished themselves in the republic of letters, that induced him to resume a subject, which he had so long laid aside. The three following years all the other chapters of that Book, except the third, the sixth, and the tenth, which have been but lately added (rather as illustrations and confirmations of some parts of the work, than as essential to it) were composed, and submitted to the judgment of the same ingenious friends. All that follows on the subject of Elocution, hath also undergone the same review. Nor has there been any material alteration made on these, or any addition to them, except in a few instances of notes, examples, and verbal corrections, since they were composed.

It is also proper to observe here, that since transcribing the present Work for the press, a manu-

manuscript was put into his hands by Doctor Beattie, at the very time that, in order to be favoured with the Doctor's opinion of this Performance, the Author gave him the first Book for his perusal. Doctor Beattie's Tract is called *An Essay on Laughter and Ludicrous Writing*. Whilst the Author carefully perused that Essay, it gave him a very agreeable surprise to discover, that on a question so nice and curious, there should, without any previous communication, be so remarkable a coincidence of sentiments in every thing wherein their subjects coincide. A man must have an uncommon confidence in his own faculties, (I might have said in his own infallibility) who is not sensibly more satisfied of the justness of their procedure, especially in abstract matters, when he discovers such a concurrence with the ideas and reasoning of writers of discernment. The subject of that piece is indeed Laughter in general, with an inquiry into those qualities in the object, by which it is excited. The investigation is conducted with the greatest accuracy, and the theory confirmed and illustrated by such a variety of pertinent examples, as give us access to scrutinize his doctrine

doctrine on every side, and view it in almost every possible light. He does not enter into the specific characters whereby wit and humour are discriminated, which are the chief considerations here. His design leads him to consider rather those particulars wherein they all agree, than those wherein they differ. He treats of ludicrous objects and ludicrous writing, with a view to account for the superior copiousness and refinement of modern ridicule. When philosophical acuteness is happily united with so great richness of fancy and mastery in language, the obscurity in which a subject was formerly involved, vanishes entirely, and a reader unacquainted with all other theories and hypotheses, can hardly be persuaded that there was ever any difficulty in the question. But there is reason to think, that the world will soon be favoured with an opportunity of judging for itself, in regard to the merits of that performance.

ONE reason, though not the only one, which the Author has for mentioning the manner wherein the composition of this Work has been conducted, and the time it has taken, is, is, not to enhance its value with the Public, but to apologize in some measure for that inequality in the execution and the style, with which, he is afraid, it will be thought chargeable. It is his purpose in this Work, on the one hand, to exhibit, he does not say, a correct map, but a tolerable sketch of the human mind; and aided by the lights which the poet and the orator so amply furnish, to disclose its secret movements, tracing its principal channels of perception and action, as near as possible, to their source: and, on the other hand, from the science of human nature, to ascertain, with greater precision, the radical principles of that art, whose object it is, by the use of language, to operate on the soul of the hearer, in the way of informing, convincing, pleasing, moving, or persuading. In the prosecution of a design so extensive, there are two extremes to be shunned. One is, too much abstraction in investigating causes; the other, too much minuteness in specifying effects. By the first, the perspicuity of a performance may be endangered; by the second, its dignity may be sacrificed. The Author does not flatter himself so far as to imagine, that he hath succeeded perfectly in his endeavours to avoid either extreme. In a work of this kind, it is impossible, that every thing should be alike perspicuous to every reader, or that all the parts should be equally elevated. Variety in this respect, as well as in others, is perhaps, on the whole, more pleasing and more instructive, than too scrupulous an uniformity. To the eye the interchange of hill and dale beautifies the prospect; and to the ear there is no music in monotony. The Author can truly say, that he has endeavoured, as much as he could, in the most abstruse questions, to avoid obscurity; and in regard to such of his remarks as may be thought too minute and particular, if just, they will not, he hopes, on a re-examination, be deemed of no consequence. Those may serve to illustrate a general observation, which are scarcely worth notice as subjects either of censure or of praise. Nor is there any thing in this Book, which, in his opinion, will create even the smallest difficulty to persons accustomed to inquire into the faculties of the mind. Indeed, the much greater part of it will, he is perfuaded, be level to the capacity of all thofe readers (not perhaps the moſt numerous claſs) who think reflection of fome uſe in reading, and who do not read merely with the intention of killing time.

He begs leave to add, that, though his ſubject be Eloquence, yet, as the nature of his work is didactical, wherein the underſtanding only is addreſſed, the ſtyle in general admits no higher qualities than purity and perſpicuity. Theſe were therefore his higheſt aim. The beſt ornaments out of place are not only unbecoming but offenſive. Nor can any thing be farther from his thoughts than to pretend to an exemption from ſuch poſitive faults in expreſſion, as, on the article of Elocution, he hath ſo freely criticized in the beſt Engliſh authors. He is entirely ſenſible, that an impropriety or other negligence in ſtyle will eſcape the notice of the writer, which hardly eſcapes that of any body elſe. Next to the purpoſe of illuſtrating the principles and canons which he here ſubmits to the judgment of the Public, the two following motives weighed moſt with the Author, in inducing him to uſe ſo much freedom in regard

gard to the writings of those for whom he has the highest veneration. One is, to show that we ought in writing as in other things, carefully to beware of implicit attachment and servile imitation, even when they seem to be claimed by the most celebrated names. The other is, to evince, that we are in danger of doing great injustice to a work, by deciding hastily on its merit from a collection of such oversights. If the critic be rigorous in marking whatever is amiss in this way, what author may abide the trial? But though such slips are not to be regarded as the sole or even principal test of demerit in literary productions, they ought not to be altogether overlooked. Whatever is faulty in any degree it were better to avoid. And there are consequences regarding the language in general, as well as the success of particular works, which should preserve verbal criticism from being considered as beneath the attention of any author. An author so far from having reason to be offended, is doubtless obliged to the man who, free from captious petulance, candidly points out his errors of what kind soever they be.

CONTENTS

OF THE FIRST VOLUME.

INTRODUCTION.　　　Page 1

BOOK I.
The Nature and Foundations of Eloquence.

CHAP. I. *Eloquence in the largest acceptation defined, its more general Forms exhibited, with their different Objects, Ends and Characters.* — 25

CHAP. II. *Of Wit, Humour, and Ridicule.* 41
　Sect. I. *Of wit.* — — 42
　Sect. II. *Of humour.* — — 57
　Sect. III. *Of ridicule.* — — 68

CHAP. III. *The Doctrine of the preceding Chapter defended.* — — 83
　Sect. I. *Aristotle's account of the ridiculous explained.* — — 84
　Sect. II. *Hobbes's account of laughter examined.* 87

CHAP. IV. *Of the Relation which Eloquence bears to Logic and to Grammar.* — — 95

CHAP. V. *Of the different Sources of Evidence, and the different Subjects to which they are respectively adapted.* — — Page 103
  Sect. I. *Of intuitive evidence.* — — ib.
    Part I. *Mathematical axioms.* — — ib.
    Part II. *Consciousness.* — — 107
    Part III. *Common sense* — — 109
  Sect. II. *Of deductive evidence.* — 120
    Part I. *Division of the subject into scientific and moral, with the principal distinctions between them.* — — — ib.
    Part II. *The nature and origin of experience.* 129
    Part III. *The subdivisions of moral reasoning.* 136
      1. *Experience.* — — — ib.
      2. *Analogy.* — — — 143
      3. *Testimony.* — — — 146
      4. *Calculations of chances.* — — 151
    Part IV. *The superiority of scientific evidence re-examined.* — — — 155

CHAP. VI. *Of the Nature and Use of the scholastic Art of syllogizing.* — — — 163

CHAP. VII. *Of the Consideration which the Speaker ought to have of the Hearers as Men in general.* 186
  Sect. I *As endowed with understanding.* 189
  Sect. II. *As endowed with imagination.* 190
  Sect. III. *As endowed with memory.* — 195
  Sect. IV. *As endowed with passions.* — 199

SECT. V. *The circumstances that are chiefly instrumental in operating on the passions.* Page 209
   Part I. *Probability.* — — ib.
   Part II. *Plausibility.* — — 210
   Part III. *Importance.* — — 220
   Part IV. *Proximity of time* — — 221
   Part V. *Connexion of place.* — — 224
   Part VI. *Relation to the persons concerned* 226
   Part VII. *Interest in the consequences.* 227

SECT. VI. *Other passions as well as moral sentiments useful auxiliaries.* — — 230

SECT. VII. *How an unfavourable passion must be calmed.* — — — 235

CHAP. VIII. *Of the Consideration which the Speaker ought to have of the Hearers as such Men in particular.* — — — 240

CHAP. IX. *Of the consideration which the Speaker ought to have of himself.* — — 242

CHAP. X. *The different kinds of public speaking in use among the moderns, compared, with a view to their different advantages in respect of eloquence,*
                                          248
   SECT. I. *In regard to the speaker.* — 249
   SECT. II. *In regard to the persons addressed.* 253
   SECT. III. *In regard to the subject.* — 259
   SECT. IV. *In regard to the occasion.* — 264
   SECT. V. *In regard to the end in view.* — 266

CHAP. XI. *Of the cause of that pleasure which we receive from objects or representations that excite pity and other painful feelings.* — Page 277

   SECT. I. *The different solutions hitherto given by philosophers, examined.* — 280
      Part I. *The first hypothesis.* — ib.
      Part II. *The second hypothesis.* — 283
      Part III. *The third hypothesis.* — 290
      Part IV. *The fourth hypothesis.* — 302
   SECT. II. *The Author's hypothesis on this subject.* 314

BOOK II.
The Foundations and essential Properties of Elocution.

CHAP. I. *The Nature and Characters of the Use which gives Law to Language.* — — 339
   SECT. I. *Reputable use.* — — 345
   SECT. II. *National use.* — — 353
   SECT. III. *Present use.* — — 357

CHAP. II. *The nature and use of verbal criticism, with its principal canons.* — — 367
   SECT. I. *Good use not always uniform in her decisions.* — — — 371
      Canon the first. — — 374
      Canon the second. — — 378
      Canon the third. — — 382
      Canon the fourth. — — 383
      Canon the fifth. — — 385

SECT. II. *Every thing favoured by good use, not on that account worthy to be retained.* Page 387
    Canon the sixth. — — 391
    Canon the seventh. — — — 397
    Canon the eighth. — — — 399
    Canon the ninth. — — — 400

CHAP. III. *Of grammatical purity.* — 407
  SECT. I. *The barbarism.* — — 410
    Part I. *By the use of obsolete words.* — ib.
    Part II. *By the use of new words.* — 412
    Part III. *By the use of good words new-modelled.* — — — 419
  SECT. II *The solecism.* — — 430
  SECT. III. *The Impropriety.* — — 456
    Part I. *Impropriety in single words.* — 457
    Part II. *Impropriety in phrases.* — 481
CHAP. IV. *Some grammatical doubts in regard to English construction stated and examined.* — 488

INTRODUCTION.

ALL art is *founded in science*, and the science is of little value which does not serve as a foundation to some beneficial art. On the most sublime of all sciences, *theology* and *ethics*, is built the most important of all arts, *the art of living*. The abstract mathematical sciences serve as a ground-work to the arts of the land-measurer and the accountant; and in conjunction with natural philosophy, including geography and astronomy, to those of the architect, the navigator, the dialist, and many others. Of what consequence anatomy is to surgery, and that part of physiology which teaches the laws of gravitation and of motion, is to the artificer, is a matter too obvious to need illustration. The general remark might, if necessary, be exemplified throughout the whole circle of arts, both useful and elegant. Valuable knowledge therefore always leads to some practical skill, and is perfected in it. On the other hand, the practical skill loses much of its beauty and extensive utility,

utility, which does not originate in knowledge. There is by confequence a natural relation between the fciences and the arts, like that which fubfifts between the parent and the offspring.

I acknowledge indeed that thefe are sometimes unnaturally feparated, and that by the mere influence of example on the one hand, and imitation on the other, fome progrefs may be made in an art, without the knowledge of the principles from which it fprang. By the help of a few rules, which men are taught to ufe mechanically, a good practical arithmetician may be formed, who neither knows the reafons on which the rules he works by were firft eftablifhed, nor ever thinks it of any moment to inquire into them. In like manner, do we not frequently meet with expert artifans, who are ignorant of the fix mechanical powers, which, though in the exercife of their profeffion they daily employ, they do not underftand the principles whereby, in any inftance, the refult of their application is afcertained? The propagation of the arts may therefore be compared more juftly to that variety which takes place in the vegetable kingdom, than to the uniformity which obtains univerfally in the animal world; for, as

to

to the anomalous race of zoophytes, I do not comprehend them in the number. It is not always neceſſary that the plant ſpring from the ſeed, a ſlip from another plant will often anſwer the purpoſe. There is, however, a very conſiderable difference in the expectations that may juſtly be raiſed from the different methods followed in the acquiſition of the art. Improvements, unleſs in extraordinary inſtances of genius and ſagacity, are not to be expected from thoſe who have acquired all their dexterity from imitation and habit. One who has had an education no better than that of an ordinary mechanic, may prove an excellent manual operator, but it is only in the well-inſtructed mechanician, that you would expect to find a good machiniſt. The analogy to vegetation above ſuggeſted, holds here alſo. The off-ſet is commonly no more than a mere copy of the parent plant. It is from the ſeed only you can expect, with the aid of proper culture, to produce new varieties, and even to make improvements on the ſpecies. "Expert men," ſays Lord Bacon, "can execute and judge of particulars, one by "one, but the general counſels, and the plots "and marſhalling of affairs, come beſt from "thoſe that are learned."

INDEED, in almost every art, even as used by mere practitioners, there are certain rules, as hath been already hinted, which must carefully be followed, and which serve the artist instead of principles. An acquaintance with these is one step, and but one step towards science. Thus in the common books of arithmetic, intended solely for practice, the rules laid down for the ordinary operations, as for numeration, or numerical notation, addition, subtraction, multiplication, division, and a few others, which are sufficient for all the purposes of the accountant, serve instead of principles; and, to a superficial observer, may be thought to supersede the study of any thing further. But their utility reaches a very little way, compared with that which results from the knowledge of the foundations of the art, and of what has been, not unfitly, styled *arithmetic universal*. It may be justly said, that, without some portion of this knowledge, the practical rules had never been invented. Besides, if by these the particular questions which come exactly within the description of the rule may be solved, by the other such general rules themselves, as serve for the solution of endless particulars, may be discovered.

INTRODUCTION.

The case I own is somewhat different with those arts which are entirely founded on experiment and observation, and are not derived, like pure mathematics, from abstract and universal axioms. But even in these, when we rise from the individual to the species, from the species to the genus, and thence to the most extensive orders and classes, we arrive, though in a different way, at the knowledge of general truths, which, in a certain sense, are also scientific, and answer a similar purpose. Our acquaintance with nature and its laws is so much extended, that we shall be enabled, in numberless cases, not only to apply to the most profitable purposes the knowledge we have thus acquired, but to determine before-hand, with sufficient certainty, the success of every new application. In this progress we are like people, who, from a low and narrow bottom, where the view is confined to a few acres, gradually ascend a lofty peak or promontory. The prospect is perpetually enlarging as we mount, and when we reach the summit, the boundless horizon, comprehending all the variety of sea and land, hill and valley, town and country, arable and desert, lies under the eye at once.

Those who in medicine have scarcely risen to the discernment of any general principles, and have no other directory but the experiences gained in the first and lowest stage, or as it were at the foot of the mountain, are commonly distinguished by the name of *empirics*. Something similar may be said to obtain in the other liberal arts, for in all of them more enlargement of mind is necessary, than is required for the exercise of those called mechanical. The character directly opposite to the *empiric* is the *visionary*, for it is not in theology only that there are visionaries. Of the two extremes I acknowledge that the latter is the worse. The first founds upon facts, but the facts are few, and commonly in his reasonings, through his imperfect knowledge of the subject, misapplied. The second often argues very consequentially from principles, which, having no foundation in nature, may justly be denominated the illegitimate issue of his own imagination. He in this resembles the man of science, that he acts systematically, for there are false as well as true theorists, and is influenced by certain general propositions, real or imaginary. But the difference lies here, that in the one they are real, in the other imaginary. The system of the one is

reared

reared on the firm basis of experience, the theory of the other is no better than a castle in the air. I mention characters only in the extreme, because in this manner they are best discriminated. In real life, however, any two of these, sometimes all the three, in various proportions, may be found blended in the same person.

The arts are frequently divided into the useful, and the polite, fine, or elegant; for these words are, in this application, used synonymously. This division is not coincident with that into the mechanical and the liberal. Physic, navigation, and the art of war, though properly liberal arts, fall entirely under the denomination of the useful, whereas painting and sculpture, though requiring a good deal of manual labour, and in that respect more nearly related to the mechanical, belong to the class denominated elegant. The first division arises purely from the consideration of the end to be attained, the second from the consideration of the means to be employed. In respect of the end, an art is either useful or elegant, in respect of the means, it is either mechanical or liberal. The true foundation of the former distribution is, that certain arts are manifestly and ultimately calculated for profit or use, whilst others, on the contrary, seem to terminate in pleasing. The one supplies a real want, the other only gratifies some mental taste. Yet in strictness, in the execution of the useful arts, there is often scope for elegance, and the arts called elegant are by no means destitute of use. The principal difference is, that use is the direct and avowed purpose of the former, whereas it is more latently and indirectly effected by the latter. Under this class are commonly included, not only the arts of the painter and the statuary, but those also of the musician and the poet. Eloquence and architecture, by which last term is always understood more than building merely for accommodation, are to be considered as of a mixed nature, wherein utility and beauty have almost equal influence.

The elegant arts, as well as the useful, are founded in experience, but from the difference of their nature, there arises a considerable difference both in their origin and in their growth. Necessity, the mother of invention, drives men, in the earliest state of society, to the study and cultivation of the useful arts; it is always leisure

and

and abundance which lead men to seek gratifications no way conducive to the preservation either of the individual or of the species. The elegant arts, therefore, are doubtless to be considered as the younger sisters. The progress of the former towards perfection is, however, much slower than that of the latter. Indeed, with regard to the first, it is impossible to say, as to several arts, what is the perfection of the art; since we are incapable of conceiving how far the united discernment and industry of men, properly applied, may yet carry them. For some centuries backwards, the men of every age have made great and unexpected improvements on the labours of their predecessors. And it is very probable that the subsequent age will produce discoveries and acquisitions, which we of this age are as little capable of foreseeing, as those who preceded us in the last century were capable of conjecturing the progress that would be made in the present. The case is not entirely similar in the fine arts. These, though later in their appearing, are more rapid in their advancement. There may, indeed, be in these a degree of perfection beyond what we have experienced; but we have some conception of the very utmost to which it can proceed. For instance, where resemblance

semblance is the object, as in a picture or a statue, a perfect conformity to its archetype is a thing at least conceivable. In like manner, the utmost pleasure of which the imagination is susceptible by a poetical narrative or exhibition, is a thing, in my judgment, not inconceivable. We Britons, for example, do, by immense degrees, excel the ancient Greeks in the arts of navigation and ship-building; and how much farther we may still excel them in these, by means of discoveries and improvements yet to be made, it would be the greatest presumption in any man to say. But as it requires not a prophetic spirit to discover, it implies no presumption to affirm, that we shall never excel them so far in poetry and eloquence, if ever in these respects we come to equal them. The same thing might probably be affirmed in regard to painting, sculpture, and music, if we had here as ample a fund of materials for forming a comparison.

But let it be observed, that the remarks now made regard only the advancement of the arts themselves; for though the useful are of slower growth than the other, and their utmost perfection cannot always be so easily ascertained, yet the acquisition of any one of them by a learner,

learner, in the perfection which it has reached at the time, is a much easier matter than the acquisition of any of the elegant arts;—besides, that the latter require much more of a certain happy combination in the original frame of spirit, commonly called genius, than is necessary in the other.

Let it be observed further, that as the gratification of taste is the immediate object of the fine arts, their effect is in a manner instantaneous, and the quality of any new production in these is immediately judged by every body; for all have in them some rudiments of taste, though in some they are improved by a good, in others corrupted by a bad education, and in others almost suppressed by a total want of education. In the useful arts, on the contrary, as more time and experience are requisite for discovering the means by which our accommodation is effected, so it generally requires examination, time, and trial, that we may be satisfied of the fitness of the work for the end proposed. In these we are not near so apt to consider ourselves as judges, unless we be either artists, or accustomed to employ and examine the works of artists in that particular profession.

I mentioned some arts that have their fundamental principles in the abstract sciences of geometry and arithmetic, and some in the doctrine of gravitation and motion. There are others, as the medical and chirurgical arts, which require a still broader foundation of science in anatomy, the animal œconomy, natural history, diseases, and remedies.—Those arts, which, like poetry, are purely to be ranked among the elegant, as their end is attained by an accommodation to some internal taste, so the springs by which alone they can be regulated, must be sought for in the nature of the human mind, and more especially in the principles of the imagination. It is also in the human mind that we must investigate the source of some of the useful arts. Logic, whose end is the discovery of truth, is founded in the doctrine of the understanding, and ethics, (under which may be comprehended economics, politics, and jurisprudence) are founded in that of the will.

This was the idea of Lord Verulam*, perhaps the most comprehensive genius in philosophy

---

* Doctrina circa *intellectum*, atque illa altera circa *voluntatem* hominis, in natalibus suis tanquam gemellæ sunt. Etenim *illuminationis puritas* et *arbitrii libertas* simul inceperunt, simul corruerunt.

phy that has appeared in modern times. But these are not the only arts which have their foundation in the science of human nature. Grammar too, in its general principles, has a close connexion with the understanding, and the theory of the association of ideas.

But there is no art whatever that hath so close a connexion with all the faculties and powers of the mind, as eloquence, or the art of speaking, in the extensive sense in which I employ the term. For, in the first place, that it ought to be ranked among the polite or fine arts, is manifest from this, that in all its exertions, with little or no exception, (as will appear afterwards) it requires the aid of the imagination. Thereby it not only pleases, but by pleasing commands attention, rouses the passions, and often at last subdues the most stubborn resolution. It is also a useful art. This is certainly the case, if the power of speech be a useful faculty, as it

---

corruerunt. Neque datur in universitate rerum tam intima sympathia quam illa *Veri* et *Boni.*—Venimus jam ad doctrinam circa usum et objecta facultatum animæ humanæ. Illa duas habet partes easque notissimas, et consensu receptas, *Logicam* et *Ethicam*——Logica de intellectu et ratione, Ethica de voluntate, appetitu, et affectibus disserit. Altera decreta, altera actiones progignit. De Aug. Sci. l. v. c. 1.

professedly

profeſſedly teaches us how to employ that faculty with the greateſt probability of ſucceſs. Further, if the logical art, and the ethical, be uſeful, eloquence is uſeful, as it inſtructs us how theſe arts muſt be applied for the conviction and the perſuaſion of others. It is indeed the grand art of communication, not of ideas only, but of ſentiments, paſſions, diſpoſitions, and purpoſes. Nay, without this, the greateſt talents, even wiſdom itſelf, loſe much of their luſtre, and ſtill more of their uſefulneſs. *The wiſe in heart*, ſaith Solomon, *ſhall be called prudent, but the ſweetneſs of the lips increaſeth learning* †. By the former a man's own conduct may be well regulated, but the latter is abſolutely neceſſary for diffuſing valuable knowledge, and enforcing right rules of action upon others.

Poetry indeed is properly no other than a particular mode or form of certain branches of oratory. But of this more afterwards. Suffice it only to remark at preſent, that the direct end of the former, whether to delight the fancy as in epic, or to move the paſſions as in tragedy, is avowedly in part the aim, and ſometimes the

† Prov. xvi. 21.

imme-

immediate and proposed aim, of the orator. The same medium language is made use of, the same general rules of composition, in narration, description, argumentation, are observed; and the same tropes and figures, either for beautifying or for invigorating the diction, are employed by both. In regard to versification, it is more to be considered as an appendage, than as a constituent of poetry. In this lies what may be called the more mechanical part of the poet's work, being at most but a sort of garnishing, and by far too unessential to give a designation to the kind. This particularity in form, to adopt an expression of the naturalists, constitutes only a variety, and not a different species.

Now though a considerable proficiency in the practice of the oratorical art may be easily and almost naturally attained, by one in whom clearness of apprehension is happily united with sensibility of taste, fertility of imagination, and a certain readiness in language, a more thorough investigation of the latent energies, if I may thus express myself, whereby the instruments employed by eloquence produce their effect upon the hearers, will serve considerably both to improve the taste, and to enrich the fancy.

By

By the former effect we learn to amend and avoid faults in compoſing and ſpeaking, againſt which the beſt natural, but uncultivated parts, give no ſecurity; and by the latter, the proper mediums are ſuggeſted, whereby the neceſſary aids of topics, arguments, illuſtrations, and motives, may be procured. Beſides, this ſtudy, properly conducted, leads directly to an acquaintance with ourſelves; it not only traces the operations of the intellect and imagination, but diſcloſes the lurking ſprings of action in the heart. In this view it is perhaps the ſureſt and the ſhorteſt, as well as the pleaſanteſt way of arriving at the ſcience of the human mind. It is an humble attempt to lead the mind of the ſtudious inquirer into this track, that the following ſheets are now ſubmitted to the examination of the public.

When we conſider the manner in which the rhetorical art hath ariſen, and been treated in the ſchools, we muſt be ſenſible, that in this, as in the imitative arts, the firſt handle has been given to criticiſm by actual performances in the art. The principles of our nature will, without the aid of any previous and formal inſtruction, ſufficiently account for the firſt attempts. As ſpeakers

speakers existed before grammarians, and reasoners before logicians; so doubtless there were orators before there were rhetoricians, and poets before critics. The first impulse towards the attainment of every art is from nature. The earliest assistance and direction that can be obtained in the rhetorical art, by which men operate on the minds of others, arises from the consciousness a man has of what operates on his own mind, aided by the sympathetic feelings, and by that practical experience of mankind, which individuals, even in the rudest state of society, are capable of acquiring. The next step is to observe and discriminate, by proper appellations, the different attempts, whether modes of arguing, or forms of speech, that have been employed for the purposes of explaining, convincing, pleasing, moving, and persuading. Here we have the beginnings of the critical science. The third step is to compare, with diligence, the various effects, favourable or unfavourable, of those attempts, carefully taking into consideration every attendant circumstance, by which the success appears to have been influenced, and by which one may be enabled to discover to what particular purpose each attempt is adapted, and in what circumstances only to be used. The fourth and last is to canvas those principles in our nature, to which the various attempts are adapted, and by which, in any instance, their success, or want of success, may be accounted for. By the first step the critic is supplied with materials. By the second, the materials are distributed and classed, the forms of argument, the tropes and figures of speech, with their divisions and subdivisions, are explained. By the third, the rules of composition are discovered, or the method of combining and disposing the several materials, so as that they may be perfectly adapted to the end in view. By the fourth, we arrive at that knowledge of human nature, which, beside its other advantages, adds both weight and evidence to all precedent discoveries and rules.

The second of the steps abovementioned, which, by the way, is the first of the rhetorical art, for all that precedes is properly supplied by Nature, appeared to the author of Hudibras, the utmost pitch that had even to his time been attained:

INTRODUCTION. 19

> For all a rhetorician's rules
> Teach nothing but to name his tools*.

In this, however, the matter hath been exaggerated by the satyrist. Considerable progress had been made by the ancient Greeks and Romans, in devising the proper rules of composition, not only in the two sorts of poesy, epic, and dramatic, but also in the three sorts of orations, which were in most frequent use among them, the deliberative, the judiciary, and the demonstrative. And I must acknowledge, that, as far as I have been able to discover, there has been little or no improvement in this respect made by the moderns. The observations and rules transmitted to us from these distinguished names in the learned world, Aristotle, Cicero, and Quintilian, have been for the most part only translated by later critics, or put into a modish dress and new arrangement. And as to the fourth and last step, it may be said to bring us into a new country, of which, though there have been some succesful incursions occasionally made upon its frontiers, we are not yet in full possession.

* P 1. l 1.

THE performance which, of all those I happen to be acquainted with, seems to have advanced farthest in this way, is the *Elements of Criticism*. But the subject of the learned and ingenious author of that work, is rather too multifarious to admit so narrow a scrutiny as would be necessary for a perfect knowledge of the several parts. Every thing that is an object of taste, *sculpture, painting, music, architecture,* and *gardening,* as well as *poetry* and *eloquence,* come within his plan. On the other hand, though his subject be more multiform, it is in respect of its connexion with the mind less extensive than that here proposed. All those particular arts are examined only on that side, wherein there is found a pretty considerable coincidence with one another, namely as objects of taste, which, by exciting sentiments of grandeur, beauty, novelty, and the like, are calculated to delight the imagination. In this view, eloquence comes no farther under consideration, than as a fine art, and adapted, like the others above mentioned, to please the fancy, and to move the passions. But to treat it also as an useful art, and closely connected with the

the understanding and the will, would have led to a discussion foreign to his purpose.

I AM aware, that, from the deduction given above, it may be urged, that the fact as here represented, seems to subvert the principle formerly laid down, and that as practice in the art has given the first scope for criticism, the former cannot justly be considered as deriving light and direction from the latter; that, on the contrary, the latter ought to be regarded as merely affording a sort of intellectual entertainment to speculative men. It may be said, that this science, however entertaining, as it must derive all its light and information from the actual examples in the art, can never in return be subservient to the art, from which alone it has received whatever it has to bestow. This objection, however specious, will not bear a near examination. For let it be observed, that though in all the arts the first rough draughts, or imperfect attempts, that are made, precede every thing that can be termed criticism, they do not precede every thing that can be termed knowledge, which every human creature that is not an idiot, is every day, from his birth, acquiring, by experience and obfervation. This knowledge muſt of neceſſity precede even thoſe rudeſt and earlieſt eſſays; and if in the imperfect and indigeſted ſtate in which knowledge muſt always be found in the mind that is rather ſelf-taught than totally untaught, it deſerves not to be dignified with the title of ſcience, neither does the firſt awkward attempt in practice merit to be honoured with the name of Art. As is the one, ſuch is the other. It is enough for my purpoſe, that ſomething muſt be known, before any thing in this way, with a view to an end, can be undertaken to be done.

At the ſame time it is acknowledged, that as man is much more an active than a contemplative being, and as generally there is ſome view to action, eſpecially in uncultivated minds, in all their obſervations and inquiries, it cannot be doubted that, in compoſition, the firſt attempts would be in the art, and that afterwards from the compariſon of different attempts with one another, and the conſideration of the ſucceſs with which they had been ſeverally attended, would ariſe gradually the rules of criticiſm.

ticism. Nor can it, on the other hand, be pleaded with any appearance of truth, that observations derived from the productions of an art, can be of no service for the improvement of that art, and consequently of no benefit to future artists. On the contrary, it is thus that every art, liberal or mechanical, elegant or useful, except those founded in pure mathematics, advances toward perfection. From observing similar but different attempts and experiments, and from comparing their effects, general remarks are made, which serve as so many rules for directing future practice; and from comparing such general remarks together, others still more general are deduced. A few individual instances serve as a foundation to those observations, which, when once sufficiently established, extend their influence to instances innumerable. It is in this way that, on experiments comparatively few, all the physiological sciences have been reared; it is in this way that those comprehensive truths were first discovered, which have had such an unlimited influence on the most important arts, and given man so vast a dominion over the elements, and even the most refractory powers of nature. It is evident, therefore,

fore, that the artist and the critic are reciprocally subservient, and the particular province of each is greatly improved by the assistance of the other.

But it is not necessary here to enter farther into this subject; what I shall have occasion afterwards to advance on the acquisition of experience, and the manner of using it, will be a sufficient illustration.

THE PHILOSOPHY OF RHETORIC.

BOOK I.

The Nature and Foundations of Eloquence.

CHAP. I.

Eloquence in the largest acceptation defined, its more general forms exhibited, with their different objects, ends, and characters.

IN speaking there is always some end proposed, or some effect which the speaker intends to produce in the hearer. The word *eloquence* in its greatest latitude denotes, ' That art or talent by which the discourse is adapted to its end*.'

ALL

---

* " Dicere secundum virtutem orationis. Scientia bene
" dicendi." Quintilian. The word *eloquence*, in common
con-

ALL the ends of speaking are reducible to four; every speech being intended to enlighten the understanding, to please the imagination, to move the passions, or to influence the will.

ANY one discourse admits only of one of these ends as the principal. Nevertheless, in discoursing on a subject, many things may be introduced, which are more immediately and apparently directed to some of the other ends of speaking, and not to that which is the chief intent of the whole. But then these other and immediate ends are in effect but means, and must be rendered conducive to that which is the primary intention. Accordingly, the propriety or the impropriety of the introduction of such secondary ends, will always be inferred from their subserviency or want of subserviency to that end, which is, in respect of them, the ultimate. For example, a discourse addressed to the understanding, and calculated to illustrate

conversation, is seldom used in such a comprehensive sense. I have, however, made choice of this definition on a double account. 1st, It exactly corresponds to Tully's idea of a perfect orator, "Optimus est orator qui dicendo animos audien-
"tium et docet, et delectat, et permovet." 2dly, It is best adapted to the subject of these papers. See the note on page 33.

or evince some point purely speculative, may borrow aid from the imagination, and admit metaphor and comparison, but not the bolder and more striking figures, as that called vision or fiction*, prosopopœia, and the like; which are not so much intended to elucidate a subject, as to excite admiration. Still less will it admit an address to the passions, which, as it never fails to disturb the operation of the intellectual faculty, must be regarded by every intelligent hearer as foreign at least, if not insidious. It is obvious, that either of these, far from being subservient to the main design, would distract the attention from it.

There is indeed one kind of address to the understanding, and only one, which, it may not be improper to observe, disdains all assistance whatever from the fancy. The address I mean, is mathematical demonstration. As this doth not, like moral reasoning, admit degrees of evidence, its perfection in point of eloquence,

---

* By vision or fiction is understood, that rhetorical figure of which Quintilian says, "Quas φαῆασιας Græci vocant, nos " sanè *visiones* appellamus, per quas imagines rerum absen- " tium ita repræsentantur animo, ut eas cernere oculis ac " præsentes habere videamur."

if so uncommon an application of the term may be allowed, consists in perspicuity. Perspicuity here results entirely from propriety and simplicity of diction, and from accuracy of method, where the mind is regularly, step by step, conducted forwards in the same track, the attention no way diverted, nothing left to be supplied, no one unnecessary word or idea introduced*. On the contrary, an harangue framed for affecting the hearts or influencing the resolves of an assembly, needs greatly the assistance both of intellect and of imagination.

In general it may be asserted, that each preceding species, in the order above exhibited, is preparatory to the subsequent; that each subsequent species is founded on the preceding, and that thus they ascend in a regular progression. Knowledge, the object of the intel-

---

* Of this kind Euclid hath given us the most perfect models, which have not, I think, been sufficiently imitated by later mathematicians: In him you find the exactest arrangement inviolably observed, the properest and simplest, and by consequence, the plainest expressions constantly used, nothing deficient, nothing superfluous, in brief, nothing which in more, or fewer, or other words, or words otherwise disposed, could have been better expressed.

lect, furnisheth materials for the fancy; the fancy culls, compounds, and, by her mimic art, disposes these materials so as to affect the passions; the passions are the natural spurs to volition or action, and so need only to be right directed. This connexion and dependency will better appear from the following observations.

When a speaker addresseth himself to the understanding, he proposes the *instruction* of his hearers, and that, either by explaining some doctrine unknown, or not distinctly comprehended by them, or by proving some position disbelieved or doubted by them.—In other words, he proposes either to dispel ignorance or to vanquish error. In the one, his aim is their *information*; in the other, their *conviction*. Accordingly the predominant quality of the former is *perspicuity*, of the latter, *argument*. By that we are made to know, by this to believe.

The imagination is addressed by exhibiting to it a lively and beautiful representation of a suitable object. As in this exhibition, the task of the orator may, in some sort, be said, like that of the painter, to consist in imitation, the merit of the work results entirely from these two sources; dignity, as well in the subject or thing

thing imitated, as in the manner of imitation; and resemblance, in the portrait or performance. Now the principal scope for this class being in narration and description, poetry, which is one mode of oratory, especially epic poetry, must be ranked under it. The effect of the dramatic, at least of tragedy, being upon the passions, the drama falls under another species, to be explained afterwards. But that kind of address of which I am now treating, attains the summit of perfection in the *sublime*; or those great and noble images, which, when in suitable colouring presented to the mind, do, as it were, distend the imagination with some vast conception, and quite ravish the soul.

The sublime, it may be urged, as it raiseth admiration, should be considered as one species of address to the passions. But this objection, when examined, will appear superficial. There are few words in any language (particularly such as relate to the operations and feelings of the mind) which are strictly univocal. Thus admiration, when persons are the object, is commonly used for a high degree of esteem; but when otherwise applied, it denotes solely an internal taste. It is that pleasurable sensation which

which instantly ariseth on the perception of magnitude, or of whatever is great and stupendous in its kind. For there is a greatness in the degrees of quality in spiritual subjects, analogous to that which subsists in the degrees of quantity in material things. Accordingly, in all tongues, perhaps without exception, the ordinary terms, which are considered as literally expressive of the latter, are also used promiscuously to denote the former. Now admiration, when thus applied, doth not require to its production, as the passions generally do, any reflex view of motives or tendencies, or of any relation either to private interest, or to the good of others; and ought therefore to be numbered among those original feelings of the mind, which are denominated by some the reflex senses, being of the same class with a taste for beauty, an ear for music, or our moral sentiments. Now the immediate view of whatever is directed to the imagination (whether the subject be things inanimate or animal forms, whether characters, actions, incidents, or manners) terminates in the gratification of some internal taste; as a taste for the wonderful, the fair, the good; for elegance, for novelty, or for grandeur.

But it is evident, that this creative faculty, the fancy, frequently lends her aid in promoting still nobler ends. From her exuberant stores most of those tropes and figures are extracted, which, when properly employed, have such a marvellous efficacy in rousing the passions, and by some secret, sudden, and inexplicable association, awakening all the tenderest emotions of the heart. In this case, the address of the orator is not ultimately intended to astonish by the loftiness of his images, or to delight by the beauteous resemblance which his painting bears to nature, nay, it will not permit the hearers even a moment's leisure for making the comparison, but, as it were, by some magical spell, hurries them, ere they are aware, into love, pity, grief, terror, desire, aversion, fury, or hatred. It therefore assumes the denomination of *pathetic**, which is the characteristic of the third species of discourse, that addressed to the passions.

Finally, that kind, the most complex of all, which is calculated to influence the will,

---

* I am sensible that this word is commonly used in a more limited sense, for that only which excites commiseration. *Perhaps* the word *impassioned* would answer better.

and

and persuade to a certain conduct, as it is in reality an artful mixture of that which proposes to convince the judgment, and that which interests the passions, its distinguishing excellency results from these two, the argumentative and the pathetic incorporated together. These acting with united force, and, if I may so express myself, in concert, constitute that passionate eviction, that *vehemence* of contention, which is admirably fitted for persuasion, and hath always been regarded as the supreme qualification in an orator[*]. It is this which beats down every

[*] This animated reasoning the Greek rhetoricians termed δεινότης, which, from signifying the principal excellency in an orator, came at length to denote oratory itself. And as vehemence and eloquence became synonymous, the latter, suitably to this way of thinking, was sometimes defined the *art of persuasion*. But that this definition is defective, appears even from their own writings, since in a consistency with it their rhetorics could not have comprehended those orations called *demonstrative*, the design of which was not to persuade, but to please. Yet it is easy to discover the origin of this defect, and that both from the nature of the thing, and from the customs which obtained among both Greeks and Romans. First, from the nature of the thing, for to persuade presupposes in some degree, and therefore may be understood to imply, all the other talents of an orator, to enlighten, to evince, to paint, to astonish, to inflame: but this doth not hold universally, one may explain with clearness, and prove with energy, who is incapable of the sublime, the pathetic,

every obstacle, and procures the speaker an irresistible power over the thoughts and purposes of his audience. It is this which hath been so justly celebrated as giving one man an ascendant over others, superior even to what despotism itself can bestow, since by the latter the more ignoble part, only the body and its members, are enslaved, whereas, from the dominion of the former, nothing is exempted, neither judgment nor affection, not even the inmost recesses, the most latent movements of the soul. What opposition is he not prepared

---

and the vehement; besides, this power of persuasion, or, as Cicero calls it, " posse voluntates hominum impellere quò " velis, unde velis, deducere," as it makes a man master of his hearers, is the most considerable in respect of consequences. Secondly, from ancient customs. All their public orations were ranked under three classes, the demonstrative, the judiciary, and the deliberative. In the two last it was impossible to rise to eminence, without that important talent, the power of persuasion. These were in much more frequent use than the first, and withal the surest means of advancing both the fortune and the fame of the orator; for as on the judiciary the lives and estates of private persons depended, on the deliberative hung the resolves of senates, the fate of kingdoms, nay of the most renowned republics the world ever knew. Consequently, to excel in these, must have been the direct road to riches, honours, and preferment. No wonder then that persuasion should almost wholly engross the rhetorician's notice.

to conquer, on whose arms reason hath conferred solidity and weight, and passion such a sharpness as enables them, in defiance of every obstruction, to open a speedy passage to the heart?

It is not, however, every kind of pathos, which will give the orator so great an ascendency over the minds of his hearers. All passions are not alike capable of producing this effect. Some are naturally inert and torpid; they deject the mind, and indispose it for enterprise. Of this kind are sorrow, fear, shame, humility. Others, on the contrary, elevate the soul, and stimulate to action. Such are hope, patriotism, ambition, emulation, anger. These, with the greatest facility, are made to concur in direction with arguments exciting to resolution and activity; and are, consequently, the fittest for producing, what, for want of a better term in our language, I shall henceforth denominate the *vehement*. There is, besides, an intermediate kind of passions, which do not so congenially and directly either restrain us from acting, or incite us to act; but, by the art of the speaker, can, in an oblique manner, be made conducive to either. Such are joy, love, esteem, compassion.

Neverthelefs, all thefe kinds may find a place in fuafory difcourfes, or fuch as are intended to operate on the will. The firft is propereft for diffuading; the fecond, as hath been already hinted, for perfuading, the third is equally accommodated to both.

Guided by the above reflections, we may eafily trace that connexion in the various forms of eloquence, which was remarked, on diftinguifhing them by their feveral objects. The imagination is charmed by a finifhed picture, wherein even drapery and ornament are not neglected, for here the end is pleafure. Would we penetrate farther, and agitate the foul, we muft exhibit only fome vivid ftrokes, fome expreffive features, not decorated as for fhow (all oftentation being both defpicable and hurtful here), but fuch as appear the natural expofition of thofe bright and deep impreffions, made by the fubject upon the fpeaker's mind; for here the end is not pleafure, but emotion. Would we not only touch the heart, but win it entirely to co-operate with our views, thofe affecting lineaments muft be fo interwoven with our argument, as that, from the paffion excited, our reafoning may derive importance, and so be fitted for commanding attention, and, by the justness of the reasoning, the passion may be more deeply rooted and enforced, and that thus, both may be made to conspire in effectuating that persuasion which is the end proposed. For here, if I may adopt the schoolmen's language, we do not argue to gain barely the assent of the understanding, but, which is infinitely more important, the consent of the will *.

To prevent mistakes, it will not be beside my purpose further to remark, that several of the terms above explained, are sometimes used by rhetoricians and critics in a much larger and more vague signification, than has been given them here. Sublimity and vehemence, in particular, are often confounded, the latter being considered as a species of the former. In this manner has this subject been treated by that great master Longinus, whose acceptation of the term *sublime* is extremely indefinite, importing an eminent degree of almost any excellence

* This subordination is beautifully and concisely expressed by Herfan in Rollin. " Je conclus que la veritable eloquence est celle qui persuade, qu'elle ne persuade ordinairement qu'on touchant, qu'elle ne touche que par des choses et par des idées palpables."

of speech, of whatever kind. Doubtless, if things themselves be understood, it does not seem material what names are assigned them. Yet it is both more accurate, and proves no inconsiderable aid to the right understanding of things, to discriminate by different signs such as are truly different. And that the two qualities above mentioned are of this number is undeniable, since we can produce passages full of vehemence, wherein no image is presented, which, with any propriety, can be termed great or sublime †. In matters of criticism, as in the

abstract

---

† For an instance of this, let that of Cicero against Antony suffice. " Tu istis faucibus, istis lateribus, ista gladia-
" toria totius corporis firmitate, tantum vini in Hippiæ nup-
" tiis exhauseras, ut tibi necesse esset in populi Romani con-
" spectu vomere postridie. Orem non modo visu fœdam,
" sed etiam auditu! Si hoc tibi inter cœnam, in tuis im-
" manibus illis poculis accidisset, quis non turpe duceret? In
" cætu vero populi Romani, negotium publicum gerens, ma-
" gister equitum, cui ructare turpe esset, is vomens, frustis
" esculentis vinum redolentibus, gremium suum et totum
" tribunal implevit." Here the vivacity of the address, in turning from the audience to the person declaimed against, the energy of the expressions, the repetition, exclamation, interrogation, and climax of aggravating circumstances, accumulated with rapidity upon one another, display in the strongest light, the turpitude of the action, and thus at once convince the judgment, and fire the indignation. It is therefore justly styled vehement. But what is the image it presents? The reverse in every respect of the sublime; what, instead of gazing on with admiration, we should avert our

eyes

abstract sciences, it is of the utmost consequence to ascertain, with precision, the meanings of words, and, as nearly as the genius of the language in which one writes will permit, to make them correspond to the boundaries assigned by Nature to the things signified. That the lofty and the vehement, though still distinguishable, are sometimes combined, and act with united force, is not to be denied. It is then only that the orator can be said to fight with weapons, which are at once sharp, massive, and refulgent, which, like Heaven's artillery, dazzle while they strike, which overpower the sight and the heart in the same instant.• How admirably do the two forenamed qualities, when happily blended, correspond in the rational to the thunder and lightning in the natural world, which are not more awfully majestical in sound and aspect, than irresistible in power ‡.

THUS

eyes from with abhorrence. For, however it might pass in a Roman senate, I question whether Ciceronian eloquence itself could excuse the uttering of such things in any modern assembly, not to say a polite one. With vernacular expressions, answering to these, " vomere, ructare fructis esculentis vi-" num redolentibus," our more delicate ears would be immoderately shocked. In a case of this kind, the more lively the picture is, so much the more abominable it is.

‡ A noted passage in Cicero's oration for Cornelius Balbus, will serve as an example of the union of sublimity with ve-

hemence

Thus much shall suffice for explaining the spirit, the intent, and the distinguishing qualities

hemence. Speaking of Pompey, who had rewarded the valour and public services of our orator's client, by making him a Roman citizen, he says, " Utrum enim, inscientem vultis " contra fœdera fecisse, an scientem? Si scientem, O nomen " nostri imperii, O populi Romani excellens dignitas, O " Cneii Pompeii sic late longèque diffusa laus, ut ejus gloriæ " domicilium communis imperii finibus terminetur O na- " tiones, urbes, populi, reges, tetrarchæ, tyranni, testes Cneii " Pompeii non solum virtutis in bello, sed etiam religionis in " pace. vos denique mutæ regiones imploro, et sola terra- " rum ultimarum vos maria, portus, insulæ, littoraque, quæ " est enim ora, quæ sedes, qui locus, in quo non extent hu- " jus cùm fortitudinis, tum vero humanitatis, tum animi, tum " consilii, impressa vestigia? Hunc quisquam incredibili qua- " dam atque inaudita gravitate, virtute, constantia prædi- " tum, fœdera scientem neglexisse, violasse, rupisse, dicere " audebit?" Here every thing conspires to aggrandize the hero, and exalt him to something more than mortal in the minds of the auditory, at the same time, every thing inspires the most perfect veneration for his character, and the most entire confidence in his integrity and judgment. The whole world is exhibited as no more than a sufficient theatre for such a superior genius to act upon. How noble is the idea! All the nations and potentates of the earth are, in a manner, produced as witnesses of his valour and his truth. Thus the orator at once fills the imagination with the immensity of the object, kindles in the breast an ardour of affection and gratitude, and by so many accumulated evidences, convinces the understanding, and silences every doubt. Accordingly, the effect which the words above quoted, and some other things advanced in relation to the same personage, had upon the audience, as we learn from Quintilian, was quite extraordinary. They extorted from them such demonstrations of
their

lities of each of the forementioned sorts of addrefs, all which agree in this, an accommodation to affairs of a serious and important nature.

CHAP. II.

Of wit, humour, and ridicule.

THIS article, concerning eloquence in its largest acceptation, I cannot properly dismiss without making some observations on another genus of oratory, in many things similar to the former, but which is naturally suited to light and trivial matters.

This also may be branched into three sorts, corresponding to those already discussed, directed to the fancy, the passions, and the will, for that which illuminates the understanding, serves

their applause and admiration, as he acknowledges to have been but ill-suited to the place and the occasion. He excuses it, however, because he considers it, not as a voluntary, but as a necessary consequence of the impression made upon the minds of the people His words are remarkable, " Atque ego " illos credo qui aderant, nec sensisse quid facerent, nec sponte " judicioque plausisse, sed velut mente captos, et quo essent " in loco ignaros, erupisse in hunc voluntatis affectum," lib. viii. cap 3. Without doubt, a considerable share of the effect ought to be ascribed to the immense advantage which the action and pronunciation of the orator would give to his expression.

as a common foundation to both, and has here nothing peculiar. This may be styled the eloquence of conversation, as the other is more strictly the eloquence of declamation*. Not, indeed, but that wit, humour, ridicule, which are the essentials of the former, may often be succesfully admitted into public harangues. And, on the other hand, sublimity, pathos, vehemence, may sometimes enter the precincts of familiar converse. To justify the use of such distinctive appellations, it is enough that they refer to those particulars which are predominant in each, though not peculiar to either.

Section I.

Of wit.

To consider the matter more nearly, it is the design of wit to excite in the mind an agreeable surprise, and that arising, not from any thing marvellous in the subject, but solely from the imagery she employs, or the strange assemblage of related ideas presented to the mind. This

---

* In the latter of these the ancients excel; in the former, the moderns Demosthenes and Cicero, not to say, Homer and Virgil, to this day, remain unrivalled, and in all antiquity, Lucian himself not excepted, we cannot find a match for Swift and Cervantes.

end

end is effected in one or other of these three ways first, in debasing things pompous or seemingly grave: I say *seemingly* grave, because to vilify what is *truly* grave, has something shocking in it, which rarely fails to counteract the end: secondly, in aggrandising things little and frivolous: thirdly, in setting ordinary objects, by means not only remote but apparently contrary, in a particular and uncommon point of view *. This will be better understood from the following observations and examples.

THE

---

* I know no language which affords a name for this species of imagery, but the English. The French *esprit* or *bel esprit*, though on some occasions rightly translated *wit*, hath commonly a signification more extensive and generical. It must be owned, indeed, that in conformity to the style of French critics, the term *wit*, in English writings, hath been sometimes used with equal latitude. But this is certainly a perversion of the word from its ordinary sense, through an excessive deference to the manner and idiom of our ingenious neighbours. Indeed, when an author varies the meaning in the same work, he not only occasions perplexity to his reader, but falls himself into an apparent inconsistency. An error of this kind in Mr. Pope has been lately pointed out by a very ingenious and judicious critic. "In the essay on criticism it is said,

"True wit is nature to advantage dress'd:

"But immediately after this the poet adds,

"For works may have more wit than does 'em good.

"Now let us substitute the definition in the place of the thing,
"and it will stand thus: A work may have more of *nature*
"*dress'd*

The materials employed by wit in the grotesque pieces she exhibits, are partly derived from those common fountains of whatever is directed to the imaginative powers, the ornaments of elocution, and the oratorical figures, simile, apostrophé, antithesis, metaphor; partly from those she in a manner appropriates to herself, irony, hyperbole, allusion, parody, and (if the reader will pardon my descending so low) paronomasia †, and pun. The limning of wit differs from the rhetorical painting above described in two respects. One is, that in the latter there is not only a resemblance requisite in that particular on which the comparison is founded, but there must also be a general similitude in the nature and quality of that which is the basis of the imagery, to that which is the theme of discourse. In respect of dignity, or the impression they make upon the mind, they must be things

---

" *dress'd to advantage*, than will do it good. This is impos-
" sible, and it is evident, that the confusion arises from the
" poet's having annexed two different ideas to the same
" word." Webb's Remarks on the Beauties of Poetry,
Dialogue II.

† Paronomasia is properly that figure which the French call *jeu de mots*. Such as " Inceptio est amentium, haud aman-
" tium" Ter. Andr. " Which tempted our attempt."
Milt. b. i. " To beg'rd the Almighty's throne, beseeching
" or besieging " B. v.

homo-

homogeneous. What has magnificence, must invariably be portrayed by what is magnificent; objects of importance by objects important; such as have grace by things graceful: Whereas the witty, though requiring an exact likeness in the first particular, demands, in the second, a contrariety rather, or remoteness. This enchantress exults in reconciling contradictions, and in hitting on that special light and attitude, wherein you can discover an unexpected similarity in objects, which, at first sight, appear the most dissimilar and heterogeneous. Thus high and low are coupled, humble and superb, momentous and trivial, common and extraordinary. Addison, indeed, observes ‡, that wit is often produced, not by the resemblance, but by the opposition of ideas. But this, of which, however, he hath not given us an instance, doth not constitute a different species, as the repugnancy in that case will always be found between objects in other respects resembling, for it is to the contrast of dissimilitude and likeness, remoteness and relation in the same objects, that its peculiar effect is imputable. Hence we hear of the flashes and the sallies of wit, phrases which imply suddenness, surprise, and contra-

‡ Spectator

riety.

riety. These are illustrated in the first by a term which implies an instantaneous emergence of light in darkness; in the second, by a word which denotes an abrupt transition to things distant. For we may remark in passing, that though language be older than criticism, those expressions adopted by the former to elucidate matters of taste, will be found to have a pretty close conformity to the purest discoveries of the latter.

Nay, of so much consequence here are surprise and novelty, that nothing is more tasteless, and sometimes disgusting, than a joke that has become stale by frequent repetition. For the same reason, even a pun or happy allusion will appear excellent when thrown out extemporé in conversation, which would be deemed execrable in print. In like manner, a witty repartee is infinitely more pleasing than a witty attack. For though, in both cases, the thing may be equally new to the reader or hearer, the effect on him is greatly injured, when there is access to suppose, that it may be the slow production of study and premeditation. This, however, holds most with regard to the inferior tribes of witticisms, of which their readiness is the best recommendation.

The

The other respect in which wit differs from the illustrations of the graver orator, is the way wherein it affects the hearer. Sublimity elevates, beauty charms, wit diverts. The first, as hath been already observed, enraptures, and as it were, dilates the soul; the second diffuseth over it a serene delight; the third tickles the fancy, and throws the spirits into an agreeable vibration.

To these reflections I shall subjoin examples in each of the three sorts of wit above explained.

It will, however, be proper to premise, that if the reader should not at first be sensible of the justness of the solutions and explications to be given, he ought not hastily to form an unfavourable conclusion. Wherever there is taste, the witty and the humorous make themselves perceived, and produce their effect instantaneously; but they are of so subtle a nature, that they will hardly endure to be touched, much less to undergo a strict analysis and scrutiny. They are like those volatile essences, which, being too delicate to bear the open air, evaporate almost as soon as they are exposed to it. Accordingly, the wittiest things will sometimes be made to appear insipid, and the most ingenious frigid, by scrutinising them too narrowly. Besides, the very frame of spirit proper for being diverted with the laughable in objects, is so different from that which is necessary for philosophising on them, that there is a risk, that when we are most disposed to inquire into the cause, we are least capable of feeling the effect, as it is certain, that when the effect hath its full influence on us, we have little inclination for investigating the cause. For these reasons, I have resolved to be brief in my illustrations, having often observed, that, in such nice and abstract inquiries, if a proper hint do not suggest the matter to the reader, he will be but more perplexed by long and elaborate discussions.

Of the first sort, which consists in the debasement of things great and eminent, Butler, amongst a thousand other instances, hath given us those which follow:

> And now had Phœbus in the lap
> Of Thetis, taken out his nap.
> And, like a lobster boil'd, the morn
> From black to red began to turn *

Here the low allegorical style of the first couplet, and the simile used in the second, afford us a just

* Hudibras, part ii. canto 2.

notion

notion of this lowest species which is distinguished by the name of *the ludicrous*. Another specimen from the same author you have in these lines

> Great on the bench, great in the saddle,
> That could as well bind o'er as swaddle,
> Mighty he was at both of these,
> And styl'd of *war*, as well as *peace*
> So some rats of amphibious nature,
> Are either for the *land* or *water* *.

In this coarse kind of drollery, those laughable translations or paraphrases of heroic and other serious poems, wherein the authors are said to be travestied, chiefly abound.

To the same class those instances must be referred, in which, though there is no direct comparison made, qualities of real dignity and importance are degraded, by being coupled with things mean and frivolous, as in some respect standing in the same predicament. An example of this I shall give from the same hand.

> For when the restless Greeks sat down
> So many years, before Troy town,
> And were renown'd, as Homer writes,
> For well-soal'd boots †, no less than fights ‡.

---

* Ibid Part I Canto 1.

† In allusion to the Ευκνημιδες Αχαιοι, an expression which frequently occurs both in the Iliad and in the Odyssey.

‡ Ibid. Part I. Canto 2.

Vol. I.   E   I shall

I shall only observe further, that this sort, whose aim is to debase, delights in the most homely expressions, provincial idioms, and cant phrases.

The second kind, consisting in the aggrandisement of little things, which is by far the most splendid, and displays a soaring imagination, these lines of Pope will serve to illustrate:

> As Berecynthia, while her offspring vie
> In homage to the mother of the sky,
> Surveys around her in the blest abode,
> An hundred sons, and every son a god:
> Not with less glory mighty Dulness crown'd,
> Shall take thro' Grubstreet her triumphant round;
> And her Parnassus glancing o'er at once,
> Behold a hundred sons, and each a dunce *.

This whole similitude is spirited. The parent of the celestials is contrasted by the daughter of night and chaos; heaven by Grubstreet; gods by dunces. Besides, the parody it contains on a beautiful passage in Virgil, adds a particular lustre to it †. This species we may term *the*

---

* Dunciad. B.   † The passage is this,
Felix prole virum, qualis Berecynthia mater
Invehitur curru Phrygias turrita per urbes,
Læta deûm partu, centum complexa nepótes,
Omnes cœlicolas, omnes supera alta tenentes. Æneis.

thrasonical,

thrasonical, or *the mock-majestic*. It affects the most pompous language, and sonorous phraseology, as much as the other affects the reverse, the vilest and most grovelling dialect.

I shall produce another example from the same writer, which is, indeed, inimitably fine. It represents a lady employed at her toilet, attended by her maid, under the allegory of the celebration of some solemn and religious ceremony. The passage is rather long for a quotation, but as the omission of any part would be a real mutilation, I shall give it entire.

 And now unveil'd, the toilet stands display'd,
 Each silver vase in mystic order laid.
 First, rob'd in white, the nymph intent adores,
 With head uncover'd, the cosmetic powers
 A heavenly image in the glass appears,
 To that she bends, to that her eyes she rears;
 Th' inferior priestess, at her altar's side,
 Trembling, begins the sacred rites of pride;
 Unnumber'd treasures opes at once, and here
 The various offerings of the world appear,
 From each she nicely culls with curious toil,
 And decks the goddess with the glittering spoil.
 This casket India's glowing gems unlocks,
 And all Arabia breathes from yonder box.
 The tortoise here and elephant unite
 Transform'd to combs, the speckled and the white.
 Here files of pins extend their shining rows,
 Puffs, powders, patches, bibles, billet doux.

> Now awful beauty puts on all its arms,
> The fair each moment rises in her charms,
> Repairs her smiles, awakens every grace,
> And calls forth all the wonders of her face;
> Sees by degrees a purer blush arise,
> And keener lightnings quicken in her eyes *.

To this class also we must refer the application of grave reflections to mere trifles. For that *great* and *serious* are naturally associated by the mind, and likewise little and trifling, is sufficiently evinced by the common modes of expression on these subjects, used in every tongue. An opposite instance of such an application we have from Philips,

> My galligaskins, that have long withstood
> The winter's fury and encroaching frosts,
> By time subdued, *(What will not time subdue!)*
> An horrid chasm disclose †.

Like to this, but not equal, is that of Young,

> One day his wife, *(for who can wives reclaim!)*
> Level'd her barbarous needle at his fame ‡.

To both the preceding kinds, the term *burlesque* is applied, but especially to the first.

Of the third species of wit, which is by far the most multifarious, and which results from

---
* Rape of the Lock, Canto 1.
† Splendid Shilling.   ‡ Universal Passion.

what

what I may call the queerness or singularity of the imagery, I shall give a few specimens that will serve to mark some of its principal varieties. To illustrate all would be impossible.

The first I shall exemplify, is where there is an apparent contrariety in the things she exhibits as connected. This kind of contrast we have in these lines of Garth,

> Then Hydrops next appears amongst the throng;
> Bloated and big she slowly sails along
> But like a miser in excess she's poor,
> And pines for thirst amidst her watery store *.

The wit in these lines doth not so much arise from the comparison they contain of the dropsy to a miser, (which falls under the description that immediately succeeds) as from the union of contraries they present to the imagination, poverty in the midst of opulence, and thirst in one who is already drenched in water.

A second sort, is where the things compared are what with dialecticians would come under the denomination of *disparates*, being such as can be ranked under no common genus. Of this I shall subjoin an example from Young,

---

* Dispensary.

> Health chiefly keeps an Atheist in the dark,
> A fever argues better than a Clarke
> Let but the logic in his pulse decay,
> The Grecian he'll renounce, and learn to pray [*]

Here, by implication, health is compared to a sophister, or darkener of the understanding, a fever to a metaphysical disputant, a regular pulse to false logic, for the word logic in the third line is used ironically. In other words, we have here modes and substances, the affections of body, and the exercise of reason strangely, but not insignificantly linked together, strangely, else the sentiment, however just, could not be denominated witty, significantly, because an unmeaning jumble of things incongruous would not be wit, but nonsense.

A THIRD variety in this species springs from confounding artfully the proper and the metaphorical sense of an expression. In this way, one will assign as a motive, what is discovered to be perfectly absurd, when but ever so little attended to, and yet, from the ordinary meaning of the words, hath a specious appearance on a single glance. Of this kind you have an instance in the subsequent lines,

---

[*] Universal Passion.

> While thus the lady talk'd, the knight
> Turn'd th' outside of his eyes to white,
> As men of inward light are wont
> To turn their optics in upon't †.

For whither can they turn their eyes more properly than to the light?

A FOURTH variety, much resembling the former, is when the argument or comparison (for all argument is a kind of comparison) is founded on the supposal of corporeal or personal attributes in what is strictly not susceptible of them, as in this,

> But Hudibras gave him a twitch
> As quick as lightning in the breech,
> Just in the place where honour's lodg'd,
> As wise philosophers have judg'd,
> Because a kick in that place, more
> Hurts honour than deep wounds before ‡.

Is demonstration itself more satisfactory? Can any thing be hurt but where it is? However, the mention of this as the sage deduction of philosophers, is no inconsiderable addition to the wit. Indeed, this particular circumstance belongs properly to the first species mentioned, in which, high and low, great and little, are coupled. Another example not unlike the preceding you have in these words,

---

† Hudibras, Part III. Canto 1.
‡ Ibid. Part II. Canto 3.

> What makes morality a crime,
> The most notorious of the time,
> Morality, which both the saints,
> And wicked too cry out against?
> 'Cause grace and virtue are within
> Prohibited degrees of kin.
> And therefore no true saint allows
> They shall be suffer'd to espouse *.

When the two foregoing instances are compared together, we should say of the first, that it has more of simplicity and nature, and is therefore more pleasing; of the second, that it has more of ingenuity and conceit, and is consequently more surprising.

The fifth and only other variety I shall observe, is that which ariseth from a relation not in the things signified, but in the signs, of all relations, no doubt, the slightest. Identity here gives rise to puns and clinches. Resemblance to quibbles, cranks, and rhimes. Of these, I imagine, it is quite unnecessary to exhibit specimens. The wit here is so dependent on the sound, that it is commonly incapable of being transfused into another language, and as, among persons of taste and discernment, it is in less request than the other sorts above enumerated,

---
* Hudibras, Part III. Canto 1.

those who abound in this, and never rise to any thing superior, are distinguished by the diminutive appellation of witlings.

Let it be remarked in general, that from one or more of the three last mentioned varieties, those plebeian tribes of witticism, the conundrums, the rebuses, the riddles, and some others, are lineally, though perhaps not all legitimately, descended. I shall only add, that I have not produced the forenamed varieties as an exact enumeration of all the subdivisions, of which the third species of wit is susceptible. It is capable, I acknowledge, of being almost infinitely diversified; and it is principally to its various exhibitions, that we apply the epithets *sportive, spritely, ingenious,* according as they recede more or less from those of the declaimer.

Section II.

Of humour.

As wit is the painting, humour is the pathetic, in this inferior sphere of eloquence. The nature and efficacy of humour may be thus unravelled. A just exhibition of any ardent or durable passion, excited by some adequate cause, instantly attacheth sympathy, the common tie of human souls, and thereby communicates the passion to the breast of the hearer. But when the emotion is either not violent or not durable, and the motive not any thing real, but imaginary, or at least quite disproportionate to the effect, or when the passion displays itself preposterously, so as rather to obstruct than to promote its aim, in these cases a natural representation, instead of fellow-feeling, creates amusement, and universally awakens contempt. The portrait in the former case we call *pathetic*, in the latter *humorous* *. It was said, that the emotion

---

* It ought to be observed, that this term is also used to express any lively strictures of such specialties in temper and conduct, as have neither moment enough to interest sympathy, nor incongruity enough to excite contempt. In this case, humour not being addressed to passion, but to fancy, must be considered as a kind of moral painting, and differs from wit only in these two things first, in that, character alone is the subject of the former, whereas all things whatever fall within the province of the latter; secondly, humour paints more simply by direct imitation, wit more variously by illustration and imagery. Of this kind of humour merely graphical, Addison hath given us numberless examples in many of the characters he hath so finely drawn, and little incidents he hath so pleasantly related in his Tatlers and Spectators. I might remark of the word *humour*, as I did of the term *wit*, that we scarcely find in other languages a word exactly corresponding. The Latin *facetiæ* seems to come the nearest Thus Cicero, " Huic generi orationis aspergentur etiam sales, qui in dicendo mirum quantum valent. quorum duo genera sunt, " unum

tion must be either not violent or not durable. This limitation is necessary, because a passion extreme in its degree, as well as lasting, cannot yield diversion to a well-disposed mind, but generally affects it with pity, not seldom with a mixture of horror and indignation. The sense of the ridiculous, though invariably the same, is in this case totally surmounted by a principle of our nature, much more powerful.

THE passion which humour addresseth as its object, is, as hath been signified above, contempt. But it ought carefully to be noted, that every address, even every pertinent address to contempt, is not humorous. This passion is not less capable of being excited by the severe and tragic, than by the merry and comic manner. The subject of humour is always character, but not every thing in character; its foibles ge-

---

" unum facetiarum, alterum dicacitatis, utetur utroque, sed
" altero in narrando aliquid venuste, altero in jaciendo mit-
" tendoque ridiculo; cujus genera plura sunt." *Orator*, 48. Here one would think, that the philosopher must have had in his eye the different provinces of wit and humour, calling the former *dicacitas*, the latter *facetiæ*. It is plain, however, that, both by him and other Latin authors, these two words are often confounded. There appears, indeed, to be more uniformity in the use that is made of the second term, than in the application of the first.

nerally,

nerally, such as caprices, little extravagancies, weak anxieties, jealousies, childish fondness, pertness, vanity, and self-conceit. One finds the greatest scope for exercising this talent in telling familiar stories, or in acting any whimsical part in an assumed character. Such an one, we say, has the talent of humouring a tale, or any queer manner which he chooseth to exhibit. Thus we speak of the passions in tragedy, but of the humorous in comedy; and even to express passion as appearing in the more trivial occurrences of life, we commonly use this term, as when we talk of good humour, ill humour, peevish or pleasant humour; hence it is that a capricious temper we call humoursome, the person possessed of it a humorist, and such facts or events as afford subject for the humorous, we denominate comical.

INDEED, comedy is the proper province of humour. Wit is called in solely as an auxiliary, humour predominates. The comic poet bears the same analogy to the author of the mock-heroic, that the tragic poet bears to the author of the epic. The epos recites, and advancing with a step majestic and sedate, engageth all the nobler powers of imagination, a sense of grandeur,

deur, of beauty, and of order, tragedy perfonates, and thus employing a more rapid and animated diction, feizeth directly upon the heart. The little epic, a narrative intended for amufement, and addreffed to all the lighter powers of fancy, delights in the excurfions of wit. the production of the comic mufe being a reprefentation, is circumfcribed by narrower bounds, and is all life and activity throughout. Thus Buckingham fays with the greateft juftnefs of comedy,

Humour is all Wit fhould be only brought
To turn agreeably fome proper thought *.

The pathetic and the facetious not only differ in fubject and effect, as will appear upon the moft fuperficial review of what hath been faid, but alfo in the manner of imitation. In this the man of humour defcends to a minutenefs which the orator difdains. The former will often fuccefsfully run into downright mimicry, and exhibit peculiarities in voice, gefture, and pronunciation, which in the other would be intolerable. The reafon of the difference is this: That we may divert, by exciting fcorn and contempt, the individual muft be expofed; that we

---

* Effay on Poetry.

may move, by interesting the more generous principles of humanity, the language and sentiments, not so much of the individual, as of human nature, must be displayed. So very different, or rather opposite, are these two in this respect, that there could not be a more effectual expedient for undoing the charm of the most affecting representation, than an attempt in the speaker to mimic the personal singularities of the man for whom he desires to interest us On the other hand, in the humorous, where the end is diversion, even over-acting, if moderate, is not improper.

It was observed already, that, though contempt be the only passion addressed by humour, yet this passion may with propriety and success be assailed by the severer eloquence, where there is not the smallest tincture of humour. This it will not be beside our purpose to specify, in order the more effectually to shew the difference. Lord Bolingbroke, speaking of the state of these kingdoms from the time of the Restoration, has these words: " The two brothers,
" Charles and James, when in exile, became
" infected with popery to such degrees as
" their different characters admitted of. Charles
" had

" had parts, and his good understanding served
" as an antidote to repel the poison. James,
" the simplest man of his time, drank off the
" whole chalice. The poison met, in his com-
" position, with all the fear, all the credulity,
" and all the obstinacy of temper proper to in-
" crease its virulence, and to strengthen its effect.
" ————Drunk with superstitious and even
" enthusiastic zeal, he ran headlong into his
" own ruin, whilst he endeavoured to precipi-
" tate ours. His parliament and his people did
" all they could to save themselves, by winning
" him. But all was vain. He had no principle
" on which they could take hold. Even his
" good qualities worked against them; and his
" love of his country went halves with his bi-
" gotry. How he succeeded we have heard
" from our fathers. The revolution of one
" thousand six hundred and eighty-eight saved
" the nation, and ruined the king *." Nothing can be more contemptuous, and at the
same time less derisive, than this representation. We should readily say of it, that it is
strongly animated, and happily expressed; but
no man who understands English would say, it
is humorous. I shall add one example from Dr.

* A Letter to Sir William Wyndham.

Swift.

Swift. "I should be exceedingly sorry to find
"the legislature make any new laws against the
"practice of duelling, because the methods are
"easy and many, for a wise man to avoid a
"quarrel with honour, or engage in it with in-
"nocence. And I can discover no political
"evil in suffering bullies, sharpers, and rakes,
"to rid the world of each other by a method of
"their own, where the law hath not been able
"to find an expedient †."

For a specimen of the humorous, take as a contrast to the two last examples, the following delineation of a fop:

>   Sir Plume (of amber snuff-box justly vain,
> And the nice conduct of a clouded cane)
> With earnest eyes and round unthinking face,
> He first the snuff box open'd, then the case,
> And thus broke out, "My Lord, Why,—what the devil?
> "Z—ds!—damn the lock!—'fore Gad, you must be civil!
> "Plague on't!—'tis past a jest,—nay prithee,—pox!
> "Give her the hair."—He spoke and rapp'd his box.
> "It grieves me much," replied the peer again,
> "Who speaks so well, should ever speak in vain;
> "But ——— ‡

This, both in the descriptive and the dramatic part, particularly in the draught it contains of the

---

† Swift on Good Manners.
‡ Rape of the Lock, Canto 4.

baronet's mind, aspect, manner, and eloquence, (if we except the sarcastic term *justly*, the double sense of the word *open'd*, and the fine irony couched in the reply) is purely facetious. An instance of wit and humour combined, where they reciprocally set off and enliven each other, Pope hath also furnished us with in another part of the same exquisite performance.

> Whether the nymph shall break Diana's law,
> Or some frail china jar receive a flaw,
> Or stain her honour, or her new brocade,
> Forget her prayers, or miss a masquerade;
> Or lose her heart, or necklace, at a ball;
> Or whether heaven has doom'd that Shock must fall †.

This is humorous, in that it is a lively sketch of the female estimate of mischances, as our poet's commentator rightly terms it, marked out by a few striking lineaments. It is likewise witty, for, not to mention the play on words like that remarked in the former example, a trope familiar to this author, you have here a comparison of—a woman's chastity to a piece of porcelain,—her honour to a gaudy robe,—her prayers to a fantastical disguise,—her heart to a trinket, and all these together to her lap-dog, and that founded on one lucky circumstance (a malicious

---

† Rape of the Lock, Canto 2.

critic would perhaps discern or imagine more) by which these things, how unlike soever in other respects, may be compared, the impression they make on the mind of a fine lady.

HUDIBRAS, so often above quoted, abounds in wit in almost all its varieties; to which the author's various erudition hath not a little contributed. And this, it must be owned, is more suitable to the nature of his poem. At the same time it is by no means destitute of humour, as appears particularly in the different exhibitions of character given by the knight and his squire. But in no part of the story is this talent displayed to greater advantage than in the consultation of the lawyer*, to which I shall refer the reader, as the passage is too long for my transcribing. There is, perhaps, no book in any language wherein the humorous is carried to a higher pitch of perfection, than in the adventures of the celebrated knight of La Mancha. As to our English dramatists, who does not acknowledge the transcendent excellence of Shakespeare in this province, as well as in the pathetic? Of the later comic writers, Congreve has an exuberance of wit, but Farquhar has more humour.

* Part III. Canto 3.

It may, however, with too much truth, be affirmed of English comedy in general, (for there are some exceptions) that, to the discredit of our stage, as well as of the national delicacy and discernment, obscenity is made too often to supply the place of wit, and ribaldry the place of humour.

Wit and humour, as above explained, commonly concur in a tendency to provoke laughter, by exhibiting a curious and unexpected affinity, the first generally by comparison, either direct or implied, the second by connecting in some other relation, such as causality or vicinity, objects apparently the most dissimilar and heterogeneous, which incongruous affinity, we may remark by the way, gives the true meaning of the word *oddity*, and is the proper object of laughter.

The difference between these and that grander kind of eloquence treated in the first part of this chapter, I shall, if possible, still farther illustrate, by a few similitudes borrowed from the optical science. The latter may be conceived as a plain mirrour, which faithfully reflects the object, in colour, figure, size, and posture. Wit, on the contrary, Proteus-like, transforms itself into a variety of shapes. It is now a convex speculum, which gives a just representation in form and colour, but withal reduces the greatest objects to the most despicable littleness; now a concave speculum, which swells the smallest trifles to an enormous magnitude; now again a speculum of a cylindrical, a conical, or an irregular make, which, though in colour, and even in attitude, it reflects a pretty strong resemblance, widely varies the proportions. Humour, when we consider the contrariety of its effects, contempt and laughter, (which constitute what in one word is termed *derision*) to that sympathy and love often produced by the pathetic, may in respect of these be aptly compared to a concave mirrour, when the object is placed beyond the focus, in which case it appears by reflection, both diminished and inverted, circumstances which happily adumbrate the contemptible and the ridiculous.

Section III.

Of ridicule.

The intention of raising a laugh is either merely to divert by that grateful titillation which it excites, or to influence the opinions and purposes of the hearers. In this also, the risible faculty, when suitably directed, hath often proved ed a very potent engine. When this is the view of the speaker, as there is always an air of reasoning conveyed under that species of imagery, narration or description, which stimulates laughter, these, thus blended, obtain the appellation of *ridicule*, the poignancy of which hath a similar effect in futile subjects, to that produced by what is called the vehement in solemn and important matters.

Nor doth all the difference between these lie in the dignity of the subject. Ridicule is not only confined to questions of less moment, but is fitter for refuting error than for supporting truth, for restraining from wrong conduct, than for inciting to the practice of what is right. Nor are these the sole restrictions, it is not properly levelled at the false, but at the *absurd* in tenets; nor can the edge of ridicule strike with equal force every species of misconduct: it is not the criminal part which it attacks, but that which we denominate silly or foolish. With regard to doctrine, it is evident that it is not falsity or mistake, but palpable error or absurdity, (a thing hardly confutable by mere argument) which is the object of contempt; and consequently those dogmas are beyond the reach of cool reasoning which are within the rightful confines of ridicule. That they are generally conceived to be so, appears from the sense universally assigned to expressions like these, 'Such 'a position is ridiculous.—It doth not deserve a 'serious answer.' Every body knows that they import more than 'It is false,' being, in other words, 'This is such an extravagance as is not 'so much a subject of argument as of laughter.' And that we may discover what it is, with regard to conduct, to which ridicule is applicable; we need only consider the different departments of tragedy and of comedy. In the last, it is of mighty influence; into the first, it never legally obtains admittance. Those things which principally come under its lash are awkwardness, rusticity, ignorance, cowardice, levity, foppery, pedantry, and affectation of every kind. But against murder, cruelty, parricide, ingratitude, perfidy*, to attempt to raise a laugh, would shew such an unnatural insensibility in the speaker,

---

* To this black catalogue an ancient Pagan of Athens or of Rome would have added *adultery*, but the modern refinements of us Christians (if without profanation we can so apply the name) absolutely forbid it, as nothing on our theatre is a more common subject of laughter than this. Nor is the laugh raised against the adulterer, else we might have some plea for our morals, if none for our taste, but to the indelible reproach of the taste, the sense, and the virtue of the nation, in his favour.

as

as would be excessively disgustful to any audience. To punish such enormities, the tragic poet must take a very different route.

Now from this distinction of vices or faults into two classes, there hath sprung a parallel division in all the kinds of poesy which relate to manners. The epopée, a picturesque, or graphical poem, is either heroic, or what is called mock-heroic, and by Aristotle iambic [*], from the measure in which poems of this kind were at first composed. The drama, an animated poem, is either in the buskin, or in the sock, for farce deserves not a place in the subdivision, being at most but a kind of dramatical apologue, whereof the characters are monstrous, the intrigue unnatural, the incidents often impossible, and which, instead of humour, has adopted a spurious bantling called *fun*. To satisfy us that satire, whose end is persuasion, admits also the like distribution, we need only recur to the different methods pursued by the two famous Latin satirists, Juvenal and Horace. The one declaims, the other derides. Accordingly, as Dryden justly observes [†], vice is the quarry of the

---

[*] Poet. 4.   [†] Origin and progress of Satire.

former, folly of the latter ‡. Thus, of the three graver forms, the aim, whether avowed or latent, always is, or ought to be the improvement of morals, of the three lighter, the refinement of manners *. But though the latter have for their peculiar object manners, in the limited and distinctive sense of that word, they may, with propriety, admit many things which directly conduce to the advancement of morals, and ought never to admit any thing which hath a contrary tendency. Virtue is of primary importance, both for the happiness of individuals, and for the well-being of society; an external

‡ The differences and relations to be found in the several forms of poetry mentioned, may be more concisely marked by the following scheme, which brings them under the view at once,

	Serious.	Facetious.		
The object, { Fancy Passion Will	— Great epic — Tragedy — High satire	— Little epic — Comedy — Low satire } The end morals.	} The means, { Insinuation Conformation Persuasion.	The poet, { Narrator. Representer. Reasoner.

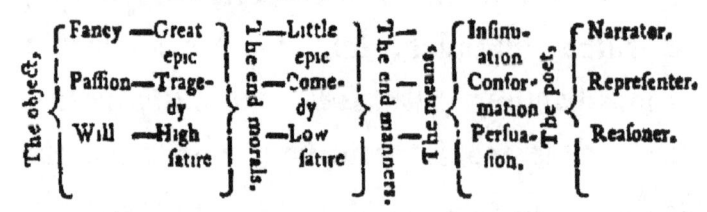

} The end manners.

* These observations will enable us to understand that of the poet,

——— Ridiculum acri
Fortius et melius magnas plerumque secat res. Hor.

Great and signal, it must be owned, are the effects of ridicule; but the subject must always appear to the ridiculer, and to those affected by his pleasantry, under the notion of littleness and futility, two essential requisites in the object of contempt and risibility.

polish

polish is at best but a secondary accomplishment, ornamental indeed when it adds a lustre to virtue, pernicious when it serves only to embellish profligacy, and in itself comparatively of but little consequence, either to private or to public felicity*.

* Whether this attention has been always given to morals, particularly in comedy, must be left to the determination of those who are most conversant in that species of scenic representations. One may, however, venture to prognosticate, that if in any period it shall become fashionable to shew no regard to virtue in such entertainments, if the hero of the piece, a fine gentleman to be sure, adorned as usual with all the superficial and exterior graces which the poet can confer, and crowned with success in the end, shall be an unprincipled libertine, a man of more spirit, forsooth, than to be checked in his pursuits by the restraints of religion, by a regard to the common right of mankind, or by the laws of hospitality and private friendships, which were accounted sacred among Pagans and those whom we denominate Barbarians, then, indeed, the stage will become merely the school of gallantry and intrigue, thither the youth of both sexes will resort, and will not resort in vain, in order to get rid of that troublesome companion modesty, intended by Providence as a guard to virtue, and a check against licentiousness; there vice will soon learn to provide herself in a proper stock of effrontery, and a suitable address for effecting her designs, and triumphing over innocence, then, in fine, if religion, virtue, principle, equity, gratitude, and good faith, are not empty sounds, the stage will prove the greatest of nuisances, and deserve to be styled, the principal corrupter of the age. Whether such an era hath ever happened in the history of the theatre, in this or any other country, or is likely to happen, I do not take upon me to decide.

ANOTHER remarkable difference, the only one which remains to be observed, between the vehement or contentious and the derisive, consists in the manner of conducting them. As in each there is a mixture of argument, this in the former ought, in appearance at least, to have the ascendant, but not in the latter. The attack of the declaimer is direct and open; argument therefore is his avowed aim. On the contrary, the passions which he excites, ought never to appear to the auditors as the effects of his intention and address, but both in him and them, as the native, the unavoidable consequences of the subject treated, and of that conviction which his reasoning produces in the understanding. Although, in fact, he intends to move his auditory, he only declares his purpose to convince them. To reverse this method, and profess an intention to work upon their passions, would be in effect to tell them that he meant to impose upon their understandings, and to bias them by his art, and consequently, would be to warn them to be on their guard against him. Nothing is better founded than the famous aphorism of rhetoricians, that the perfection of art consists in concealing art*. On

* Artis est celare artem,

the other hand, the assault of him who ridicules is from its very nature covert and oblique. What we profess to contemn, we scorn to confute. It is on this account that the reasoning in ridicule, if at all delicate, is always conveyed under a species of disguise. Nay, sometimes, which is more astonishing, the contempt itself seems to be dissembled, and the rallier assumes an air of arguing gravely in defence of that which he actually exposeth as ridiculous. Hence, undoubtedly, it proceeds, that a serious manner commonly adds energy to a joke. The fact, however, is, that in this case the very dissimulation is dissembled. He would not have you think him in earnest, though he affects the appearance of it; knowing that otherwise his end would be frustrated. He wants that you should perceive that he is dissembling, which no real dissembler ever wanted. It is, indeed, this circumstance alone, which distinguishes an ironical expression from a lie. Accordingly, through the thinness of the veil employed, he takes care that the sneer shall be discovered. You are quickly made to perceive his aim, by means of the strange arguments he produces, the absurd consequences he draws, the odd embarrasments, which in his personated character he is

involved

involved in, and the still odder methods he takes to disentangle himself. In this manner doctrines and practices are treated, when exposed by a continued run of irony, a way of refutation which bears a strong analogy to that species of demonstration termed by mathematicians, apagogical, as reducing the adversary to what is contradictory or impracticable. This method seems to have been first introduced into moral subjects, and employed with success, by the father of ancient wisdom, Socrates. As the attack of ridicule, whatever form it adopts, is always indirect, that of irony may be said to be reverted. It resembles the manner of fighting ascribed to the ancient Parthians, who were ever more formidable in flight than in onset; who looked towards one quarter, and fought towards the opposite; whose bodies moved in one direction, and their arrows in the contrary *.

It remains now to confirm and illustrate this branch of the theory, by suitable examples. And, not to encumber the reader with a needless multiplicity of excerptions, I shall first recur

---

* Miles sagittas et celerem fugam
Parthi—————perhorrescit. Hor.
Fidentemque fuga Parthum versisque sagittis. Virg.

to those already produced. The first, second, and fifth passages from Butler, the first from Pope, the first from Young, and the quotation from the Dispensary, though witty, have no ridicule in them. Their whole aim is to divert by the oddness of the imagery. This merits a careful and particular attention, as on the accuracy of our conceptions here, depends, in a great measure, our forming a just notion of the relation which ridicule bears to wit, and of the distinction that subsists between them. Let this, therefore, be carefully remembered, that where nothing reprehensible, or supposed to be reprehensible, either in conduct or in sentiment is, struck at, there is properly no satire, (or, as it is sometimes termed emphatically enough, pointed wit) and consequently no ridicule.

The example that first claims a particular notice here, is one from Young's Satires,

Health chiefly keeps an Atheist in the dark.

The wittiness of this passage was already illustrated, I shall now endeavour to shew the argument couched under it, both which together constitute the ridicule. 'Atheism is unreasonable.' Why? 'The Atheist neither founds his unbelief on 'reason, nor will attend to it. Was ever an
'Infidel

'Infidel in health convinced by reasoning; or
'did he ever in sickness need to be reasoned with
'on this subject? The truth then is, that the
'daring principles of the libertine are solely sup-
'ported by the vigour and healthiness of his
'constitution, which incline him to pleasure,
'thoughtlessness, and presumption; according-
'ly you find, that when this foundation is sub-
'verted, the whole fabric of Infidelity falls to
'pieces.' There is rarely, however, so much
of argument in ridicule as may be discovered
in this passage. Generally, as was observed already, it is but hinted in a single word or phrase, or appears to be glanced at occasionally, without any direct intention. Thus in the third quotation from Butler there is an oblique thrust at Homer, for his manner of recurring so often in poems of so great dignity, to such mean and trifling epithets. The fourth and the sixth satirize the particular fanatical practice, and fanatical opinion, to which they refer. To assign a preposterous motive to an action, or to produce an absurd argument for an opinion, is an innuendo, that no good motive or argument can be given*. The citations from the Rape of the Lock

* We have an excellent specimen of this sort of ridicule, in Montesquieu's Spirit of Laws, B. xv. C. 5. where the practice of

Lock are no otherwise to be considered as ridicule, than as a lively exhibition of some follies, either in disposition or in behaviour, is the strongest dissuasive from imitating them. In this way humour rarely fails to have some raillery in it, in like manner as the pathetic often persuades without argument, which, when obvious, is supplied by the judgment of the hearer †. The second example seems intended to disgrace the petty quaintness of a fop's manner, and the emptiness of his conversation, as being a huddle of oaths and nonsense. The third finely satirizes the value which the ladies too often put upon the merest trifles. To these I shall add one instance more from Hudibras, where it is said of priests and exorcists,

> Supplied with spiritual provision,
> And magazines of ammunition,
> With crosses, relics, crucifixes,
> Beads, pictures, rosaries, and pixes,
> The tools of working out salvation,
> By mere mechanic operation ‡.

---

of Europeans in enslaving the negroes, is ironically justified, in a manner which does honour to the author's humanity and love of justice, at the same time that it displays a happy talent in ridicule.

† Ridicule resulting from a simple, but humorous narration, is finely illustrated in the first ten or twelve provincial letters.

‡ Part III. Canto 1.

The

The reasoning here is sufficiently insinuated by the happy application of a few words, such as mechanic tools to the work of salvation, crosses, relics, beads, pictures, and other such trumpery, to spiritual provision. The justness of the representation of their practice, together with the manifest incongruity of the things, supply us at once with the wit and the argument. There is in this poem a great deal of ridicule; but the author's quarry is the frantic excesses of enthusiasm, and the base artifices of hypocrisy, he very rarely, as in the above passage, points to the idiot gew-gaws of superstition. I shall only add one instance from Pope, which has something peculiar in it,

> Then sighing thus, " And am I now threescore?
> " Ah why, ye gods! should two and two make four?"

This, though not in the narrative, but in the dramatic style, is more witty than humorous. The absurdity of the exclamation in the second line is too gross to be natural to any but a madman, and therefore hath not humour. Nevertheless, its resemblance to the common complaint of old age contained in the first, of which it may be called the analysis, renders it at once both an ingenious exhibition of such complaint

---

† Dunciad.

in its real import, and an argument of its folly. But notwithstanding this example, it holds in general, that when any thing nonsensical in principle is to be assailed by ridicule, the natural ally of reason is wit; when any extravagance or impropriety in conduct, humour seldom fails to be of the confederacy. It may be further observed, that the words *banter* and *raillery* are also used to signify ridicule of a certain form, applied, indeed, more commonly to practices than to opinions, and oftener to the little peculiarities of individuals, than to the distinguishing customs or usages of sects and parties. The only difference in meaning, as far as I have remarked, between the two terms, is that the first generally denotes a coarser, the second a finer sort of ridicule; the former prevails most among the lower classes of the people, the latter only among persons of breeding.

I shall conclude this chapter with observing, that though the gayer and more familiar eloquence now explained, may often properly, as was remarked before, be admitted into public orations on subjects of consequence, such, for instance, as are delivered in the senate or at the bar, and even sometimes, though more sparingly,

sparingly, on the bench; it is seldom or never of service in those which come from the pulpit. It is true, that an air of ridicule in disproving or dissuading, by rendering opinions or practices contemptible, hath occasionally been attempted with approbation, by preachers of great name. I can only say, that when this airy manner is employed, it requires to be managed with the greatest care and delicacy, that it may not degenerate into a strain but ill adapted to so serious an occupation. For the reverence of the place, the gravity of the function, the solemnity of worship, the severity of the precepts, and the importance of the motives of religion; above all, the awful presence of God, with a sense of which, the mind, when occupied in religious exercises, ought eminently to be impressed; all these seem utterly incompatible with the levity of ridicule. They render jesting impertinence, and laughter madness. Therefore, any thing in preaching which might provoke this emotion, would justly be deemed an unpardonable offence against both piety and decorum.

In the two preceding chapters I have considered the nature of oratory in general, its various forms, whether arising from difference in

the

the object, understanding, imagination, passion, will, or in the subject, eminent and severe, light and frivolous, with their respective ends and characters. Under these are included all the primary and characteristical qualities of whatever can pertinently find a place either in writing or in discourse, or can truly be termed fine in the one, or eloquent in the other.

CHAP. III.

The doctrine of the preceding chapter defended.

BEFORE I proceed to another topic, it will perhaps be thought proper to inquire how far the theory now laid down and explained, coincides with the doctrines on this article to be found in the writings of philosophers and critics. Not that I think such inquiries and discussions always necessary; on the contrary, I imagine, they often tend but to embarrass the reader, by distracting his attention to a multiplicity of objects, and so to darken and perplex a plain question. This is particularly the case on those points on which there hath been a variety of jarring sentiments. The simplest way and the most perspicuous, and generally that which

which best promotes the discovery of truth, is to give as distinct and methodical a delineation as possible of one's own ideas, together with the grounds on which they are founded, and to leave it to the doubtful reader (who thinks it worth the trouble) to compare the theory with the systems of other writers, and then to judge for himself. I am not, however, so tenacious of this method, as not to allow, that it may sometimes, with advantage, be departed from. This holds especially when the sentiments of an author are opposed by inveterate prejudices in the reader, arising from contrary opinions early imbibed, or from an excessive deference to venerable names and ancient authorities.

Section I.

Aristotle's account of the ridiculous *explained.*

Some, on a superficial view, may imagine, that the doctrine above expounded is opposed by no less authority than that of Aristotle. If it were, I should not think that equivalent to a demonstration of its falsity. But let us hear, Aristotle hath observed, that "the ridiculous im-
"plies something deformed, and consists in those
"smaller

" smaller faults, which are neither painful nor
" pernicious, but unbeseeming · thus a face ex-
" cites laughter wherein there is deformity and
" distortion without pain." For my part, nothing can appear more coincident than this, as far as it goes, with the principles which I have endeavoured to establish. The Stagyrite here speaks of ridicule, not of laughter in general, and not of every sort of ridicule, but solely of the ridiculous in manners, of which he hath in few words given a very apposite description. To take notice of any other laughable object, would have been foreign to his purpose. Laughter is not his theme, but comedy, and laughter only so far as comedy is concerned with it. Now the concern of comedy reaches no farther than that kind of ridicule which, as I said, relates to manners. The very words with which the above quotation is introduced, evince the truth of this. " Comedy," says he, " is, as
" we remarked, an imitation of things that are
" amiss, yet it does not level at every vice *."
He had remarked in the preceding chapter, that

---

* The whole passage runs thus, Ἡ δὲ κωμῳδία ἐστίν, ὥσπερ εἴπομεν, μίμησις φαυλοτέρων μέν, οὐ μέντοι κατὰ πᾶσαν κακίαν, ἀλλὰ τοῦ αἰσχροῦ ἐστι τὸ γελοῖον μόριον· τὸ γὰρ γελοῖόν ἐστιν ἁμάρτημά τι καὶ αἶσχος ἀνώδυνον καὶ οὐ φθαρτικόν· οἷον εὐθὺς τὸ γελοῖον πρόσωπον αἰσχρόν τι καὶ διεστραμμένον ἄνευ ὀδύνης. Poet. 5.

its means of correction are " not reproach, but
" ridicule †." Nor does the clause in the end
of the sentence, concerning a countenance which
raises laughter, in the least invalidate what I have
now affirmed; for it is plain, that this is suggested in the way of similitude, to illustrate what
he had advanced, and not as a particular instance of the position he had laid down. For
we can never suppose that he would have called
distorted features " a certain fault or slip ‡," and
still less that he would have specified this, as
what might be corrected by the art of the comedian. As an instance, therefore, it would have
confuted his definition, and shewn that his account of the object of laughter must be erroneous, since this emotion may be excited, as appears from the example produced by himself,
where there is nothing faulty or vicious in any
kind or degree. As an illustration it was extremely pertinent. It shewed that the ridiculous in manners (which was all that his definition regarded) was, as far as the different nature
of the things would permit, analogous to the
laughable in other subjects, and that it supposed
an incongruous combination, where there is

† Ου ψογοι αλλα το γιλοιον δραμαΐο ποιησας.   ‡ Ἁμαρτημα τι

nothing

nothing either calamitous or destructive. But that in other objects unconnected with either character or conduct, with either the body or the soul, there might not be images or exhibitions presented to the mind, which would naturally provoke laughter, the philosopher hath nowhere, as far as I know, so much as insinuated.

SECTION II.

Hobbes's account of laughter examined.

FROM the founder of the peripatetic school, let us descend to the philosopher of Malmesbury, who hath defined laughter "a sudden glory, aris-"ing from a sudden conception of some emi-"nency in ourselves, by comparison with the "infirmity of others, or with our own former-"ly *." This account is, I acknowledge, incompatible with that given in the preceding pages, and, in my judgment, results entirely from a view of the subject, which is in some respect partial, and in some respect false. It is in some respect partial. When laughter is produced by ridicule, it is, doubtless, accompanied

* Human Nature, Chap. IX. § 13.

with some degree of contempt. Ridicule, as hath been observed already, has a double operation, first on the fancy, by presenting to it such a group as constitutes a laughable object; secondly, on the passion mentioned, by exhibiting absurdity in human character, in principles or in conduct: and contempt always implies a sense of superiority. No wonder then that one likes not to be ridiculed or laughed at. Now it is this union which is the great source of this author's error, and of his attributing to one of the associated principles, from an imperfect view of the subject, what is purely the effect of the other.

For, that the emotion called laughter, doth not result from the contempt, but solely from the perception of oddity with which the passion is occasionally, not necessarily, combined, is manifest from the following considerations. First, contempt may be raised in a very high degree, both suddenly and unexpectedly, without producing the least tendency to laugh. Of this instances have been given already from Bolingbroke and Swift, and innumerable others will occur to those who are conversant in the writings of those authors. Secondly, laughter may be,

be, and is daily produced by the perception of incongruous affociation, when there is no contempt. And this fhews that Hobbes's view of the matter is falfe as well as partial. " Men," fays he, " laugh at jefts, the wit whereof always con-
" fifteth in the elegant difcovering and convey-
" ing to our minds, fome abfurdity of ano-
" ther*." I maintain, that men alfo laugh at jefts, the wit whereof doth not confift in difcovering any abfurdity of another, for all jefts do not come within his defcription. On a careful perufal of the foregoing fheets, the reader will find that there hath been feveral inftances of this kind produced already, in which it hath been obferved, that there is wit, but no ridicule. I fhall bring but one other inftance. Many have laughed at the queernefs of the comparifon in thefe lines,

> For rhime the rudder is of verfes,
> With which, like fhips, they fteer their courfes†;

who never dreamt that there was any perfon or party, practice or opinion, derided in them. But as people are often very ingenious in their manner of defending a favourite hypothefis, if any admirer of the Hobbefian philofophy fhould pretend to difcover fome clafs of men whom

---

* Ibid.   † Hudibras, Part I. Canto 1.

the

the poet here meant to ridicule, he ought to consider, that if any one hath been tickled with the passage to whom the same thought never occurred, that single instance would be sufficient to subvert the doctrine, as it would shew that there may be laughter, where there is no triumph or glorying over any body, and consequently no conceit of one's own superiority. So that there may be, and often is, both contempt without laughter, and laughter without contempt.

Besides, where wit is really pointed, which constitutes ridicule, that it is not from what gives the conceit of our own eminence by comparison, but purely from the odd assemblage of ideas, that the laughter springs, is evident from this, that if you make but a trifling alteration on the expression, so as to destroy the wit (which often turns on a very little circumstance), without altering the real import of the sentence, (a thing not only possible but easy) you will produce the same opinion, and the same contempt; and consequently will give the same subject of triumph, yet without the least tendency to laugh: and conversely, in reading a well-written satire, a man may be much diverted by the wit,

wit, whose judgment is not convinced by the ridicule or insinuated argument, and whose former esteem of the object is not in the least impaired. Indeed, men's telling their own blunders, even blunders recently committed, and laughing at them, a thing not uncommon in very risible dispositions, is utterly inexplicable on Hobbes's system. For, to consider the thing only with regard to the laugher himself, there is to him no subject of glorying, that is not counterbalanced by an equal subject of humiliation, (he being both the person laughing, and the person laughed at) and these two subjects must destroy one another. With regard to others, he appears solely under the notion of inferiority, as the person triumphed over. Indeed, as in ridicule, agreeably to the doctrine here propounded, there is always some degree, often but a very slight degree of contempt; it is not every character, I acknowledge, that is fond of presenting to others such subjects of mirth. Wherever one shews a proneness to it, it is demonstrable that on that person sociality and the love of laughter have much greater influence, than vanity or self-conceit: since, for the sake of sharing with others in the joyous entertainment, he can submit to the mortifying circumstance

stance of being the subject. This, however, is in effect no more than enjoying the sweet which predominates, notwithstanding a little of the bitter with which it is mingled. The laugh in this case is so far from being expressive of the passion, that it is produced in spite of the passion, which operates against it, and if strong enough, would effectually restrain it.

But it is impossible that there could be any enjoyment to him on the other hypothesis, which makes the laughter merely the expression of a triumph, occasioned by the sudden display of one's own comparative excellence, a triumph in which the person derided could not partake. In this case, on the contrary, he must undoubtedly sustain the part of the weeper, (according to the account which the same author hath given of that opposite passion*, as he calls it) and " sudden'y fall out with himself, on the sudden " conception of defect." To suppose that a person in laughing enjoys the contempt of himself as a matter of exultation over his own infirmity, is of a piece with Cowley's description of envy exaggerated to absurdity, wherein she is said

---

* Hobbes's Hum. Nat. Chap. ix. § 14.

To envy at the praise herself had won †.

In the same way, a miser may be said to grudge the money that himself hath got, or a glutton the repasts; for the lust of praise as much terminates in self, as avarice or gluttony. It is a strange sort of theory which makes the frustration of a passion, and the gratification, the same thing.

As to the remark, that wit is not the only cause of this emotion, that men laugh at indecencies and mischances, nothing is more certain. A well-dressed man falling into the kennel, will raise in the spectators a peal of laughter. But this confirms, instead of weakening, the doctrine here laid down. The genuine object is always things grouped together, in which there is some striking unsuitableness. The effect is much the same, whether the things themselves are presented to the senses by external accident, or the ideas of them are presented to the imagination by wit and humour, though it is only with the latter that the subject of eloquence is concerned.

---

† Davideis, Book I.

In regard to Hobbes's system, I shall only remark further, that, according to it, a very risible man, and a very self-conceited supercilious man, should imply the same character, yet, in fact, perhaps no two characters more rarely meet in the same person. Pride, and contempt, its usual attendant, considered in themselves, are unpleasant passions, and tend to make men fastidious, always finding ground to be dissatisfied with their situation and their company. Accordingly, those who are most addicted to these passions, are not generally the happiest of mortals. It is only when the last of these hath gotten for an alloy, a considerable share of sensibility in regard to wit and humour, which serves both to moderate and to sweeten the passion, that it can be termed in any degree sociable or agreeable. It hath been often remarked of very proud persons, that they disdain to laugh, as thinking that it derogates from their dignity, and levels them too much with the common herd. The merriest people, on the contrary, are the least suspected of being haughty and contemptuous people. The company of the former is generally as much courted as that of the latter is shunned. To refer ourselves to such universal observations, is to appeal to the common sense of mankind. How admirably is the height of pride and arrogance touched in the character which Cæsar gives of Cassius!

> ——— He loves no plays
> As thou doft, Antony; he hears no music,
> Seldom he smiles, and smiles in such a sort,
> As if he mock'd himself, and scorn'd his spirit,
> That could be mov'd to smile at any thing [*].

I should not have been so particular in the refutation of the English philosopher's system in regard to laughter, had I not considered a careful discussion of this question, as one of the best means of developing some of the radical principles of this inquiry.

CHAP. IV.

Of the relation which eloquence bears to logic and to grammar.

IN contemplating a human creature, the most natural division of the subject is the common division into soul and body, or into the living principle of perception and of action, and that system of material organs, by which the other

---
[*] Shakespeare's Julius Cæsar.

receives information from without, and is enabled to exert its powers, both for its own benefit and for that of the species. Analogous to this, there are two things in every discourse which principally claim our attention, the sense and the expression, or in other words, the thought, and the symbol by which it is communicated. These may be said to constitute the soul and the body of an oration, or indeed, of whatever is signified to another by language. For, as in man, each of these constituent parts hath its distinctive attributes, and as the perfection of the latter consisteth in its fitness for serving the purposes of the former, so it is precisely with those two essential parts of every speech, the sense and the expression. Now it is by the sense that rhetoric holds of logic, and by the expression that she holds of grammar.

The sole and ultimate end of logic, is the eviction of truth, one important end of eloquence; though, as appears from the first chapter, neither the sole, nor always the ultimate, is the conviction of the hearers. Pure logic regards only the subject, which is examined solely for the sake of information. Truth, as such, is the proper aim of the examiner. Eloquence not only confiders the fubject, but alfo the fpeaker and the hearers, and both the fubject and the fpeaker for the fake of the hearers, or rather for the fake of the effect intended to be produced in them. Now to convince the hearers, is always either propofed by the orator as his end in addreffing them, or fuppofed to accompany the accomplifhment of his end. Of the five forts of difcourfes above mentioned, there are only two wherein conviction is the avowed purpofe. One is that addreffed to the underftanding, in which the fpeaker propofeth to prove fome pofition difbelieved or doubted by the hearers; the other is that which is calculated to influence the will, and perfuade to a certain conduct, for it is by convincing the judgment, that he propofeth to intereft the paffions, and fix the refolution. As to the three other kinds of difcourfes enumerated, which addrefs the underftanding, the imagination, and the paffions, conviction, though not the end, ought ever to accompany the accomplifhment of the end. It is never formally propofed as an end where there are not fuppofed to be previous doubts or errors to conquer. But when due attention is not paid to it, by a proper management of the fubject, doubts, difbelief, and miftake will be raifed by the discourse itself, where there were none before, and these will not fail to obstruct the speaker's end, whatever it be. In explanatory discourses, which are of all kinds the simplest, there is a certain precision of manner which ought to pervade the whole, and which, though not in the form of argument, is not the less satisfactory, since it carries internal evidence along with it. In harangues pathetic or panegyrical, in order that the hearers may be moved or pleased, it is of great consequence to impress them with the belief of the reality of the subject. Nay, even in those performances where truth, in regard to the individual facts related, is neither sought nor expected, as in some sorts of poetry, and in romance, truth still is an object to the mind, the general truths regarding character, manners, and incidents. When these are preserved, the piece may justly be denominated true, considered as a picture of life; though false, considered as a narrative of particular events. And even these untrue events must be counterfeits of truth, and bear its image, for in cases wherein the proposed end can be rendered consistent with unbelief, it cannot be rendered compatible with incredibility. Thus, in order to satisfy the mind, in most cases, truth, and in every case, what bears the semblance of truth, must be presented to it. This holds equally, whatever be the declared aim of the speaker. I need scarcely add, that to prove a particular point, is often occasionally necessary in every sort of discourse, as a subordinate end conducive to the advancement of the principal. If then it is the business of logic to evince the truth, to convince an auditory, which is the province of eloquence, is but a particular application of the logician's art. As logic therefore forges the arms which eloquence teacheth us to wield, we must first have recourse to the former, that being made acquainted with the materials of which her weapons and armour are severally made, we may know their respective strength and temper, and when and how each is to be used.

Now, if it be by the sense or soul of the discourse that rhetoric holds of logic, or the art of thinking and reasoning, it is by the expression or body of the discourse, that she holds of grammar, or the art of conveying our thoughts, in the words of a particular language. The observation of one analogy naturally suggests another. As the soul is of heavenly extraction, and the body of earthly, so the sense of the discourse ought to have its source in the invariable nature of truth and right; whereas the expression can derive its energy only from the arbitrary conventions of men, sources as unlike, or rather as widely different, as the breath of the Almighty and the dust of the earth. In every region of the globe, we may soon discover, that people feel and argue in much the same manner, but the speech of one nation is quite unintelligible to another. The art of the logician is accordingly, in some sense, universal, the art of the grammarian is always particular and local. The rules of argumentation laid down by Aristotle, in his Analytics, are of as much use for the discovery of truth in Britain or in China, as they were in Greece; but Priscian's rules of inflection and construction, can assist us in learning no language but Latin. In propriety there cannot be such a thing as an universal grammar, unless there were such a thing as an universal language. The term hath sometimes, indeed, been applied to a collection of observations on the similar analogies that have been discovered in all tongues, ancient and modern, known to the authors of such collections. I do not mention this liberty in the use of the term with a view to censure it. In the application

cation of technical or learned words, an author hath greater scope, than in the application of those which are in more frequent use, and is only then thought censurable, when he exposeth himself to be misunderstood. But it is to my purpose to observe, that as such collections convey the knowledge of no tongue whatever, the name *grammar*, when applied to them, is used in a sense quite different from that which it has in the common acceptation; perhaps as different, though the subject be language, as when it is applied to a system of geography.

Now the grammatical art hath its completion in syntax; the oratorical, as far as the body or expression is concerned, in style. Syntax regards only the composition of many words into one sentence; style, at the same time that it attends to this, regards further, the composition of many sentences into one discourse. Nor is this the only difference, the grammarian, with respect to what the two arts have in common, the structure of sentences, requires only purity; that is, that the words employed belong to the language, and that they be construed in the manner, and used in the signification, which custom hath rendered necessary for conveying the sense.

The orator requires also beauty and strength. The highest aim of the former, is the lowest aim of the latter: where grammar ends, eloquence begins.

Thus the grammarian's department bears much the same relation to the orator's, which the art of the mason bears to that of the architect. There is, however, one difference, that well deserves our notice. As in architecture it is not necessary that he who designs, should execute his own plans, he may be an excellent artist in this way, who would handle very awkwardly the hammer and the trowel. But it is alike incumbent on the orator, to design and to execute. He must therefore be master of the language he speaks or writes, and must be capable of adding to grammatic purity, those higher qualities of elocution, which will render his discourse graceful and energetic.

So much for the connexion that subsists between rhetoric and these parent arts, logic and grammar.

CHAP.

CHAP. V.

Of the different sources of Evidence, and the different subjects to which they are respectively adapted.

LOGICAL truth consisteth in the conformity of our conceptions to their archetypes in the nature of things. This conformity is perceived by the mind, either immediately on a bare attention to the ideas under review, or mediately by a comparison of these with other related ideas. Evidence of the former kind is called intuitive; of the latter, deductive.

SECTION I.

Of Intuitive Evidence.

PART I. *Mathematical axioms.*

OF intuitive evidence there are different sorts. One is that which results purely from *intellection**. Of this kind is the evidence of these propositions,

---

* I have here adopted the term *intellection* rather than *perception*, because, though not so usual, it is both more apposite, and less equivocal. *Perception* is employed alike to denote every immediate object of thought, or whatever is apprehended by the mind, our sensations themselves, and those qualities in body, suggested by our sensations, the ideas of these upon reflection,

whether

positions, 'One and four make five Things equal to the same thing, are equal to one another. The whole is greater than a part,' and in brief, all axioms in arithmetic and geometry. These are in effect but so many different expositions of our own general notions, taken in different views. Some of them are no other than definitions, or equivalent to definitions To say, 'One and four make *five*,' is precisely the same as to say, 'We give the name *five* to one added to four.' In fact, they are all, in some respect, reducible to this axiom, 'Whatever is, is.' I do not say, they are deduced from it, for they have in like manner that original and intrinsic evidence, which makes them, as soon as the terms are understood, to be perceived intuitively. And if they are not thus perceived, no deduction of reason will ever confer on them any additional evidence. Nay, in point of time, the discovery of the less general truths has the priority, not from their superior evidence, but solely from

---

whether remembered or imagined, together with those called general notions, or abstract ideas. It is only the last of these kinds which are considered as peculiarly the object of the understanding, and which, therefore, require to be distinguished by a peculiar name. Obscurity arising from an uncommon word, is easily surmounted, whereas ambiguity, by misleading us, ere we are aware, confounds our notion of the subject altogether.

this confideration, that the lefs general are fooner objects of perception to us, the natural progrefs of the mind in the acquifition of its ideas, being from particular things to univerfal notions, and not inverfely. But I affirm, that, though not deduced from that axiom, they may be confidered as particular exemplifications of it, and coincident with it, inafmuch as they are all implied in this, that the properties of our clear and adequate ideas can be no other than what the mind clearly perceives them to be.

But, in order to prevent miftakes, it will be neceffary further to illuftrate this fubject. It might be thought, that if axioms were propofitions perfectly identical, it would be impoffible to advance a ftep, by their means, beyond the fimple ideas firft perceived by the mind. And it muft be owned, if the predicate of the propofition were nothing but a repetition of the fubject, under the fame afpect, and in the fame or fynonymous terms, no conceivable advantage could be made of it for the furtherance of knowledge. Of fuch propofitions as thefe, for inftance, 'Seven are feven,' 'eight are eight,' and ' ten added to eleven, are equal to ten added ' to eleven,' it is manifeft, that we could never

avail

avail ourselves for the improvement of science. Nor does the change of the term make any alteration in point of utility. The propositions 'Twelve are a dozen,' 'twenty are a score,' unless considered as explications of the words *dozen* and *score*, are equally insignificant with the former. But when the thing, though in effect coinciding, is considered under a different aspect; when what is single in the subject, is divided in the predicate, and conversely; or when what is a whole in the one, is regarded as a part of something else in the other; such propositions lead to the discovery of innumerable, and apparently remote relations. One added to four may be accounted no other than a definition of the word *five*, as was remarked above. But when I say, ' Two added to three are equal to ' five,' I advance a truth, which, though equally clear, is quite distinct from the preceding. Thus, if one should affirm, ' Twice fifteen make ' thirty,' and again, ' Thirteen added to seven-' teen make thirty,' no body would pretend that he had repeated the same proposition in other words. The cases are entirely similar. In both, the same thing is predicated of ideas which, taken severally, are different. From these again result other equations, as, ' One added to four

' are

'are equal to two added to three,' and 'twice fif-
'teen are equal to thirteen added to seventeen.'

Now it is by the aid of such simple and elementary principles, that the arithmetician and the algebraist proceed to the most astonishing discoveries. Nor are the operations of the geometrician essentially different. By a very few steps you are made to perceive the equality, or rather the coincidence of the sum of the two angles, formed by one straight line falling on another, with two right angles. By a process equally plain, you are brought to discover, first, that if one side of a triangle be produced, the external angle will be equal to both the internal and opposite angles, and then, that all the angles of a triangle are equal to two right angles. So much for the nature and use of the first kind of intuitive evidence, resulting from pure intellection.

PART II, *Consciousness.*

THE next kind is that which ariseth from *consciousness.* Hence every man derives the perfect assurance that he hath of his own existence. Nor is he only in this way assured that he exists, but that he thinks, that he feels, that he sees, that

he

he hears, and the like. Hence his absolute certainty in regard to the reality of his sensations and passions, and of every thing whose essence consists in being perceived. Nor does this kind of intuition regard only the truth of the original feelings or impressions, but also many of the judgments that are formed by the mind, on comparing these one with another. Thus the judgments we daily and hourly form, concerning resemblances or disparities in visible objects, or size in things tangible, where the odds is considerable, darker or lighter tints in colours, stronger or weaker tastes or smells, are all self-evident, and discoverable at once. It is from the same principle, that in regard to ourselves we judge infallibly concerning the feelings, whether pleasant or painful, which we derive from what are called the internal senses, and pronounce concerning beauty or deformity, harmony or discord, the elegant or the ridiculous. The difference between this kind of intuition and the former, will appear on the slightest reflection. The former concerns only abstract notions or ideas, particularly in regard to number and extension, the objects purely of the understanding, the latter concerns only the existence of the mind itself, and its actual feelings,

ings, impressions or affections, pleasures or pains, the immediate subjects of sense, taking that word in the largest acceptation. The former gives rise to those universal truths, first principles or axioms, which serve as the foundation of abstract science; whereas the latter, though absolutely essential to the individual, yet, as it only regards particular perceptions, which represent no distinct genus or species of objects, the judgments resulting thence cannot form any general positions to which a chain of reasoning may be fastened, and consequently are not of the nature of axioms, though both similar and equal in respect of evidence.

PART III. *Common sense.*

THE third sort is that which ariseth from what hath been termed properly enough, *common sense* †, as being an original source of knowledge

† The first among the moderns who took notice of this principle as one of the genuine springs of our knowledge, was Buffier, a French philosopher of the present century, in a book intitled *Traité des premiéres véritez*, one who, to an uncommon degree of acuteness in matters of abstraction, added that solidity of judgment which hath prevented in him, what had proved the wreck of many great names in philosophy, his understanding becoming the dupe of his ingenuity. This doctrine hath lately, in our own country, been set in the clearest light, and

supported

ledge common to all mankind. I own, indeed, that in different persons it prevails in different degrees supported by invincible force of argument, by two very able writers in the science of man, Dr. Reid in his *Inquiry into the human mind*, and Dr. Beattie in his *Essay on the immutability of truth*. I beg leave to remark in this place, that, though for distinction's sake, I use the term *common sense* in a more limited signification than either of the authors last mentioned, there appears to be no real difference in our sentiments of the thing itself. I am not ignorant that this doctrine has been lately attacked by Dr. Priestley in a most extraordinary manner, a manner which no man who has any regard to the name either of Englishman, or of philosopher, will ever desire to see imitated, in this or any other country. I have read the performance, but have not been able to discover the author's sentiments in relation to the principal point in dispute. He says expressly, [Examination of Dr. Reid's Inquiry, &c p. 119.] " Had these writers," Messieurs Reid, Beattie, and Oswald, " assumed, as the elements " of their common sense, certain truths which are so plain, that " no man could doubt of them, (without entering into the " ground of our assent to them) their conduct would have been " liable to very little objection.' And is not this the very thing which these writers have done? What he means to signify by the parenthesis, " (without entering into the ground of " our assent to them)" it is not easy to guess. By a ground of assent to any proposition, is commonly understood, a reason or argument in support of it. Now, by his own hypothesis, there are truths so plain, that no man can doubt of them. If so, what ground of assent beyond their own plainness ought we to seek, what besides this can we ever hope to find, or what better reason needs be given for denominating such truths, the dictates of common sense? If something plainer could be found to serve as evidence of any of them, then this plainer truth would be admitted as the first principle, and the other would be considered as deduced by reasoning. But notwithstanding the

degrees of strength, but no human creature hath been found originally and totally destitute of it,

who

the mistake in the instance, the general doctrine of primary truths would remain unhurt. It seems, however, that though their conduct would have been liable to very little, it would have been liable to some objection. "All that could have been "said would have been, that, without any necessity, they had "made an innovation in the received use of a term." I have a better opinion of these gentlemen than to imagine, that if the thing which they contend for, be admitted, they will enter into a dispute with any person about the name; though, in my judgment, even as to this, it is not they but he who is the innovator. He proceeds, "For no person ever denied, "that there are self-evident truths, and that these must be af- "sumed, as the foundation of all our reasoning. I never met "with any person, who did not acknowledge this, or heard of "any argumentative treatise that did not go upon the suppofi- "tion of it." Now, if this be the case, I would gladly know, what is the great point he controverts. Is it, whether such self-evident truths shall be denominated principles of common sense, or be distinguished by some other appellation? Was it worth any man's while to write an octavo of near 400 pages for the discussion of such a question as this? And if, as he assures us, they have said more than is necessary, in proof of a truth which he himself thinks indisputable, was it no more than necessary in Dr. Priestley, to compose so large a volume in order to convince the world, that too much had been said already on the subject? I do not enter into the examination of his objections, to some of the particular principles produced as primary truths. An attempt of this kind would be foreign to my purpose; besides that the authors he has attacked, are better qualified for defending their own doctrine, and, no doubt, will do it, if they think there is occasion. I shall only subjoin two remarks on this book. The first is, that the author, through

the

who is not accounted a monster in his kind; for such, doubtless, are all idiots and changelings.

the whole, confounds two things totally distinct, certain associations of ideas, and certain judgments implying belief, which, though in some, are not in all, cases, and therefore not necessarily connected with association. And if so, merely to account for the association, is in no case to account for the belief with which it is attended. Nay, admitting his plea, [page 86] that by the principle of association, not only the ideas, but the concomitant belief may be accounted for, even this does not invalidate the doctrine he impugns. For, let it be observed, that it is one thing to assign a cause which, from the mechanism of our nature, has given rise to a particular tenet of belief, and another thing to produce a reason by which the understanding has been convinced. Now, unless this be done as to the principles in question, they must be considered as primary truths in respect of the understanding, which never deduced them from other truths, and which is under a necessity in all her moral reasonings, of founding upon them. In fact, to give any other account of our conviction of them, is to confirm, instead of confuting the doctrine, that in all argumentation they must be regarded as primary truths, or truths which reason never inferred through any medium, from other truths previously perceived. My second remark is, that though this examiner has, from Dr. Reid, given us a catalogue of first principles, which he deems unworthy of the honourable place assigned them, he has no where thought proper to give us a list of those self-evident truths which, by his own account, and in his own express words, "must be assumed as the foundation of " all our reasoning." How much light might have been thrown upon the subject by the contrast? Perhaps we should have been enabled, on the comparison, to discover some distinctive characters in his genuine axioms, which would have preserved us from the danger of confounding them with their spurious ones.

Nothing

lings. By madness, a disease which makes terrible havoc on the faculties of the mind, it may be in a great measure, but is never entirely lost.

It is purely hence that we derive our assurance of such truths as these ' Whatever has a begin-
' ning has a cause. When there is in the effect,
' a manifest adjustment of the several parts to a
' certain end, there is intelligence in the cause.
' The course of nature will be the same to-mor-
' row, that it is to-day, or, the future will re-
' semble the past. There is such a thing as body;
' or, there are material substances independent of
' the mind's conceptions. There are other in-
' telligent beings in the universe beside me. The
' clear representations of my memory in regard
' to past events, are indubitably true' These, and a great many more of the same kind it is impossible for any man by reasoning to evince, as might easily be shewn, were this a proper place

Nothing is more evident than that, in whatever regards matter of fact, the mathematical axioms will not answer. These are purely fitted for evolving the abstract relations of quantity. This he in effect owns himself [page 39]. It would have been obliging then, and would have greatly contributed to shorten the controversy, if he had given us, at least, a specimen of those self-evident principles, which, in his estimation, are the *non plus ultra* of moral reasoning.

for the discussion. And it is equally impossible, without a full conviction of them, to advance a single step in the acquisition of knowledge, especially in all that regards mankind, life, and conduct.

I AM sensible, that some of these, to men not accustomed to inquiries of this kind, will appear at first not to be primary principles, but conclusions from other principles; and some of them will be thought to coincide with the other kinds of intuition above mentioned. Thus the first, ' Whatever hath a beginning hath a cause,' may be thought to stand on the same footing with mathematical axioms. I acknowledge, that in point of evidence they are equal, and it is alike impossible in either case, for a rational creature to with-hold his assent. Nevertheless, there is a difference in kind. All the axioms in mathematics are but the enunciations of certain properties in our abstract notions, distinctly perceived by the mind, but have no relation to any thing without themselves, and can never be made the foundation of any conclusion concerning actual existence: whereas, in the axiom last specified, from the existence of one thing we intuitively conclude the existence of another.

This

This proposition, however, so far differs, in my apprehension, from others of the same order, that I cannot avoid considering the opposite assertion as not only false, but contradictory, but I do not pretend to explain the ground of this difference.

The faith we give to memory may be thought, on a superficial view, to be resolvable into consciousness, as well as that we give to the immediate impressions of sense. But on a little attention one may easily perceive the difference. To believe the report of our senses doth, indeed, commonly imply, to believe the existence of certain external and corporeal objects, which give rise to our particular sensations. This, I acknowledge, is a principle which doth not spring from consciousness, (for consciousness cannot extend beyond sensation) but from common sense, as well as the assurance we have in the report of memory. But this was not intended to be included under the second branch of intuitive evidence. By that firm belief in sense, which I there resolved into consciousness, I meant no more than to say, I am certain that I see, and feel, and think, what I actually see, and feel, and think. As in this I pronounce only concerning my own present feelings, whose essence consists in being felt, and of which I am at present conscious, my conviction is reducible to this axiom, or coincident with it, 'It is impossible for a thing to be and not to be at the same time.' Now when I say, I trust entirely to the clear report of my memory, I mean a good deal more than, 'I am certain that my memory gives such a report, or represents things in such a manner,' for this conviction I have indeed from consciousness, but I mean, 'I am certain that things happened heretofore at such a time, in the precise manner in which I now remember that they then happened.' Thus there is a reference in the ideas of memory to former sensible impressions, to which there is nothing analogous in sensation. At the same time, it is evident, that remembrance is not always accompanied with this full conviction. To describe, in words, the difference between those lively signatures of memory, which command an unlimited assent, and those fainter traces which raise opinion only, or even doubt, is perhaps impracticable; but no man stands in need of such assistance to enable him in fact to distinguish them, for the direction of his own judgment and conduct. Some may imagine,

that

that it is from experience we come to know what faith in every case is due to memory. But it will appear more fully afterwards, that unless we had implicitly relied on the distinct and vivid informations of that faculty, we could not have moved a step towards the acquisition of experience. It must, however, be admitted, that experience is of use in assisting us to judge concerning the more languid and confused suggestions of memory; or, to speak more properly, concerning the reality of those things, of which we ourselves are doubtful, whether we remember them or not.

In regard to the primary truths of this order, it may be urged, that it cannot be affirmed of them all at least, as it may of the axioms in mathematics, or the assurances we have from consciousness, that the denial of them implies a manifest contradiction. It is, perhaps, physically possible, that the course of nature will be inverted the very next moment, that my memory is no other than a delirium, and my life a dream; that all is mere illusion; that I am the only being in the universe, and that there is no such thing as body. Nothing can be juster than the reply given by Buffier, " It must be owned,"

says he*, " that to maintain propositions, the re-
" verse of the primary truths of common sense,
" doth not imply a contradiction, it only im-
" plies insanity." But if any person, on account of this difference in the nature of these
two classes of axioms, should not think the term
intuitive so properly applied to the evidence of
the last mentioned, let him denominate it, if
he please, instinctive: I have no objection to
the term; nor do I think it derogates in the
least from the dignity, the certainty, or the importance of the truths themselves. Such instincts are no other than the oracles of eternal
wisdom.

For, let it be observed farther, that axioms
of this last kind are as essential to moral reasoning, to all deductions concerning life and existence, as those of the first kind are to the sciences of arithmetic and geometry. Perhaps it
will appear afterwards, that, without the aid of
some of them, these sciences themselves would
be utterly inaccessible to us. Besides, the mathematical axioms can never extend their influence beyond the precincts of abstract knowledge,
in regard to number and extension, or assist us

* Premiéres Véritez, Part I. Chap. 11.

in the discovery of any matter of fact; whereas, with knowledge of the latter kind, the whole conduct and business of human life is principally and intimately connected. All reasoning necessarily supposes that there are certain principles in which we must acquiesce, and beyond which we cannot go, principles clearly discernible by their own light, which can derive no additional evidence from any thing besides. On the contrary supposition, the investigation of truth would be an endless and a fruitless task; we should be eternally proving, whilst nothing could ever be proved, because, by the hypothesis, we could never ascend to premises which require no proof. "If there be no first truths," says the author lately quoted, "there can be no "second truths, nor third, nor indeed any "truth at all*."

So much for intuitive evidence, in the extensive meaning which hath here been given to that term, as including every thing whose evidence results from the simple contemplation of the ideas or perceptions which form the proposition under consideration, and requires not the intervention of any third idea as a medium of

* Ib. Dessein de l'ouvrage.

proof. This, for order's sake, I have distributed into three classes, the truths of pure intellection, of consciousness, and of common sense. The first may be denominated metaphysical, the second physical, the third moral; all of them natural, original, and unaccountable.

Section II.

Of deductive evidence.

Part I. *Division of the subject into scientific and moral, with the principal distinctions between them.*

All rational or deductive evidence is derived from one or other of these two sources: from the invariable properties or relations of general ideas, or from the actual, though perhaps, variable connexions, subsisting among things. The former we call demonstrative, the latter moral. Demonstration is built on pure intellection, and consisteth in an uninterrupted series of axioms. That propositions formerly demonstrated are taken into the series, doth not in the least invalidate this account; inasmuch as these propositions are all resolvable into axioms, and are admitted as links in the chain;

not

not because necessary, but merely to avoid the useless prolixity which frequent and tedious repetitions of proofs formerly given would occasion. Moral evidence is founded on the principles we have from consciousness and common sense, improved by experience; and as it proceeds on this general presumption or moral axiom, that the course of nature in time to come, will be similar to what it hath been hitherto, it decides, in regard to particulars, concerning the future from the past, and concerning things unknown, from things familiar to us. The first is solely conversant about number and extension, and about those other qualities which are measurable by these. Such are duration, velocity, and weight. With regard to such qualities as pleasure and pain, virtue and vice, wisdom and folly, beauty and deformity, though they admit degrees, yet, as there is no standard or common measure, by which their differences and proportions can be ascertained and expressed in numbers, they can never become the subject of demonstrative reasoning. Here rhetoric, it must be acknowledged, hath little to do. Simplicity of diction, and precision in arrangement, whence results perspicuity, are, as was observed already*,

---

* Chap. I. Part 1.

all

all the requisites. The proper province of rhetoric is the second, or moral evidence; for to the second belong all decisions concerning fact, and things without us.

But that the nature of moral evidence may be better understood, it will not be amiss to remark a few of the most eminent differences between this and the demonstrative.

The first difference that occurs is in their subjects. The subject of the one is, as hath been observed, abstract independent truth, or the unchangeable and necessary relations of ideas; that of the other, the real, but often changeable and contingent connexions that subsist among things actually existing. Abstract truths, as the properties of quantity, have no respect to time or to place, no dependence on the volition of any being, or on any cause whatever, but are eternally and immutably the same. The very reverse of all this generally obtains with regard to fact. In consequence of what has been now advanced, assertions opposite to truths of the former kind, are not only false, but absurd. They are not only not true, but it is impossible they should be true, whilst the meanings of the words (and consequently the ideas compared) remain the same. This doth not hold commonly

monly in any other kind of evidence. Take, for instance, of the first kind, the following affirmations, 'The cube of two is the half of sixteen.' 'The square of the hypotenuse is equal to the sum of the squares of the sides.' 'If equal things be taken from equal things, the remainders will be equal.' Contrary propositions, as, 'The cube of two is more than the half of sixteen.' 'The square of the hypotenuse is less than the sum of the squares of the sides.' 'If equal things be taken from equal things, the remainders will be unequal,' are chargeable, not only with falsity, but with absurdity, being inconceivable and contradictory. Whereas, to these truths which we acquire by moral evidence, 'Cæsar overcame Pompey.' 'The sun will rise to-morrow.' 'All men will die,' the opposite assertions, though untrue, are easily conceivable without changing, in the least, the import of the words, and therefore do not imply a contradiction.

THE second difference I shall remark is, that moral evidence admits degrees, demonstration doth not. This is a plain consequence of the preceding difference. Essential or necessary truth, the sole object of the latter, is incompatible with degree. And though actual truth, or matter of

fact,

fact, be the ultimate aim of the former, likelihood alone, which is susceptible of degree, is usually the utmost attainment. Whatever is exhibited as demonstration, is either mere illusion, and so no evidence at all, or absolutely perfect. There is no medium. In moral reasoning we ascend from possibility, by an insensible gradation, to probability, and thence, in the same manner, to the summit of moral certainty. On this summit, or on any of the steps leading to it, the conclusion of the argument may rest. Hence the result of that is, by way of eminence, denominated science, and the evidence itself is termed scientific; the result of this is frequently (not always) intitled to no higher denomination than opinion. Now, in the mathematical sciences, no mention is ever made of opinions.

The third difference is, that in the one there never can be any contrariety of proofs, in the other, there not only may be, but almost always is. If one demonstration were ever capable of being refuted, it could be solely by another demonstration, this being the only sort of evidence adapted to the subject, and the only sort by which the former could be matched. But, to suppose that contraries are demonstrable,

is

is to suppose that the same proposition is both true and false, which is a manifest contradiction. Consequently, if there should ever be the appearance of demonstration on opposite sides, that on one side must be fallacious and sophistical. It is not so with moral evidence, for unless in a few singular instances, there is always real, not apparent evidence on both sides. There are contrary experiences, contrary presumptions, contrary testimonies, to balance against one another. In this case, the probability, upon the whole, is in the proportion which the evidence on the side that preponderates bears to its opposite. We usually say, indeed, that the evidence lies on such a side of the question, and not on the reverse, but by this expression is only meant the overplus of evidence, on comparing both sides. In like manner, when we affirm of an event, that it is probable, we say the contrary is only possible, although, when they are severally considered, we do not scruple to say, This is more probable than that; or, The probabilities on one side, outweigh those on the other.

The fourth and last difference I shall observe is, that scientific evidence is simple, consisting of only one coherent series, every part of which depends on the preceding; and, as it were, suspends the following: moral evidence is generally complicated, being in reality a bundle of independent proofs. The longest demonstration is but one uniform chain, the links whereof, taken severally, are not to be regarded as so many arguments, and consequently, when thus taken, they conclude nothing, but taken together, and in their proper order, they form one argument, which is perfectly conclusive. It is true, the same theorem may be demonstrable in different ways, and by different mediums; but as a single demonstration clearly understood, commands the fullest conviction, every other is superfluous. After one demonstrative proof, a man may try a second, purely as an exercise of ingenuity, or the better to assure himself that he hath not committed an oversight in the first. Thus it may serve to warrant the regular procedure of his faculties, but not to make an addition to the former proof, or supply any deficiency perceived in it. So far is it from answering this end, that he is no sooner sensible of a defect in an attempt of this nature, than the whole is rejected as good for nothing, and carrying with it no degree of evidence whatever.

In moral reasoning, on the contrary, there is often a combination of many distinct topics of argument, noway dependent on one another. Each hath a certain portion of evidence belonging to itself, each bestows on the conclusion a particular degree of likelihood, of all which accumulated, the credibility of the fact is compounded. The former may be compared to an arch, no part of which can subsist independently of the rest. If you make any breach in it, you destroy the whole. The latter may be compared to a tower, the height whereof is but the aggregate of the heights of the several parts reared above one another, and so may be gradually diminished, as it was gradually raised.

So much for the respective natures of scientific and of moral evidence, and those characteristical qualities which discriminate them from each other. On a survey of the whole, it seems indubitable, that if the former is infinitely superior in point of authority, the latter no less excells in point of importance. Abstract truth, as far as it is the object of our faculties, is almost entirely confined to quantity, concrete or discrete. The sphere of Demonstration is narrow, but within her sphere she is a despotic sovereign,

vereign, her sway is uncontroulable. Her rival, on the contrary, hath less power, but wider empire. Her forces, indeed, are not always irresistible; but the whole world is comprised in her dominions. Reality or fact comprehends the laws and the works of nature, as well as the arts and the institutions of men; in brief, all the beings which fall under the cognizance of the human mind, with all their modifications, operations, and effects. By the first, we must acknowledge, when applied to things, and combined with the discoveries of the second, our researches into nature in a certain line are facilitated, the understanding is enlightened, and many of the arts, both elegant and useful, are improved and perfected. Without the aid of the second, society must not only suffer, but perish. Human nature itself could not subsist. This organ of knowledge, which extends its influence to every precinct of philosophy, and governs in most, serves also to regulate all the ordinary, but indispensable concernments of life. To these it is admirably adapted, notwithstanding its inferiority in respect of dignity, accuracy, and perspicuity. For it is principally to the acquisitions procured by experience, that we owe the use of language, and the knowledge of almost every

every thing that makes the soul of a man differ from that of a new-born infant. On the other hand, there is no despot so absolute, as not to be liable to a check on some side or other, and that the prerogatives of demonstration are not so very considerable, as on a cursory view one is apt to imagine; that this, as well as every other operation of the intellect, must partake in the weakness incident to all our mental faculties, and inseparable from our nature, I shall afterwards take an opportunity particularly to evince.

PART II. *The nature and origin of Experience.*

I SHOULD now consider the principal tribes comprehended under the general name of moral evidence; but, that every difficulty may be removed, which might retard our progress in the proposed discussion, it will be necessary, in the first place, to explore more accurately those sources in our nature, which give being to experience, and consequently to all those attainments, moral and intellectual, that are derived from it. These sources are two, sense and memory. The senses, both external and internal, are the original inlets of perception. They inform the mind of the facts which, in the present instant,

instant, are situated within the sphere of their activity, and no sooner discharge their office in any particular instance, than the articles of information exhibited by them, are devolved on the memory. Remembrance instantly succeeds sensation, insomuch that the memory becomes the sole repository of the knowledge received from sense; knowledge which, without this repository, would be as instantaneously lost as it is gotten, and could be of no service to the mind. Our sensations would be no better than the fleeting pictures of a moving object on a camera obscura, which leave not the least vestige behind them. Memory therefore is the only original voucher extant, of those past realities for which we had once the evidence of sense. Her ideas are, as it were, the prints that have been left by sensible impressions. But from these two faculties, considered in themselves, there results to us the knowledge only of individual facts, and only of such facts as either heretofore have come, or at present do come, under the notice of our senses.

Now, in order to render this knowledge useful to us, in discovering the nature of things, and in regulating our conduct, a further process of the mind is necessary, which deserves to be be carefully attended to, and may be thus illustrated. I have observed a stone fall to the ground when nothing intervened to impede its motion. This single fact produces little or no effect on the mind beyond a bare remembrance. At another time I observe the fall of a tile, at another of an apple, and so of almost every kind of body in the like situation. Thus my senses first, and then my memory, furnish me with numerous examples, which, though different in every other particular, are similar in this, that they present a body moving downwards till obstructed either by the ground or by some intervenient object. Hence my first notion of gravitation. For, with regard to the similar circumstances of different facts, as by the repetition such circumstances are more deeply imprinted, the mind acquires a habit of retaining them, omitting those circumstances peculiar to each, wherein their differences consist. Hence, if objects of any kind in a particular manner circumstanced, are remembered to have been usually, and still more, if uniformly, succeeded by certain particular consequences, the idea of the former in the supposed circumstance introduced into the mind, immediately associates the idea of the latter; and if the object itself so circumstanced, be presented to the senses, the mind instantly anticipates the appearance of the customary consequence. This holds also inversely. The retention and association above explained, are called Experience. The anticipation is in effect no other than a particular conclusion from that experience. Here we may remark, by the way, that though memory gives birth to experience, which results from the comparison of facts remembered, the experience or habitual association remains, when the individual facts on which it is founded are all forgotten. I know from an experience, which excludes all doubt, the power of fire in melting silver, and yet may not be able at present to recollect a particular instance in which I have seen this effect produced, or even in which I have had the fact attested by a credible witness.

Some will perhaps object, that the account now given makes our experimental reasoning look like a sort of mechanism necessarily resulting from the very constitution of the mind. I acknowledge the justness of the remark, but do not think that it ought to be regarded as an objection. It is plain that our reasoning in this way, if you please to call it so, is very early, and

and precedes all reflection on our faculties, and the manner of applying them. Those who attend to the progress of human nature through its different stages, and through childhood in particular, will observe, that children make great acquisitions in knowledge from experience, long before they attain the use of speech. The beasts also, in their sphere, improve by experience, which hath in them just the same foundations of sense and memory as in us, and hath, besides, a similar influence on their actions. It is precisely in the same manner, and with the same success, that you might train a dog, or accustom a child, to expect food on your calling to him in one tone of voice, and to dread your resentment, when you use another. The brutes have evidently the rudiments of this species of rationality, which extends as far in them as the immediate purposes of self-preservation require, and which, whether you call it reason or instinct, they both acquire and use in the same manner as we do. That it reaches no farther in them, seems to arise from an original incapacity of classing, and (if I may use the expression) generalising their perceptions; an exercise which to us very quickly becomes familiar, and is what chiefly fits us for the use of language. Indeed, in the extent of this capacity, as much perhaps as in any thing, lies also the principal natural superiority of one man over another.

But that we may be satisfied, that to this kind of reasoning, in its earliest and simplest form, little or no reflection is necessary, let it be observed, that it is now universally admitted by opticians, that it is not purely from sight, but from sight aided by experience, that we derive our notions of the distance of visible objects from the eye. The sensation, say they, is instantaneously followed by a conclusion or judgment founded on experience. The point is determined from the different phases of the object, found in former trials, to be connected with different distances, or from the effort that accompanies the different conformations we are obliged to give the organs of sight, in order to obtain a distinct vision of the object. Now if this be the case, as I think hath been sufficiently evinced of late, it is manifest, that this judgment is so truly instantaneous, and so perfectly the result of feeling and association, that the forming of it totally escapes our notice. Perhaps in no period of life will you find a person, that, on the first mention of it, can be easily persuaded, that he

derives

derives this knowledge from experience. Every man will be ready to tell you, that he needs no other witnesses than his eyes, to satisfy him that objects are not in contact with his body, but are at different distances from him as well as from one another. So passive is the mind in this matter, and so rapid are the transitions which, by this ideal attraction, she is impelled to make, that she is, in a manner, unconscious of her own operations. There is some ground to think, from the exact analogy which their organs bear to ours, that the discovery of distance from the eye, is attained by brutes in the same manner as by us. As to this, however, I will not be positive. But though, in this way, the mind acquires an early perception of the most obvious and necessary truths, without which the bodily organs would be of little use; in matters less important, her procedure is much slower, and more the result of voluntary application; and as the exertion is more deliberate, she is more conscious of her own activity, or at least remembers it longer. It is then only that in common style we honour her operation with the name of *reasoning*; though there is no essential difference between the two cases. It is true, indeed, that the conclusions in the first way, by which also in infancy we learn language, are commonly more to be regarded as infallible, than those effected in the second.

PART III. *The subdivisions of Moral Reasoning.*

BUT to return to the proposed distribution of moral evidence. Under it I include these three tribes, experience, analogy, and testimony. To these I shall subjoin the consideration of a fourth, totally distinct from them all, but which appears to be a mixture of the demonstrative and the moral, or rather, a particular application of the former, for ascertaining the precise force of the latter. The evidence I mean, is that resulting from calculations concerning chances.

I. *Experience.*

THE first of these I have named peculiarly the evidence of experience, not with philosophical propriety, but in compliance with common language, and for distinction's sake. Analogical reasoning is surely reasoning from a more indirect experience. Now, as to this first kind, our experience is either uniform or various. In the one case, provided the facts on which it is founded be sufficiently numerous, the conclusion is said to be morally certain. In the other, the conclusion built on the greater number of instances, is said to be probable, and more or less so, according to the proportion which the instances on that side bear to those on the opposite. Thus we are perfectly assured, that iron thrown into the river will sink, that deal will float; because these conclusions are built on a full and uniform experience. That, in the last week of December next, it will snow in any part of Britain specified, is perhaps probable, that is, if, on inquiry or recollection, we are satisfied that this hath more frequently happened than the contrary: that some time in that month it will snow, is more probable, but not certain; because, though this conclusion be founded on experience, that experience is not uniform: lastly, that it will snow some time during winter, will, I believe, on the same principles, be pronounced certain.

It was affirmed, that experience, or the tendency of the mind to associate ideas under the notion of causes, effects, or adjuncts, is never contracted by one example only. This assertion, it may be thought, is contradicted by the principle on which physiologists commonly proceed, who

who confider one accurate experiment in fupport of a particular doctrine as fufficient evidence. The better to explain this phænomenon, and the farther to illuftrate the nature of experience, I fhall make the following obfervations. Firft, whereas fenfe and memory are converfant only about individuals, our earlieft experiences imply, or perhaps generate, the notion of a fpecies, including all thofe individuals, which have the moft obvious and univerfal refemblance. From Charles, Thomas, William, we afcend to the idea of man, from Britain, France, Spain, to the idea of kingdom. As our acquaintance with nature enlarges, we difcover refemblances of a ftriking and important nature, between one fpecies and another, which naturally begets the notion of a genus. From comparing men with beafts, birds, fifhes, and reptiles, we perceive, that they are all alike poffeffed of life, or a principle of fenfation and action, and of an organifed body, and hence acquire the idea of animal, in like manner from comparing kingdoms with republics and ariftocracies, we obtain the idea of nation, and thence again rife in the fame track to ideas ftill more comprehenfive. Further, let it be remembered, that by experience we not only decide concerning the future from the

past,

past, but concerning things uncommon from things familiar, which resemble them.

Now to apply this observation; a botanist in traversing the fields, lights on a particular plant, which appears to be of a species he is not acquainted with. The flower he observes is monopetalous, and the number of flowers it carries is seven. Here are two facts that occur to his observation, let us consider in what way he will be disposed to argue from them. From the first he does not hesitate to conclude, not only as probable, but as certain, that this individual, and all of the same species, invariably produce monopetalous flowers. From the second, he by no means concludes, as either certain or even probable, that the flowers which either this plant, or others of the same species, carry at once, will always be seven. This difference, to a superficial inquirer, might seem capricious, since there appears to be one example, and but one in either case, on which the conclusion can be founded. The truth is, that it is not from this example only that he deduces these inferences. Had he never heretofore taken the smallest notice of any plant, he could not have reasoned at all from these remarks. The mind recurs instantly, from

the

the unknown to all the other known species of the same genus, and thence to all the known genera of the same order or tribe, and having experienced in the one instance, a regularity in every species, genus, and tribe, which admits no exception; in the other, a variety as boundless as is that of season, soil, and culture, it learns hence to mark the difference.

AGAIN, we may observe, that, on a closer acquaintance with those objects wherewith we are surrounded, we come to discover that they are mostly of a compound nature, and that not only as containing a complication of those qualities called accidents, as gravity, mobility, colour, extension, figure, solidity, which are common almost to all matter, not only as consisting of different members, but as comprehending a mixture of bodies, often very different in their nature and properties, as air, fire, water, earth, salt, oil, spirit, and the like. These, perhaps, on deeper researches, will be found to consist of materials still simpler. Moreover, as we advance in the study of Nature, we daily find more reason to be convinced of her constancy in all her operations, that like causes in like circumstances always produce like effects, and inversely like

effects

effects always flow from like causes. The inconstancy which appears at first in some of Nature's works, a more improved experience teacheth us to account for in this manner. As most of the objects we know, are of a complex nature, on a narrower scrutiny we find, that the effects ascribed to them, ought often solely to be ascribed to one or more of the component parts; that the other parts noway contribute to the production; that, on the contrary, they sometimes tend to hinder it. If the parts in the composition of similar objects were always in equal quantity, their being compounded would make no odds, if the parts, though not equal, bore always the same proportion to the whole, this would make a difference; but such as in many cases might be computed. In both respects, however, there is an immense variety. Perhaps every individual differs from every other individual of the same species, both in the quantities and in the proportions of its constituent members and component parts. This diversity is also found in other things, which, though hardly reducible to species, are generally known by the same name. The atmosphere in the same place at different times, or at the same time in different places, differs in density, heat, humidity, and the number,

ber, quality, and proportion of the vapours or particles with which it is loaden. The more then we become acquainted with elementary natures, the more we are ascertained by a general experience of the uniformity of their operations. And though perhaps it be impossible for us to attain the knowledge of the simplest elements of any body, yet, when any thing appears so simple, or rather so exactly uniform, as that we have observed it invariably to produce similar effects, on discovering any new effect, though but by one experiment, we conclude from the general experience of the efficient, a like constancy in this energy as in the rest. Fire consumes wood, melts copper, and hardens clay. In these instances it acts uniformly, but not in these only. I have always experienced hitherto, that whatever of any species is consumed by it once, all of the same species it will consume upon trial at any time. The like may be said of what is melted, or hardened, or otherwise altered, by it. If then, for the first time, I try the influence of fire on any fossil, or other substance, whatever be the effect, I readily conclude, that fire will always produce a similar effect on similar bodies. This conclusion is not founded on this single instance, but on this instance compared with a general experience

perience of the regularity of this element in all its operations.

So much for the first tribe, the evidence of experience, on which I have enlarged the more, as it is, if not the foundation, at least the criterion of all moral reasoning whatever. It is, besides, the principal organ of truth in all the branches of physiology, (I use the word in its largest acceptation,) including natural history, astronomy, geography, mechanics, optics, hydrostatics, meteorology, medicine, chymistry. Under the general term I also comprehend natural theology and psychology, which, in my opinion, have been most unnaturally disjoined by philosophers. Spirit, which here comprises only the Supreme Being and the human soul, is surely as much included under the notion of natural object, as body is, and is knowable to the philosopher purely in the same way, by observation and experience.

II. *Analogy*.

The evidence of analogy, as was hinted above, is but a more indirect experience, founded on some remote similitude. As things, however, are often more easily comprehended by the aid of example,

example, than by definition, I shall in that manner illustrate the difference between experimental evidence, and analogical. The circulation of the blood in one human body is, I shall suppose, experimentally discovered. Nobody will doubt of this being a sufficient proof from experience, that the blood circulates in every human body. Nay further, when we consider the great similarity which other animal bodies bear to the human body, and that both in the structure and in the destination of the several organs and limbs; particularly when we consider the resemblance in the blood itself, and blood vessels, and in the fabric and pulsation of the heart and arteries, it will appear sufficient experimental evidence of the circulation of the blood in brutes, especially in quadrupeds. Yet, in this application, it is manifest, that the evidence is weaker than in the former. But should I from the same experiment infer the circulation of the sap in vegetables, this would be called an argument only from analogy. Now all reasonings from experience are obviously weakened in proportion to the remoteness of the resemblance subsisting between that on which the argument is founded, and that concerning which we form the conclusion.

The same thing may be considered in a different way. I have learned from experience, that like effects sometimes proceed from objects which faintly resemble, but not near so frequently as from objects which have a more perfect likeness. By this experience I am enabled to determine the degrees of probability from the degrees of similarity, in the different cases. It is presumable that the former of these ways has the earliest influence, when the mind, unaccustomed to reflection, forms but a weak association, and consequently but a weak expectation of a similar event from a weak resemblance. The latter seems more the result of thought, and is better adapted to the ordinary forms of reasoning.

It must be allowed, that analogical evidence is at best but a feeble support, and is hardly ever honoured with the name of proof. Nevertheless, when the analogies are numerous, and the subject admits not evidence of another kind, it doth not want its efficacy. It must be owned, however, that it is generally more successful in silencing objections, than in evincing truth, and on this account may more properly be styled the defensive arms of the orator, than the offensive. Though it rarely refutes, it frequently repels refutation,

futation, like those weapons which, though they cannot kill the enemy, will ward his blows *.

III. *Testimony.*

THE third tribe is the evidence of testimony, which is either oral or written. This also hath been thought by some, but unjustly, to be solely and originally derived from the same source, experience †. The utmost, in regard to this, that can be affirmed with truth, is, that the evidence of testimony is to be considered as strictly logical, no farther than human veracity in general, or the veracity of witnesses of such a character, and in such circumstances in particular, is supported, or, perhaps more properly, hath not been refuted by experience. But that testimony, antecedently to experience, hath a natural influence on belief, is undeniable. In this it resembles memory, for though the defects and

---

* Dr. Butler, in his excellent treatise called *The analogy of Religion natural and revealed, to the constitution and course of nature,* hath shewn us, how useful this mode of reasoning may be rendered, by the application he hath so successfully made of it, for refuting the cavils of infidelity.

† I had occasion to make some reflections on this subject formerly. See Dissertation on Miracles, Part 1. Sect. 1. There are several ingenious observations on the same subject in Reid's Inquiry, Ch. vi. Sect. 23.

misrepresentations of memory are corrected by experience, yet that this faculty hath an innate evidence of its own, we know from this; that if we had not previously given an implicit faith to memory, we had never been able to acquire experience. This will appear from a revisal of its nature, as explained above. Nay, it must be owned, that in what regards single facts, testimony is more adequate evidence than any conclusions from experience. The immediate conclusions from experience are general, and run thus 'This is the ordinary course of nature.' 'Such an event may reasonably be expected, 'when all the attendant circumstances are simi- 'lar.' When we descend to particulars, the conclusion necessarily becomes weaker, being more indirect. For though all the *known* circumstances be similar, all the *actual* circumstances may not be similar; nor is it possible in any case to be assured, that all the actual circumstances are known to us. Accordingly, experience is the foundation of philosophy; which consists in a collection of general truths, systematically digested. On the contrary, the direct conclusion from testimony is particular, and runs thus: 'This is the fact in the instance specified. Testimony, therefore, is the foundation of history, which is occupied about individuals. Hence we derive our acquaintance with past ages, as from experience we derive all that we can discover of the future. But the former is dignified with the name of knowledge, whereas the latter is regarded as matter of conjecture only. When experience is applied to the discovery of the truth in a particular incident, we call the evidence presumptive, ample testimony is accounted a positive proof of the fact. Nay, the strongest conviction built merely on the former is sometimes overturned by the slightest attack of the latter. Testimony is capable of giving us absolute certainty (Mr. Hume himself being judge*) even of the most miraculous fact, or of what is contrary to uniform experience. For, perhaps, in no other instance can experience be applied to individual events, with so much certainty, as in what relates to the revolutions of the heavenly bodies. Yet, even this evidence, he admits, may not only be counterbalanced, but destroyed, by testimony.

But to return. Testimony is a serious intimation from another, of any fact or observation, as being what he remembers to have seen or heard

* Essay of Miracles, p. 2.

or experienced. To this, when we have no positive reasons of mistrust or doubt, we are, by an original principle of our nature, (analogous to that which compels our faith in memory) led to give an unlimited assent. As on memory alone is founded the merely personal experience of the individual, so on testimony, in concurrence with memory, is founded the much more extensive experience, which is not originally our own, but derived from others *. By the first, I question not, a man might acquire all the knowledge necessary for mere animal support, in that rudest state of human nature (if ever such a state existed) which was without speech, and without society; to the last, in conjunction with the other, we are indebted for every thing which distinguishes the man from the brute, for language, arts, and civilization. It hath been observed, that from experience we learn to confine our belief in human testimony, within the proper bounds. Hence we are taught to consider many attendant circumstances, which serve either to corroborate or to invalidate its evidence. The reputation of the attester, his manner of address, the nature of the fact attested, the occasion of giving the

* Dissertation on Miracles, Part I. Sect. 2.

testimony, the possible or probable design in giving it, the disposition of the hearers to whom it was given, and several other circumstances, have all considerable influence in fixing the degree of credibility. But of these I shall have occasion to take notice afterwards. It deserves likewise to be attended to on this subject, that in a number of concurrent testimonies, (in cases wherein there could have been no previous concert) there is a probability distinct from that which may be termed the sum of the probabilities resulting from the testimonies of the witnesses, a probability which would remain even though the witnesses were of such a character as to merit no faith at all. This probability ariseth purely from the concurrence itself. That such a concurrence should spring from chance, is as one to infinite, that is, in other words, morally impossible. If therefore concert be excluded, there remains no other cause but the reality of the fact.

Now to this species of evidence, testimony, we are first immediately indebted for all the branches of philology, such as history, civil, ecclesiastic, and literary; grammar, languages, jurisprudence, and criticism, to which I may add revealed religion, as far as it is to be considered

sidered as a subject of historical and critical inquiry, and so discoverable by natural means: and secondly, to the same source we owe, as was hinted above, a great part of that light which is commonly known under the name of experience, but which is, in fact, not founded on our own personal observations, or the notices originally given by our own senses, but on the attested experiences and observations of others. So that as hence we derive entirely our knowledge of the actions and productions of men, especially in other regions, and in former ages, hence also we derive, in a much greater measure than is commonly imagined, our acquaintance with Nature and her works.——Logic, rhetoric, ethics, œconomics, and politics, are properly branches of pneumatology, though very closely connected with the philological studies above enumerated.

IV. *Calculations of chances.*

THE last kind of evidence I proposed to consider, was that resulting from calculations of chances. Chance is not commonly understood either in philosophic or in vulgar language to imply the exclusion of a cause, but our ignorance of the cause. It is often employed to denote a bare possibility of an event, when nothing is known either to produce or to hinder it. But in this meaning it can never be made the subject of calculation. It then only affords scope to the calculator, when a cause is known for the production of an effect, and when that effect must necessarily be attended with this or that or the other circumstance; but no cause is known to determine us to regard one particular circumstance, in preference to the rest, as that which shall accompany the supposed effect. The effect is then considered as necessary, but the circumstance as only casual or contingent. When a die is thrown out of the hand, we know that its gravity will make it fall; we know also, that this, together with its cubical figure, will make it lie so, when intercepted by the table, as to have one side facing upwards. Thus far we proceed on the certain principles of a uniform experience, but there is no principle which can lead me to conclude, that one side rather than another will be turned up. I know that this circumstance is not without a cause; but is, on the contrary, as really effected by the previous tossing which it receives in the hand or in the box, as its fall and the manner of its lying are by its gravity and figure. But the various turns or motions

tions given it, in this manner, do inevitably escape my notice, and so are held for nothing. I say, therefore, that the chance is equal for every one of the six sides. Now, if five of these were marked with the same figure, suppose a dagger [†], and only one with an asterisk [*], I should, in that case, say, there were five chances that the die would turn up the dagger, for one that it would turn up the asterisk. For the turning up each of the six sides being equally possible, there are five cases in which the dagger, and only one in which the asterisk, would be uppermost.

This differs from experience, inasmuch as I reckon the probability here, not from numbering and comparing the events, after repeated trials, but without any trial, from balancing the possibilities on both sides. But though different from experience, it is so similar, that we cannot wonder that it should produce a similar effect upon the mind. These different positions being considered as equal, if any of five shall produce one effect, and but the sixth another, the mind weighing the different events, resteth in an expectation of that in which the greater number of chances concur, but still accompanied with a degree of hesitancy, which appears proportioned

tioned to the number of chances on the opposite side. It is much after the same manner that the mind, on comparing its own experiences, when five instances favour one side, to one that favours the contrary, determines the greater credibility of the former. Hence in all complicated cases, the very degree of probability may be arithmetically ascertained. That two dice marked in the common way will turn up seven, is thrice as probable as that they will turn up eleven, and six times as probable as that they will turn up twelve*. The degree of probability is here determined demonstratively. It is indeed true, that such mathematical calculations may be founded on experience, as well as upon chances. Examples of this we have in the computations that have been made of the value of annuities, insurances, and several other commercial articles. In such cases, a great number of instances is necessary, the greatest exactness in collecting them on each side, and due care that there be no discoverable peculiarity in any

---

* Call one die A, the other B. The chances for 7 are

  A 1. B 6. | A 4. B 3.
  A 2. B 5. | A 5. B 2.
  A 3. B 4. | A 6. B 1.

  The chances for 11 are
    A 6. B 5.
    A 5. B 6.

The only chance for 12 is A 6. B 6. The 1st is to the 2d, as 6 to 2, to the 3d, as 6 to 1.

of them, which would render them unfit for supporting a general conclusion.

PART IV. *The superiority of scientific evidence re-examined.*

AFTER the enumeration made in the first part of this section, of the principal differences between scientific evidence and moral, I signified my intention of resuming the subject afterwards, as far at least as might be necessary to shew, that the prerogatives of demonstration are not so considerable, as on a cursory view one is apt to imagine. It will be proper now to execute this intention. I could not attempt it sooner, as the right apprehension of what is to be advanced, will depend on a just conception of those things which have lately been explained. In the comparison referred to, I contrasted the two sorts of evidence, as they are in themselves, without considering the influence which the necessary application of our faculties in using both, has, and ought to have, on the effect. The observations then made in that abstracted view of the subject, appear to be well founded. But that view, I acknowledge, doth not comprehend the whole with which we are concerned.

It was observed of memory, that as it instantly succeeds sensation, it is the repository of all the stores from which our experience is collected, and that without an implicit faith in the clear representations of that faculty, we could not advance a step in the acquisition of experimental knowledge. Yet we know that memory is not infallible; nor can we pretend, that in any case there is not a physical possibility of her making a false report. Here, it may be said, is an irremediable imbecillity in the very foundation of moral reasoning. But is it less so in demonstrative reasoning? This point deserves a careful examination.

It was remarked concerning the latter, that it is a proof consisting of an uninterrupted series of axioms. The truth of each is intuitively perceived as we proceed. But this process is of necessity gradual, and these axioms are all brought in succession. It must then be solely by the aid of memory, that they are capable of producing conviction in the mind. Nor by this do I mean to affirm, that we can remember the preceding steps, with their connexions, so as to have them all present to our view at one instant, for then we should, in that instant, perceive the whole

whole intuitively. Our remembrance, on the contrary, amounts to no more than this, that the perception of the truth of the axiom to which we are advanced in the proof, is accompanied with a strong impression on the memory, of the satisfaction that the mind received from the justness and regularity of what preceded. And in this we are under a necessity of acquiescing; for the understanding is no more capable of contemplating and perceiving at once, the truth of all the propositions in the series, than the tongue is capable of uttering them at once. Before we make great progress in geometry, we come to demonstrations, wherein there is a reference to preceding demonstrations; and in these perhaps to others that preceded them. The bare reflection, that as to these we once were satisfied, is accounted by every learner, and teacher too, as sufficient. And if it were not so, no advancement at all could be made in this science. Yet, here again, the whole evidence is reduced to the testimony of memory. It may be said that, along with the remembrance now mentioned, there is often in the mind, a conscious power of recollecting the several steps, whenever it pleases, but the power of recollecting them severally and successively, and the actual instantaneous recollection

tion of the whole, are widely different. Now what is the consequence of this induction? It is plainly this, that, in spite of the pride of mathesis, no demonstration whatever can produce, or reasonably ought to produce, a higher degree of certainty, than that which results from the vivid representations of memory, on which the other is obliged to lean. Such is here the natural subordination, however rational and purely intellectual the former may be accounted, however mysterious and inexplicable the latter. For it is manifest, that without a perfect acquiescence in such representations, the mathematician could not advance a single step beyond his definitions and axioms. Nothing therefore is more certain, however inconceivable it appeared to Dr. Priestley, than what was affirmed by Dr. Oswald, that, *the possibility of error attends the most complete demonstration.*

If from theory we recur to fact, we shall quickly find, that those most deeply versed in this sort of reasoning, are conscious of the justness of the remark now made. A geometrician, I shall suppose, discovers a new theorem, which, having made a diagram for the purpose, he attempts to demonstrate, and succeeds in the attempt.

The figure he hath constructed is very complex, and the demonstration long. Allow me now to ask, Will he be so perfectly satisfied on the first trial, as not to think it of importance to make a second, perhaps a third, and a fourth? Whence arises this diffidence? Purely from the consciousness of the fallibility of his own faculties. But to what purpose, it may be said, the reiterations of the attempt, since it is impossible for him, by any efforts, to shake off his dependence on the accuracy of his attention, and fidelity of his memory? Or, what can he have more than reiterated testimonies of his memory, in support of the truth of its former testimony? I acknowledge, that after a hundred attempts he can have no more. But even this is a great deal. We learn from experience, that the mistakes or oversights committed by the mind in one operation, are sometimes, on a review, corrected in a second, or perhaps in a third. Besides, the repetition, when no error is discovered, enlivens the remembrance, and so strengthens the conviction. But for this conviction, it is plain that we are in a great measure indebted to memory, and in some measure even to experience.

ARITH-

Arithmetical operations, as well as geometrical, are in this nature scientific; yet the most accurate accountants are very sensible of the possibility of committing a blunder, and therefore rarely fail, for securing the matter, when it is of importance, to prove what they have done, by trying to effect the same thing another way. You have employed yourself, I suppose, in resolving some difficult problem by algebra, and are convinced that your solution is just. One whom you know to be an expert algebraist, carefully peruses the whole operation, and acquaints you that he hath discovered an error in your procedure. You are that instant sensible that your conviction was not of such an impregnable nature, but that his single testimony, in consequence of the confidence you repose in his experienced veracity and skill, makes a considerable abatement in it.

Many cases might be supposed, of belief founded only on moral evidence, which it would be impossible thus to shake. A man of known probity and good sense, and (if you think it makes an addition of any moment in this case) an astronomer and philosopher, bids you look at the sun as it goes down, and tells you with a serious

rious countenance, that the sun which sets today will never again rise upon the earth. What would be the effect of this declaration? Would it create in you any doubts? I believe it might, as to the soundness of the man's intellects, but not as to the truth of what he said. Thus, if we regard only the effect, demonstration itself doth not always produce such immoveable certainty, as is sometimes consequent on merely moral evidence. And if there are, on the other hand, some well-known demonstrations, of so great authority, that it would equally look like lunacy to impugn, it may deserve the attention of the curious, to inquire how far, with respect to the bulk of mankind, these circumstances, their having stood the test of ages, their having obtained the universal suffrage of those who are qualified to examine them (things purely of the nature of moral evidence), have contributed to that unshaken faith with which they are received.

The principal difference then, in respect of the result of both kinds, is reduced to this narrow point. In mathematical reasoning, provided you are ascertained of the regular procedure of the mind, to affirm that the conclusion is false, implies a contradiction; in moral reasoning, though the procedure of the mind were quite unexceptionable, there still remains a physical possibility of the falsity of the conclusion. But how small this difference is in reality, any judicious person who but attends a little, may easily discover. The geometrician, for instance, can no more doubt, whether the book called Euclid's Elements is a human composition, whether its contents were discovered and digested into the order in which they are there disposed, by human genius and art, than he can doubt the truth of the propositions therein demonstrated. Is he in the smallest degree surer of any of the properties of the circle, than that if he take away his hand from the compasses, with which he is describing it on the wall, they will immediately fall to the ground. These things affect his mind, and influence his practice, precisely in the same manner.

So much for the various kinds of evidence, whether intuitive or deductive; intuitive evidence, as divided into that of pure intellection, of consciousness, and of common sense, under the last of which that of memory is included; deductive evidence, as divided into scientific and moral, with the subdivisions of the latter into experience, analogy, and testimony, to which hath been

been added, the confideration of a mixed fpecies concerning chances. So much for the various fubjects of difcourfe, and the forts of eviction of which they are refpectively fufceptible. This, though peculiarly the logician's province, is the foundation of all conviction, and confequently of perfuafion too. To attain either of thefe ends, the fpeaker muft always affume the character of the clofe and candid reafoner: for though he may be an acute logician who is no orator, he will never be a confummate orator who is no logician.

CHAP. VI.

Of the nature and ufe of the fcholaftic art of fyllogizing.

HAVING in the preceding chapter endeavoured to trace the outlines of natural logic, perhaps with more minutenefs than in fuch an inquiry as this was ftrictly neceffary, it might appear ftrange to pafs over in filence the dialectic of the fchools, an art which, though now fallen into difrepute, maintained for a tract of ages, the higheft reputation among the learned. What was fo long regarded, as teaching the only legitimate use and application of our rational powers in the acquisition of knowledge, ought not surely, when we are employed in investigating the nature and the different sorts of evidence, to be altogether overlooked.

It is long since I was first convinced, by what Mr. Locke hath said on the subject, that the syllogistic art, with its figures and moods, serves more to display the ingenuity of the inventor, and to exercise the address and fluency of the learner, than to assist the diligent inquirer in his researches after truth. The method of proving by syllogism, appears, even on a superficial review, both unnatural and prolix. The rules laid down for distinguishing the conclusive from the inconclusive forms of argument, the true syllogism from the various kinds of sophism, are at once cumbersome to the memory, and unnecessary in practice. No person, one may venture to pronounce, will ever be made a reasoner, who stands in need of them. In a word, the whole bears the manifest indications of an artificial and ostentatious parade of learning, calculated for giving the appearance of great profundity, to what in fact is very shallow. Such, I acknowledge, have been, of a long time, my sentiments on the subject. On a nearer inspection, I cannot say I have found reason to alter them, though I think I have seen a little further into the nature of this disputative science, and consequently into the grounds of its futility. I shall, therefore, as briefly as possible, lay before the reader a few observations on the subject, and so dismiss this article.

Permit me only to premise in general, that I proceed all along on the supposition, that the reader hath some previous acquaintance with school logic. It would be extremely superfluous in a work like this, to give even the shortest abridgment that could be made of an art so well known, and which is still to be found in many thousand volumes. On the other hand, it is not necessary that he be an adept in it, a mere smattering will sufficiently serve the present purpose.

My first observation is, that this method of arguing has not the least affinity to moral reasoning, the procedure in the one being the very reverse of that employed in the other. In moral reasoning we proceed by analysis, and ascend from particulars to universals, in syllogizing we proceed by synthesis, and descend from universals to particulars. The analytic is the only method which we can follow, in the acquisition of natural knowledge, or of whatever regards actual existences; the synthetic is more properly the method that ought to be pursued in the application of knowledge already acquired. It is for this reason it has been called the didactic method, as being the shortest way of communicating the principles of a science. But even in teaching, as often as we attempt, not barely to inform, but to convince, there is a necessity of recurring to the tract, in which the knowledge we would convey, was first attained. Now, the method of reasoning by syllogism, more resembles mathematical demonstration, wherein, from universal principles, called axioms, we deduce many truths, which, though general in their nature, may, when compared with those first principles, be justly styled particular. Whereas, in all kinds of knowledge, wherein experience is our only guide, we can proceed to general truths, solely by an induction of particulars.

Agreeably to this remark, if a syllogism be regular in mood and figure, and if the premises be true, the conclusion is infallible. The whole foundation of the syllogistic art lies in these two axioms.

axioms: 'Things which coincide with the same thing, coincide with one another;' and 'Two things, whereof one does, and one does not coincide with the same thing, do not coincide with one another.' On the former rest all the affirmative syllogisms, on the latter all the negative. Accordingly, there is no more mention here of probability and of degrees of evidence, than in the operations of geometry and algebra. It is true, indeed, that the term *probable* may be admitted into a syllogism, and make an essential part of the conclusion, and so it may also in an arithmetical computation; but this does not in the least affect what was advanced just now; for, in all such cases, the probability itself is assumed in one of the premises: whereas, in the inductive method of reasoning, it often happens, that from certain facts we can deduce only probable consequences.

I OBSERVE secondly, that though this manner of arguing has more of the nature of scientific reasoning, than of moral, it has, nevertheless, not been thought worthy of being adopted by mathematicians, as a proper method of demonstrating their theorems. I am satisfied that mathematical demonstration is capable of being moulded

moulded into the syllogistic form, having made the trial with success on some propositions. But that this form is a very incommodious one, and has many disadvantages, but not one advantage of that commonly practised, will be manifest to every one who makes the experiment. It is at once more indirect, more tedious, and more obscure. I may add, that if into those abstract sciences one were to introduce some specious fallacies, such fallacies could be much more easily sheltered under the awkward verbosity of this artificial method, than under the elegant simplicity of that which has hitherto been used.

My third remark, which, by the way, is directly consequent on the two former, shall be, that in the ordinary application of this art, to matters with which we can be made acquainted only by experience, it can be of little or no utility. So far from leading the mind, agreeably to the design of all argument and investigation, from things known to things unknown, and by things evident to things obscure, its usual progress is, on the contrary, from things less known to things better known, and by things obscure to things evident. But that it may not be thought that I do injustice to the art by this representation,

tion, I must entreat, that the few following considerations may be attended to.

When in the way of induction, the mind proceeds from individual instances to the discovery of such truths as regard a species, and from these again, to such as comprehend a genus, we may say with reason, that as we advance, there may be in every succeeding step, and commonly is, less certainty than in the preceding, but in no instance whatever can there be more. Besides, as the judgment formed concerning the less general, was anterior to that formed concerning the more general, so the conviction is more vivid arising from both circumstances; that, being less general, it is more distinctly conceived, and being earlier, it is more deeply imprinted. Now the customary procedure in the syllogistic science is, as was remarked, the natural method reversed, being from general to special, and consequently from less to more obvious. In scientific reasoning the case is very different, as the axioms or universal truths from which the mathematician argues, are so far from being the slow result of induction and experience, that they are self-evident. They are no sooner apprehended than necessarily assented to.

But to illustrate the matter by examples, take the following specimen in *Barbara*, the first mood of the first figure

> All animals feel,
> All horses are animals,
> Therefore all horses feel.

It is impossible that any reasonable man who really doubts whether a horse has feeling or is a mere automaton, should be convinced by this argument. For, supposing he uses the names *horse* and *animal*, as standing in the same relation of species and genus, which they bear in the common acceptation of the words, the argument you employ is, in effect, but an affirmation of the point which he denies, couched in such terms as include a multitude of other similar affirmations, which, whether true or false, are nothing to the purpose. Thus *all animals feel*, is only a compendious expression, for *all horses feel, all dogs feel, all camels feel, all eagles feel*, and so through the whole animal creation. I affirm, besides, that the procedure here is from things less known to things better known. It is possible that one may believe the conclusion who denies the major. but the reverse is not possible; for, to express myself in the language of the art, that may be predicated of the species, which is not predicable of the genus; but that can never be predicated of the genus which is not predicable of the species. If one, therefore, were under such an error in regard to the brutes, true logic, which is always coincident with good sense, would lead our reflections to the indications of perception and feeling, given by these animals, and the remarkable conformity which in this respect, and in respect of their bodily organs, they bear to our own species.

It may be said, that if the subject of the question were a creature much more ignoble than the horse, there would be no scope for this objection to the argument. Substitute, then, the word *oysters* for horses in the minor, and it will stand thus,

> All animals feel,
> All oysters are animals;
> Therefore all oysters feel.

In order to give the greater advantage to the advocate for this scholastic art, let us suppose the antagonist does not maintain the opposite side from any favour to Descartes' theory concerning brutes, but from some notion entertained of that particular order of beings, which is the subject of dispute. It is evident, that though he
should

should admit the truth of the major, he would regard the minor as merely another manner of expressing the conclusion; for he would conceive an animal no otherwise, than as a body endowed with sensation or feeling.

Sometimes indeed, there is not in the premises any position more generic, under which the conclusion can be comprised. In this case you always find that the same proposition is exhibited in different words; insomuch that the stress of the argument lies in a mere synonyma, or something equivalent. The following is an example:

> The Almighty ought to be worshipped,
> God is the Almighty;
> Therefore God ought to be worshipped.

It would be superfluous to illustrate that this argument could have no greater influence on the Epicurean, than the first mentioned one would have on the Cartesian. To suppose the contrary, is to suppose the conviction effected by the charm of a sound, and not by the sense of what is advanced. Thus also, the middle term and the subject frequently correspond to each other, as the definition, description, or circumlocution, and the name. Of this I shall give an example

ample in *Difamis*, as in the technical dialect, the third mood of the third figure is denominated:

> Some men are rapacious;
> All men are rational animals,
> Therefore some rational animals are rapacious.

Who does not perceive that rational animals is but a periphrasis for men?

It may be proper to subjoin one example at least in negative syllogisms. The subsequent is one in *Celarent*, the second mood of the first figure·

> Nothing violent is lasting;
> But tyranny is violent;
> Therefore tyranny is not lasting.

Here a *thing violent* serves for the genus of which *tyranny* is a species; and nothing can be clearer than that it requires much less experience to discover, whether shortness of duration be justly attributed to tyranny the species, than whether it be justly predicated of every violent thing. The application of what was said on the first example to that now given, is so obvious, that it would be losing time to attempt further to illustrate it.

Logicians have been at pains to discriminate the regular and consequential combinations of
the

the three terms, as they are called, from the irregular and inconsequent. A combination of the latter kind, if the defect be in the form, is called a paralogism, if in the sense, a sophism; though sometimes these two appellations are confounded. Of the latter, one kind is denominated *petitio principii*, which is commonly rendered in English *a begging of the question*, and is defined, the proving of a thing by itself, whether expressed in the same or in different words, or, which amounts to the same thing, assuming in the proof the very opinion or principle proposed to be proved. It is surprising that this should ever have been by those artists styled a sophism, since it is in fact so essential to the art, that there is always some radical defect in a syllogism, which is not chargeable with this. The truth of what I now affirm, will appear to any one, on the slightest review of what has been evinced in the preceding part of this chapter.

The fourth and last observation I shall make on this topic, is, that the proper province of the syllogistical science, is rather the adjustment of our language, in expressing ourselves on subjects previously known, than the acquisition of knowledge in things themselves. According to M. du du Marsais, "Reasoning consists in deducing, "inferring, or drawing a judgment from other "judgments already known, or rather, in shew- "ing that the judgment in question has been "already formed implicitly, insomuch that the "only point is to develop it, and show its iden- "tity with some anterior judgment*." Now I affirm that the former part of this definition suits all deductive reasoning, whether scientifical or moral, in which the principle deduced is distinct from, however closely related to, the principles from which the deduction is made. The latter part of the definition, which begins with the words *or rather*, does not answer as an explication of the former, as the author seems to have intended, but exactly hits the character of syllogistic reasoning, and indeed of all sorts of controversy merely verbal. If you regard only the thing signified, the argument conveys no instruction, nor does it forward us in the knowledge of things a single step. But if you regard principally the signs, it may serve to cor-

* Le raisonnement consiste à déduire, à inferer, à tirer un jugement d'autres jugemens deja connus; ou plutot à faire voir que le jugement dont il s'agit, a deja été porté d'une manière implicite, de sorte qu'il n'est plus question que de le développer, et d'en faire voir l'identité avec quelque jugement anterieur. Logique, Art 7.

rect misapplications of them, through inadvertency or otherwise.

In evincing the truth of this doctrine,—I shall begin with a simple illustration from what may happen to any one in studying a foreign tongue. I learn from an Italian and French dictionary, that the Italian word *pecora* corresponds to the French word *brebis*, and from a French and English dictionary, that the French *brebis* corresponds to the English *sheep*. Hence I form this argument,

> *Pecora* is the same with *brebis*,
> *Brebis* is the same with *sheep*,
> Therefore *pecora* is the same with *sheep*.

This, though not in mood and figure, is evidently conclusive. Nay more, if the words *pecora*, *brebis*, and *sheep*, under the notion of signs, be regarded as the terms, it has three distinct terms, and contains a direct and scientifical deduction from this axiom, ‘Things coincident ‘with the same thing, are coincident with one ‘another.’ On the other hand, let the things signified be solely regarded, and there is but one term in the whole, namely the species of quadruped, denoted by the three names above mentioned. Nor is there, in this view of the matter,
another

another judgment in all the three propositions, but this identical one, 'A sheep is a sheep.'

Nor let it be imagined, that the only right application can be in the acquisition of strange languages. Every tongue whatever gives scope for it, inasmuch as in every tongue the speaker labours under great inconveniences, especially on abstract questions, both from the paucity, obscurity, and ambiguity of the words, on the one hand, and from his own misapprehensions, and imperfect acquaintance with them, on the other. As a man may, therefore, by an artful and sophistical use of them, be brought to admit, in certain terms, what he would deny in others, this disputatious discipline may, under proper management, by setting in a stronger light the inconsistences occasioned by such improprieties, be rendered instrumental in correcting them. It was remarked above †, that such propositions as these, 'Twelve are a dozen,' 'Twenty are a score,' unless considered as explications of the words *dozen* and *score*, are quite insignificant. This limitation, however, it was necessary to add, for those positions which are identical when considered purely as relating to

† Chap. V. Sect. I Part I.

the things signified, are nowise identical when regarded purely as explanatory of the names. Suppose that through the imperfection of a man's knowledge in the language, aided by another's sophistry, and perhaps his own inattention, he is brought to admit of the one term, what he would refuse of the other, such an argument as this might be employed,

> Twelve, you allow, are equal to the fifth part of sixty;
> Now a dozen are equal to twelve,
> Therefore a dozen are equal to the fifth part of sixty.

I mark the case rather strongly, for the sake of illustration; for I am sensible, that in what regards things so definite as all names of number are, it is impossible for any who is not quite ignorant of the tongue, to be misled. But the intelligent reader will easily conceive, that in abstruse and metaphysical subjects, wherein the terms are often both extensive and indefinite in their signification, and sometimes even equivocal, the most acute and wary may be intangled in them.

In further confirmation of my fourth remark, I shall produce an example in *Camestres*, the second mood of the second figure:

All

All animals are mortal;
But angels are not mortal;
Therefore angels are not animals.

When the antagonist calls an angel an animal, it must proceed from one or other of these two causes, either from an error in regard to the nature of the angelic order, or from a mistake as to the import of the English word *animal*. If the first be the case; namely, some erroneous opinion about angels, as that they are embodied spirits, generated and corruptible like ourselves; it is evident that the forementioned syllogism labours under the common defect of all syllogisms. It assumes the very point in question. But if the difference between the disputants be, as it frequently happens, merely verbal, and the opponent uses the word *animal*, as another name for living creature, and as exactly corresponding to the Greek term*, arguments of this sort may be of service for setting the impropriety of such a misapplication of the English name in a clearer light. For let it be observed, that though Nature hath strongly marked the principal differences to be found in different orders of beings, a procedure which hath suggested to men the manner of classing things into genera and spe-

* ζων.

cies, this does not hold equally in every cafe. Hence it is, that the general terms in different languages do not always exactly correfpond. Some nations, from particular circumftances, are more affected by one property in objects, others by another. This leads to a different diftribution of things under their feveral names. Now, though it is not of importance that the words in one tongue exactly correfpond to thofe in another, it is of importance that in the fame tongue uniformity in this refpect be, as much as poffible, obferved. Errors in regard to the figns, tend not only to retard the progrefs of knowledge, but to introduce errors in regard to the things fignified. Now by fuggefting the different attributes comprifed in the definition of the term, as fo many mediums in the proof, an appeal is made to the adverfary's practice in the language. In this way fuch mediums may be prefented, as will fatisfy a candid adverfary, that the application he makes of the term in queftion, is not conformable to the ufage of the tongue.

On the other hand it is certain, that in matters of an abftract and complex nature, where the terms are comprehenfive, indefinite, not in frequent ufe, and confequently not well afcertained,

tained, men may argue together eternally, without making the smallest impression on each other, not sensible all the while, that there is not at bottom any difference between them, except as to the import of words and phrases. I do not say, however, that this is a consequence peculiar to this manner of debating, though perhaps oftener resulting from it, on account of its many nice distinctions, unmeaning subtleties, and mazy windings, than from any other manner. For it must be owned, that the syllogistic art has at, least as often been employed for imposing fallacies on the understanding, as for detecting those imposed. And though verbal controversy seems to be its natural province, it is neither the only method adapted to such discussions, nor the most expeditious.

To conclude then, what shall we denominate the artificial system, or organ of truth, as it has been called, of which we have been treating? Shall we style it, the art of reasoning? So honourable an appellation it by no means merits, since, as hath been shewn, it is ill adapted to scientific matters, and for that reason never employed by the mathematician, and is utterly incapable of assisting us in our researches into nature. Shall we then pronounce it the science of *logomachy*, or in plain English, the art of fighting with words, and about words? And in this wordy warfare, shall we say that the rules of syllogizing are the tactics? This would certainly hit the matter more nearly, but I know not how it happens, that to call any thing *logomachy* or *altercation*, would be considered as giving bad names, and when a good use may be made of an invention, it seems unreasonable to fix an odious name upon it, which ought only to discriminate the abuse. I shall therefore only title it, the scholastic art of disputation*. It is the schoolmen's science of defence.

When all erudition consisted more in an acquaintance with words, and an address in using them, than in the knowledge of things, dexterity in this exercitation conferred as much lustre on the scholar, as agility in the tilts and tournaments added glory to the knight. In proportion

---

* It answers to that branch of logic which Lord Verulam styles *Doctrina de elenchis hermeniæ*, concerning which he affirms, "Dedimus ei nomen ex usu, quia verus ejus usus est plane " redargutio, et cautio circa usum verborum. Quinimo partem " illam de prædicamentis si recte instituatur, circa cautiones " de rebus confundendis aut transponendis definitionum et divisi " onum terminis, præcipuum usum sortiri existimamus, et hoc " etiam referri ma'umus." De Aug. Sci. L. v. c. 4.

as the attention of mankind has been drawn off to the study of Nature, the honours of this contentious art have faded, and it is now almost forgotten. There is no reason to wish its revival, as eloquence seems to have been very little benefited by it, and philosophy still less.

Nay, there is but too good reason to affirm, that there are two evils at least which it has gendered. These are, first, an itch of disputing on every subject, however uncontrovertible, the other, a sort of philosophic pride, which will not permit us to think, that we believe any thing, even a self-evident principle, without a previous reason or argument. In order to gratify this passion, we invariably recur to words, and are at immense pains to lose ourselves in clouds of our own raising. We imagine we are advancing and making wonderful progress, while the mist of words in which we have involved our intellects, hinders us from discerning that we are moving in a circle all the time*.

* How ridiculous are the efforts which some very learned and judicious men have made, in order to evince that whatever begins to exist must have a cause. One argues, 'There must have 'been a cause to determine the time and place,' as though it were more evident that the accidents could not be determined without a cause, than that the existence of the thing could not

be so determined. Another insists very curiously, that if a thing had no cause, it must have been the cause of itself, a third, with equal consistency, that nothing must have been the cause. Thus, by always assuming *the absolute necessity of a cause,* they demonstrate *the absolute necessity of a cause.* For a full illustration of the futility of such pretended reasonings, see the Treatise of Human Nature, B. I. Part III. Sect. 3. I do not think they have succeeded better who have attempted to assign a reason for the faith we have in this principle, that *the future will resemble the past.* A late author imagines, that he solves the difficulty at once, by saying, that ' what is now time past, was once future; and that though ' no man has had experience of what *is* future, every man has had ' experience of what *was* future.' Would it then be more perspicuous to state the question thus, ' How come we to believe ' that *what is future,* not *what was future,* will resemble the ' past?' Of the first he says expressly, that no man has had experience, though almost in the same breath he tells us, not very confidently, ' The answer is sufficient, have we not always ' found it to be so?' an answer which appears to me not more illogical than ungrammatical. But admitting with him, that to consider time as past or future (though no distinction can be more precise) is only puzzling the question, let us inquire whether a reason can be assigned, for judging that the unknown time will resemble the known. Suppose our whole time divided into equal portions. Call these portions A, B, C, D, E, F, G. Of these the three first have been experienced, the remaining four are not. The three first I found to resemble one another, but how must I argue with regard to the rest? Shall I say, B was like A, therefore D will be like C, or, if you think it strengthens the argument, shall I say, C resembled A and B, therefore D will resemble A, B, and C. I would gladly know what sort of reasoning, scientifical or moral, this could be denominated, or what is the medium by which the conclusion is made out? Suppose, further, I get acquainted with D, formerly unknown, and find that it actually resembles A, B, and C, how can this furnish me with any knowledge of E, F, and G, things totally distinct? The resemblance I have discovered in D to A,
B,

B, and C, can never be extended to any thing that is not D, nor any part of D, namely to E, F, and G, unless you assume this as the medium, that the unknown will resemble the known, or, which is equivalent, that the future will resemble the past. So far is this principle, therefore, from being deduced from particular experiences, that it is fundamental to all particular deductions from experience, in which we could not advance a single step without it. We are often misled in cases of this nature, by a vague and popular use of words, not attending to the nicer differences in their import in different situations. If one were to ask me, 'Have you then no reason to believe that the 'future will resemble the past?' I should certainly answer, 'I 'have the greatest reason to believe it.' And if the question had been concerning a geometrical axiom, I should have returned the same answer. By *reason* we often mean, not an argument, or medium of proving, but a ground in human nature on which a particular judgment is founded. Nay further, as no progress in reasoning can be made where there is no foundation, (and first principles are here the sole foundation) I should readily admit, that the man who does not believe such propositions, if it were possible to find such a man, is perfectly irrational, and consequently not to be argued with.

CHAP.

CHAP. VII.

Of the confideration which the Speaker ought to have of the Hearers, as Men in general.

RHETORIC, as was obferved already, not only confiders the fubject, but alfo the hearers and the fpeaker *. The hearers muft be confidered in a twofold view, as men in general, and as fuch men in particular.

As men in general, it muft be allowed there are certain principles in our nature, which, when properly addreffed and managed, give no inconfiderable aid to reafon in promoting belief. Nor is it juft to conclude from this conceffion, as fome have haftily done, that oratory may be defined, 'The art of deception.' The ufe of fuch helps will be found, on a ftricter examination, to be in moft cafes quite legitimate, and even neceffary, if we would give reafon herfelf that influence which is certainly her due. In order to evince the truth confidered by itfelf, conclufive arguments alone are requifite, but in order to convince me by thefe arguments, it is moreover requifite that they be underftood, that they

* Chap. IV.

be attended to, that they be remembered by me; and in order to perfuade me by them, to any particular action or conduct, it is further requifite, that by interefting me in the fubject, they may, as it were, be felt It is not therefore the underftanding alone that is here concerned. If the orator would prove fuccefsful, it is neceffary that he engage in his fervice all thefe different powers of the mind, the imagination, the memory, and the paffions. Thefe are not the fupplanters of reafon, or even rivals in her fway; they are her handmaids, by whofe miniftry fhe is enabled to ufher truth into the heart, and procure it there a favourable reception. As handmaids they are liable to be feduced by fophiftry in the garb of reafon, and fometimes are made ignorantly to lend their aid in the introduction of falfehood. But their fervice is not on this account to be difpenfed with, there is even a neceffity of employing it founded in our nature. Our eyes and hands and feet will give us the fame affiftance in doing mifchief as in doing good; but it would not therefore be better for the world, that all mankind were blind and lame. Arms are not to be laid afide by honeft men, becaufe carried by affaffins and ruffians, they are to be ufed the rather for this very reafon. Nor

are

are those mental powers of which eloquence so much avails herself, like the art of war or other human arts, perfectly indifferent to good and evil, and only beneficial as they are rightly employed. On the contrary, they are by nature, as will perhaps appear afterwards, more friendly to truth than to falsehood, and more easily retained in the cause of virtue, than in that of vice *.

* "Notandum est en'm, affectus ipsos ad bonum apparens semper ferri, atque hac ex parte aliquid habere cum ratione commune verum illud interest, quod *affectus intuentur præcipué bonum in præsentia, ratio prospiciens in longum, etiam futurum, et in summa.* Ideoque cùm quæ in præsentia obversentur, impleant phantasiam fortius, succumbit plerumque ratio et subjugatur. Sed postquam eloquentia et suasionum vi effectum sit, ut futura et remota constituantur et conspiciantur tanquam præsentia, tum demum abeunte in partes rationis phantasiâ, ratio fit superior. Concludamus igitur, non deberi magis vitio verti *Rhetoricæ*, quod deteriorem partem cohonestare sciat, quam *Dialecticæ*, quod sophismata concinnare doceat. Quis enim nescit, contrariorum eandem rationem esse, licet usu opponantur?" De Aug. Sci. L. vi c. 3. Τα υποκειμενα πραγματα ουχ ομοιως εχει, αλλ' αιει τ' αληθη κ̃ τα βελτιω τη φυσει ευσυλλογιϛοτερα κ̃ πιθανωτερα, ως απλως ειπει —ει δ' οτι μεγαλα βλαψειεν αν ο χρωμενος αδικως τη τοιαυτη δυναμει των λογων, τουτο γε κοινον εϛι κατα παντων των αγαθων, πλην αρετης, κ̃ μαλιϛα κατα των χρησιμωτατων, οιον ισχυος, υγιειας, πλουτου, ϛρατηγιας· τοιοις γαρ αν τις ωφιλησειε τα μεγιϛα, χρωμενος δικαιως και βλαψειεν αδικως. Arist. Rhet L. I. c. I.

SECTION I.

Men considered as endowed with Understanding.

But to descend to particulars, the first thing to be studied by the speaker is, that his arguments may be understood. If they be unintelligible, the cause must be either in the sense or in the expression. It lies in the sense, if the mediums of proof be such as the hearers are unacquainted with, that is, if the ideas introduced be either without the sphere of their knowledge, or too abstract for their apprehension and habits of thinking. It lies in the sense likewise, if the train of reasoning (though no unusual ideas should be introduced) be longer, or more complex, or more intricate, than they are accustomed to. But as the fitness of the arguments in these respects, depends on the capacity, education, and attainments of the hearers, which in different orders of men are different, this properly belongs to the consideration which the speaker ought to have of his audience, not as men in general, but as such men in particular. The obscurity which ariseth from the expression will come in course to be considered in the sequel.

Section II.

Men considered as endowed with Imagination.

The second thing requisite is that they be attended to, for this purpose the imagination must be engaged. Attention is prerequisite to every effect of speaking, and without some gratification in hearing, there will be no attention, at least of any continuance. Those qualities in ideas which principally gratify the fancy, are vivacity, beauty, sublimity, novelty. Nothing contributes more to vivacity than striking resemblances in the imagery, which convey, besides, an additional pleasure of their own.

But there is still a further end to be served by pleasing the imagination, than that of awakening and preserving the attention, however important this purpose alone ought to be accounted. I will not say with a late subtile metaphysician *, that " Belief consisteth in the liveliness of our ideas." That this doctrine is erroneous, it would be quite foreign to my purpose to attempt here to evince †. Thus much however is indubitable, that belief

---

* The author of, A Treatise of Human Nature, in 3 vols.

† If one is desirous to see a refutation of this principle, let him consult Reid's Inquiry, Ch. ii. Sect. 5.

commonly enlivens our ideas, and that lively ideas have a stronger influence than faint ideas to induce belief. But so far are these two from being coincident, that even this connexion between them, though common, is not necessary. Vivacity of ideas is not always accompanied with faith, nor is faith always able to produce vivacity. The ideas raised in my mind by the Oedipus Tyrannus of Sophocles, or the Lear of Shakespeare, are incomparably more lively than those excited by a cold but faithful historiographer. Yet I may give full credit to the languid narrative of the latter, though I believe not a single sentence in those tragedies. If a proof were asked of the greater vivacity in the one case than in the other (which, by the way, must be finally determined by consciousness), let these effects serve for arguments. The ideas of the poet give greater pleasure, command closer attention, operate more strongly on the passions, and are longer remembered. If these be not sufficient evidences of greater vivacity, I own I have no apprehension of the meaning which that author affixes to the term. The connexion, however, that generally subsisteth between vivacity and belief will appear less marvellous, if we reflect that there is not so great a difference between argument

gument and illustration, as is usually imagined. The same ingenious writer says, concerning moral reasoning, that it is but a kind of comparison. The truth of this assertion any one will easily be convinced of, who considers the preceding observations on that subject.

Where then lies the difference between addressing the judgment, and addressing the fancy? and what hath given rise to the distinction between ratiocination and imagery? The following observations will serve for an answer to this query. It is evident, that though the mind receives a considerable pleasure from the discovery of resemblance, no pleasure is received when the resemblance is of such a nature as is familiar to every body. Such are those resemblances which result from the specific and generic qualities of ordinary objects. What gives the principal delight to the imagination, is the exhibition of a strong likeness, which escapes the notice of the generality of people. The similitude of man to man, eagle to eagle, sea to sea, or in brief, of one individual to another individual of the same species, affects not the fancy in the least. What poet would ever think of comparing a combat between two of his heroes to a combat between other

other two? Yet no-where else will he find so strong a resemblance. Indeed, to the faculty of imagination this resemblance appears rather under the notion of identity, although it be the foundation of the strongest reasoning from experience. Again, the similarity of one species to another of the same genus, as of the lion to the tiger, of the alder to the oak, though this too be a considerable fund of argumentation, hardly strikes the fancy more than the preceding, inasmuch as the generical properties, whereof every species participates, are also obvious. But if from the experimental reasoning we descend to the analogical, we may be said to come upon a common to which reason and fancy have an equal claim. "A comparison," says Quintilian[*], "hath almost the effect of an example." But what are rhetorical comparisons, when brought to illustrate any point inculcated on the hearers, (what are they, I say) but arguments from analogy? In proof of this let us borrow an instance from the forementioned rhetorician, "Would "you be convinced of the necessity of educa- "tion for the mind, consider of what import- "ance culture is to the ground: the field

---

[*] Instit. lib. v. cap. 11. Proximas exempli vires habet similitudo.

"which, cultivated, produceth a plentiful crop
"of useful fruits, if neglected, will be over-run
"with briars and brambles, and other useless or
"noxious weeds †." It would be no better than trifling to point out the argument couched in this passage. Now if comparison, which is the chief, hath so great an influence upon conviction, it is no wonder that all those other oratorical tropes and figures addressed to the imagination, which are more or less nearly related to comparison, should derive hence both light and efficacy *. Even antithesis implies comparison. Simile is a comparison in epitome ‡. Metaphor is an allegory in miniature. Allegory and prosopopeia are comparisons conveyed under a particular form.

† Ibid. Ut si animum dicas excolendum, similitudine utaris terræ, quæ neglecta sentes atque dumos, exculta fructus creat.

* Præterea, nescio quomodo etiam credit facilius, quæ audienti jucunda sunt, et voluptate ad fidem ducitur. Quint L. iv. c. 2.

‡ Simile and comparison are in common language frequently confounded. The difference is this. Simile is no more than a comparison suggested in a word or two, as, He fought like a lion His face shone as the sun. Comparison is a simile circumstantiated and included in one or more separate sentences.

SECTION III.

Men considered as endowed with Memory.

FURTHER, vivid ideas are not only more powerful than languid ideas in commanding and preserving attention, they are not only more efficacious in producing conviction, but they are also more easily retained. Those several powers, understanding, imagination, memory, and passion, are mutually subservient to one another. That it is necessary for the orator to engage the help of memory, will appear from many reasons, particularly from what was remarked above, on the fourth difference between moral reasoning and demonstrative*. It was there observed, that in the former the credibility of the fact is the sum of the evidence of all the arguments, often independent of one another, brought to support it. And though it was shewn that demonstration itself, without the assistance of this faculty, could never produce conviction; yet here it must be owned, that the natural connexion of the several links in the chain renders the remembrance easier. Now as nothing can operate on the mind, which is not in some respect present to it, care must be taken by the

* Chap. V. Sect. ii. P. 1.

orator, that, in introducing new topics, the vestiges left by the former on the minds of the hearers, may not be effaced. It is the sense of this necessity which hath given rise to the rules of composition.

Some will perhaps consider it as irregular, that I speak here of addressing the memory, of which no mention at all was made in the first chapter, wherein I considered the different forms of eloquence, classing them by the different faculties of the mind addressed. But this apparent irregularity will vanish, when it is observed, that, with regard to the faculties there mentioned, each of them may not only be the direct, but even the ultimate object of what is spoken. The whole scope may be at one time to inform or convince the understanding, at another to delight the imagination, at a third to agitate the passions, and at a fourth to determine the will. But it is never the ultimate end of speaking to be remembered, when what is spoken tends neither to instruct, to please, to move, nor to persuade. This therefore is of necessity no more on any occasion than a subordinate end; or, which is precisely the same thing, the means to some further end, and as such, it is more or less necessary on every occasion. The speaker's attention to this subserviency of memory is always so much the more requisite, the greater the difficulty of remembrance is, and the more important the being remembered is to the attainment of the ultimate end. On both accounts, it is of more consequence in those discourses whose aim is either instruction or persuasion, than in those whose design is solely to please the fancy, or to move the passions. And if there are any which answer none of those ends, it were better to learn to forget them, than to teach the method of making them be retained.

The author of the treatise above quoted, hath divided the principles of association in ideas into resemblance, contiguity, and causation. I do not here inquire into all the defects of this enumeration, but only observe, that even on his own system, order both in space and time ought to have been included. It appears at least to have an equal title with causation, which, according to him, is but a particular modification and combination of the other two. Causation considered as an associating principle, is, in his theory, no more than the contiguous succession of two ideas, which is more deeply imprinted on the mind by its experience of a similar contiguity and succession of the impressions from which they are copied. This therefore is the result of resemblance and vicinity united. Order in place is likewise a mode of vicinity, where this last tie is strengthened by the regularity and simplicity of figure, which qualities arise solely from the resemblance of the corresponding parts of the figure, or the parts similarly situated. Regular figures, besides the advantages which they derive from simplicity and uniformity, have this also, that they are more familiar to the mind than irregular figures, and are therefore more easily conceived. Hence the influence which order in place hath upon the memory. If any person questions this influence, let him but reflect, how much easier it is to remember a considerable number of persons, whom one hath seen ranged on benches or chairs, round a hall, than the same number seen standing promiscuously in a crowd; and how natural it is for assisting the memory in recollecting the persons, to recur to the order wherein they were placed.

As to order in time, which in composition is properly styled Method, it consisteth principally in connecting the parts in such a manner as to give

give vicinity to things in the discourse, which have an affinity; that is, resemblance, causality, or other relation in nature, and thus making their customary association and resemblance, as in the former case, co-operate with their contiguity in duration, or immediate succession in the delivery. The utility of method for aiding the memory, all the world knows. But besides this, there are some parts of the discourse, as well as figures of speech, peculiarly adapted to this end. Such are the division of the subject, the rhetorical repetitions of every kind, the different modes of transition and recapitulation.

SECTION IV.

Men considered as endowed with Passions.

To conclude; when persuasion is the end, passion also must be engaged. If it is fancy which bestows brilliancy on our ideas, if it is memory which gives them stability, passion doth more, it animates them. Hence they derive spirit and energy. To say, that it is possible to persuade without speaking to the passions, is but at best a kind of specious nonsense. The coolest reasoner always in persuading, addresseth himself to the passions some way or other. This he cannot avoid doing, if he speak to the purpose. To make me believe, it is enough to shew me that things are so; to make me act, it is necessary to shew that the action will answer some end. That can never be an end to me which gratifies no passion or affection in my nature. You assure me, 'It is for my honour.' Now you solicit my pride, without which I had never been able to understand the word. You say, 'It is 'for my interest.' Now you bespeak my self-love. 'It is for the public good.' Now you rouse my patriotism. 'It will relieve the miser-'able.' Now you touch my pity. So far therefore it is from being an unfair method of persuasion to move the passions, that there is no persuasion without moving them.

But if so much depend on passion, where is the scope for argument? Before I answer this question, let it be observed, that, in order to persuade, there are two things which must be carefully studied by the orator. The first is, to excite some desire or passion in the hearers; the second is, to satisfy their judgment, that there is a connexion between the action to which he would persuade them, and the gratification of the desire or passion which he excites. This is the

the analysis of persuasion. The former is effected by communicating lively and glowing ideas of the object, the latter, unless so evident of itself as to supersede the necessity, by presenting the best and most forcible arguments which the nature of the subject admits. In the one lies the pathetic, in the other the argumentative. These incorporated together (as was observed in the First Chapter) constitute that vehemence of contention to which the greatest exploits of eloquence ought doubtless to be ascribed. Here then is the principal scope for argument, but not the only scope, as will appear in the sequel. When the first end alone is attained, the pathetic without the rational, the passions are indeed roused from a disagreeable languor by the help of the imagination, and the mind is thrown into a state, which, though accompanied with some painful emotions, rarely fails, upon the whole, to affect it with pleasure. But, if the hearers are judicious, no practical effect is produced. They cannot by such declamation be influenced to a particular action, because not convinced that that action will conduce to the gratifying of the passion raised. Your eloquence hath fired my ambition, and makes me burn with public zeal. The consequence is, there is nothing which at present

sent I would not attempt for the sake of fame, and the interest of my country. You advise me to such a conduct, but you have not shown me how that can contribute to gratify either passion. Satisfy me in this, and I am instantly at your command. Indeed, when the hearers are rude and ignorant, nothing more is necessary in the speaker than to inflame their passions. They will not require that the connexion between the conduct he urges and the end proposed, be evinced to them. His word will satisfy. And therefore bold affirmations are made to supply the place of reasons. Hence it is that the rabble are ever the prey of quacks and impudent pretenders of every denomination.

On the contrary, when the other end alone is attained, the rational without the pathetic, the speaker is as far from his purpose as before. You have proved beyond contradiction, that acting thus is the sure way to procure such an object. I perceive that your reasoning is conclusive, but I am not affected by it. Why? I have no passion for the object. I am indifferent whether I procure it or not. You have demonstrated, that such a step will mortify my enemy. I believe it, but I have no resentment, and will not trouble
myself

myself to give pain to another. Your arguments evince that it would gratify my vanity. But I prefer my ease. Thus passion is the mover to action, reason is the guide. Good is the object of the will, truth is the object of the understanding*.

It

* Several causes have contributed to involve this subject in confusion. One is the ambiguity and imperfection of language. Motives are often called arguments, and both motives and arguments are promiscuously styled reasons. Another is, the idle disputes that have arisen among philosophers, concerning the nature of good, both physical and moral. " Truth and good " are one," says the author of the Pleasures of Imagination, an author whose poetical merit will not be questioned by persons of taste. The expression might have been passed in the poet, whose right to the use of *catachresis*, one of the many privileges comprehended under the name *poetic licence*, prescription hath fully established. But by philosophising on this passage in his notes, he warrants us to canvass his reasoning, for no such privilege hath as yet been conceded to philosophers. Indeed, in attempting to illustrate, he has, I think, confuted it, or, to speak more properly, shown it to have no meaning. He mentions two opinions concerning the connexion of truth and beauty, which is one species of good. " Some philosophers, says he, assert an " independent and invariable law in Nature, in consequence of " which *all rational beings must alike perceive beauty in some cer-* " *tain proportions, and deformity in the contrary.*" Now, though I do not conceive what is meant either by *an independent law*, or by *contrary proportions*, this, if it proves any thing, proves as clearly that deformity and truth are one, as that beauty and truth are one; for those *contrary proportions* are surely as much proportions, or, if you will, as true proportions, as *some certain proportions* are. Accordingly, if, in the conclusion deduced, you put the word *deformity* instead of *beauty*, and the word

beauty

It may be thought that when the motive is the equity, the generosity, or the intrinsic merit

beauty instead of *deformity*, the sense will be equally complete. "Others," he adds, "there are, who believe beauty to be "merely a relative and arbitrary thing, and that it is not im- "possible, in a physical sense, *that two beings of equal capa-* "*cities for truth, should perceive, one of them beauty, and the* "*other deformity, in the same relation*. And upon this sup- "position, by that truth which is always connected with beau- "ty, nothing more can be meant than the conformity of any "object to those proportions, upon which, after careful exami- "nation, *the beauty of that species is found to depend.*" This opinion, if I am able to comprehend it, differs only in one point from the preceding. It supposes the standard or law of beauty, not invariable and universal. It is liable to the same objection, and that rather more glaringly, for if the same relations must be always equally *true relations*, deformity is as really one with truth, as beauty is, since the very same relations can exhibit both appearances. In short, no hypothesis hitherto invented hath shown that by means of the discursive faculty, without the aid of any other mental power, we could ever obtain a notion of either the beautiful or the good, and till this be shown, nothing is shown to the purpose. The author aforesaid, far from at- tempting this, proceeds on the supposition, that we first per- ceive beauty, he says not how, and then having by a careful ex- amination, discovered the proportions which gave rise to the perception, denominate them *true*; so that all those elaborate disquisitions with which we are amused, amount only to a few insignificant identical propositions very improperly expressed. For out of a vast profusion of learned phrase, this is all the in- formation we can pick, that 'Beauty is ——*truly* beauty,' and that 'Good is——*truly* good.' "Moral good," says a cele- brated writer, "consisteth in *fitness*." From this account any person would at first readily conclude, that morals, according to him, are not concerned in the ends which we pursue, but
solely

rit of the action recommended, argument may be employed to evince the reasonableness of the

solely in the choice of means for attaining our ends; that if this choice be judicious, the conduct is moral; if injudicious, the contrary. But this truly pious author is far from admitting such an interpretation of his words. *Fitness* in his sense hath no relation to a further end. It is an absolute fitness, a fitness in itself. We are obliged to ask, What then is that fitness, which you call absolute? for the application of the word in every other case invariably implying the proper direction of means to an end, far from affording light to the meaning it has here, tends directly to mislead us. The only answer, as far as I can learn, that hath ever been given to this question, is neither more nor less than this, ' That alone is absolutely fit which is morally ' good:' so that in saying moral good consisteth in fitness, no more is meant than that it consisteth in moral good. Another moralist appears, who hath made a most wonderful discovery. It is, that there is not a vice in the world but lying, and that acting virtuously in any situation, is but one way or other of telling truth. When this curious theory comes to be explained, we find the practical lie results solely from acting contrary to what those moral sentiments dictate, which, instead of deducing, he every where presupposeth to be known and acknowledged by us. Thus he reasons perpetually in a circle, and without advancing a single step beyond it, makes the same things both causes and effects reciprocally. Conduct appears to be false for no other reason, but because it is immoral, and immoral for no other reason but because it is false. Such philosophy would not have been unworthy those profound ontologists, who have blest the world with the discovery that ' One being is but *one* being,' that ' A being is *truly* a being,' and that ' Every being has all ' the *properties* that it has,' and who, to the unspeakable increase of useful knowledge, have denominated these the general attributes of being, and distinguished them by the titles, *unity, truth,* and *goodness*. This, if it be any thing, is the very sublimate of science.

end,

end, as well as the fitness of the means. But this way of speaking suits better the popular dialect, than the philosophical. The term *reasonableness*, when used in this manner, means nothing but the goodness, the amiableness, or moral excellency. If therefore the hearer hath no love of justice, no benevolence, no regard to right, although he were endowed with the perspicacity of a cherub, your harangue could never have any influence on his mind. The reason is, when you speak of the fitness of the means, you address yourself only to the head; when you speak of the goodness of the end, you address yourself to the heart, of which we supposed him destitute. Are we then to class the virtues among the passions? By no means. But without entering into a discussion of the difference, which would be foreign to our purpose, let it suffice to observe, that they have this in common with passion. They necessarily imply an habitual propensity to a certain species of conduct, an habitual aversion to the contrary; a veneration for such a character, an abhorrence of such another. They are therefore, though not passions, so closely related to them, that they are properly considered as motives to action, being equally capable of giving an impulse to the will. The difference is a-kin to that, if not the same, which rhetoricians observe between *pathos* and *ethos*, passion and disposition *. Accordingly, what is addressed solely to the moral powers of the mind, is not so properly denominated the pathetic, as the *sentimental*. The term, I own, is rather modern, but is nevertheless convenient, as it fills a vacant room, and doth not, like most of our newfangled words, justle out older and worthier occupants, to the no small detriment of the language. It occupies, so to speak, the middle place between the pathetic and that which is addressed to the imagination, and partakes of both, adding to the warmth of the former, the grace and attractions of the latter.

Now the principal questions on this subject, are these two. How is a passion or disposition that is favourable to the design of the orator, to be excited in the hearers? How is an unfavourable passion or disposition to be calmed? As to the first, it was said already in general, that passion must be awakened by communicating lively ideas of the object. The reason will be obvious from the following remarks: A passion

---

* This seems to have been the sense which Quintilian had of the difference between παθος and ηθος, when he gave *amor* for an example of the first, and *charitas* of the second. The word ηθος is also sometimes used for moral sentiment.

is most strongly excited by sensation. The sight of danger, immediate or near, instantly rouseth fear, the feeling of an injury, and the presence of the injurer, in a moment kindle anger. Next to the influence of sense, is that of memory, the effect of which upon passion, if the fact be recent and remembered distinctly and circumstantially, is almost equal. Next to the influence of memory, is that of imagination; by which is here solely meant, the faculty of apprehending what is neither perceived by the senses, nor remembered. Now, as it is this power of which the orator must chiefly avail himself, it is proper to inquire what those circumstances are, which will make the ideas he summons up in the imaginations of his hearers, resemble, in lustre and steadiness, those of sensation and remembrance. For the same circumstances will infallibly make them resemble also in their effects; that is, in the influence they will have upon the passions and affections of the heart.

SECTION V.

The circumstances that are chiefly instrumental in operating on the passions.

THESE are perhaps all reducible to the seven following, probability, plausibility, importance, proximity of time, connexion of place, relation of the actors or sufferers to the hearers or speaker, interest of the hearers or speaker in the consequences †.

PART I. *Probability.*

THE first is *probability*, which is now considered only as an expedient for enlivening passion. Here again there is commonly scope for argument ‡. Probability results from evidence, and

---

† I am not quite positive as to the accuracy of this enumeration, and shall therefore freely permit my learned and ingenious friend Dr. Reid, to annex the *et cætera*, he proposes in such cases, in order to supply all defects. See Sketches of the History of Man. B. III Sk. 1. Appendix, c. II. sect. 2.

‡ In the judiciary orations of the ancients, this was the principal scope for argument. That to condemn the guilty, and to acquit the innocent, would gratify their indignation against the injurious, and their love of right was too manifest to require a proof. The fact, that there was guilt in the prisoner, or that there was innocence, did require it. It was otherwise in deliberative orations, as the conduct recommended was more remotely connected with the emotions raised.

begets

begets belief. Belief invigorates our ideas. Belief raised to the highest becomes certainty. Certainty flows either from the force of the evidence, real or apparent, that is produced; or without any evidence produced by the speaker, from the previous notoriety of the fact. If the fact be notorious, it will not only be superfluous in the speaker to attempt to prove it, but it will be pernicious to his design. The reason is plain. By proving he supposeth it questionable, and by supposing actually renders it so to his audience: he brings them from viewing it in the stronger light of certainty, to view it in the weaker light of probability: in lieu of sun-shine he gives them twilight. Of the different means and kinds of probation I have spoken already.

Part II. *Plausibility.*

The second circumstance is *plausibility,* a thing totally distinct from the former, as having an effect upon the mind quite independent of faith or probability. It ariseth chiefly from the consistency of the narration, from its being what is commonly called natural and feasible. This the French critics have aptly enough denominated in their language *vraisemblance,* the English critics more improperly in theirs *probability.*

In

In order to avoid the manifest ambiguity there is in this application of the word, it had been better to retain the word *verisimilitude*, now almost obsolete. That there is a relation between those two qualities must, notwithstanding, be admitted. This, however, is an additional reason for assigning them different names. An homonymous term, whose differing significations have no affinity to one another, is scarce ever liable to be misunderstood.

But as to the nature and extent of this relation, let it be observed, that the want of plausibility implies an internal improbability, which it will require the stronger external evidence to surmount. Nevertheless, the implausibility may be surmounted by such evidence, and we may be fully ascertained of what is in itself exceedingly implausible. Implausibility is, in a certain degree, positive evidence against a narrative; whereas plausibility implies no positive evidence for it. We know that fiction may be as plausible as truth. A narration may be possessed of this quality in the highest degree, which we not only regard as improbable, but know to be false. Probability is a light darted on the object, from the proofs, which for this reason are pertinently enough styled *evidence*. Plausibility is a native lustre issuing directly from the object. The former is the aim of the historian, the latter of the poet. That every one may be satisfied, that the second is generally not inferior to the first, in its influence on the mind, we need but appeal to the effects of tragedy, of epic, and even of romance, which in its principal characters, participates of the nature of poesy, though written in prose.

It deserves, however, to be remarked, that though plausibility alone hath often greater efficacy in rousing the passions, than probability, or even certainty, yet, in any species of composition wherein truth, or at least probability is expected, the mind quickly nauseates the most plausible tale, which is unsupported by proper arguments. For this reason it is the business of the orator, as much as his subject will permit, to avail himself of both qualities. There is one case, and but one, in which plausibility itself may be dispensed with, that is, when the fact is so incontestible, that it is impossible to entertain a doubt of it; for when implausibility is incapable of impairing belief, it hath sometimes, especially in forensic causes, even a good effect. By

presenting

presenting us with something monstrous in its kind, it raises astonishment, and thereby heightens every passion which the narrative is fitted to excite.

But to return to the explication of this quality. When I explained the nature of experience, I showed, that it consisteth of all the general truths collected from particular facts remembered; the mind forming to itself often insensibly, and as it were mechanically, certain maxims, from comparing, or rather associating the similar circumstances of different incidents*. Hence it is, that when a number of ideas relating to any fact or event, are successively introduced into my mind by a speaker; if the train he deduceth, coincide with the general current of my experience; if in nothing it thwart those conclusions and anticipations which are become habitual to me, my mind accompanies him with facility, glides along from one idea to another, and admits the whole with pleasure. If, on the contrary, the train he introduceth, run counter to the current of my experience, if in many things it shock those conclusions and anticipations which are become habitual to me, my mind at-

* Chap. V. Sect. ii. Part 2.

tends him with difficulty, suffers a sort of violence in passing from one idea to another, and rejects the whole with disdain.

> For while upon such monstrous scenes we gaze,
> They shock our faith, our indignation raise †. FRANCIS.

In the former case I pronounce the narrative natural and credible, in the latter I say it is unnatural and incredible, if not impossible; and, which is particularly expressive of the different appearances in respect of connexion made by the ideas in my mind, the one tale I call coherent, the other incoherent. When therefore the orator can obtain no direct aid from the memory of his hearers, which is rarely to be obtained, he must, for the sake of brightening, and strengthening, and, if I may be permitted to use so bold a metaphor, cementing his ideas, bespeak the assistance of experience. This, if properly employed, will prove a potent ally, by adding the grace of *verisimilitude* to the whole. It is therefore first of all requisite, that the circumstances of the narration, and the order in which they are exhibited, be what is commonly called natural, that is, congruous to general experience.

---

† Quodcunque ostendis mihi sic, incredulus odi.
HOR. De Arte Poet.

WHERE passion is the end, it is not a sufficient reason for introducing any circumstance that it is natural, it must also be pertinent. It is pertinent, when either necessary for giving a distinct and consistent apprehension of the object, at least for obviating some objection that may be started, or doubt that may be entertained concerning it; or when such as in its particular tendency promotes the general aim. All circumstances however plausible, which serve merely for decoration, never fail to divert the attention, and so become prejudicial to the proposed influence on passion.

BUT I am aware, that from the explication I have given of this quality, it will be said, that I have run into the error, if it be an error, which I intended to avoid, and have confounded it with probability, by deriving it solely from the same origin, experience. In answer to this, let it be observed, that in every plausible tale, which is unsupported by external evidence, there will be found throughout the whole, when duly canvassed, a mixture of possibilities and probabilities, and that not in such a manner as to make one part or incident probable, another barely possible, but so blended as equally to affect the whole,

whole, and every member. Take the Iliad for an example, That a haughty, choleric, and vindictive hero, such as Achilles is represented to have been, should, upon the public affront and injury he received from Agamemnon, treat that general with indignity, and form a resolution of withdrawing his troops, remaining thenceforth an unconcerned spectator of the calamities of his countrymen, our experience of the baleful influences of pride and anger, renders in some degree probable; again, that one of such a character as Agamemnon, rapacious, jealous of his pre-eminence as commander in chief, who envied the superior merit of Achilles, and harboured resentment against him, that such a one, I say, on such an occurrence as is related by the poet, should have given the provocation, will be acknowledged also to have some probability. But that there were such personages, of such characters, in such circumstances, is merely possible. Here there is a total want of evidence. Experience is silent. Properly indeed the case comes not within the verge of its jurisdiction. Its general conclusions may serve in confutation, but can never serve in proof of particular or historical facts. Sufficient testimony, and that only will answer here. The testimony of the poet in this case goes for nothing. His object we know is not truth but likelihood. Experience, however, advances nothing against those allegations of the poet, therefore we call them possible; it can say nothing for them, therefore we do not call them probable. The whole at most amounts to this, If such causes existed, such effects probably followed. But we have no evidence of the existence of the causes; therefore we have no evidence of the existence of the effects. Consequently, all the probability implied in this quality, is a hypothetical probability, which is in effect none at all. It is an axiom among dialecticians, in relation to the syllogistic art, that the conclusion always follows the weaker of the premises. To apply this to the present purpose, an application not illicit, though unusual, if one of the premises, suppose the major, contain an affirmation that is barely possible, the minor one that is probable, possibility only can be deduced in the conclusion.

These two qualities therefore, *probability* and *plausibility*, (if I may be indulged a little in the allegoric style) I shall call Sister-graces, daughters of the same father *Experience*, who is the progeny of *Memory*, the first-born and heir of *Sense*.

Senfe. These daughters *Experience* had by different mothers. The elder is the offspring of *Reason*, the younger is the child of *Fancy*. The elder regular her in features, and majestic both in shape and mien, is admirably fitted for commanding esteem, and even a religious veneration; the younger careless, blooming, sprightly, is entirely formed for captivating the heart, and engaging love. The conversation of each is entertaining and instructive, but in different ways. Sages seem to think that there is more instruction to be gotten from the just observations of the elder, almost all are agreed that there is more entertainment in the lively sallies of the younger. The principal companion and favourite of the first is *Truth*, but whether *Truth* or *Fiction* share most in the favour of the second, it were often difficult to say. Both are naturally well-disposed, and even friendly to *Virtue*, but the elder is by much the more steady of the two; the younger, though perhaps not less capable of doing good, is more easily corrupted, and hath sometimes basely turned procuress to *Vice*. Though rivals, they have a sisterly affection to each other, and love to be together. The elder, sensible that there are but few who can for any time relish her society alone, is generally

anxious

anxious that her sister be of the party; the younger, conscious of her own superior talents in this respect, can more easily dispense with the other's company. Nevertheless, when she is discoursing on great and serious subjects, in order to add weight to her words, she often quotes her sister's testimony, which she knows is better credited than her own, a compliment that is but sparingly returned by the elder. Each sister hath her admirers. Those of the younger are more numerous, those of the elder more constant. In the retinue of the former you will find the young, the gay, the dissipated, but these are not her only attendants. The middle-aged, however, and the thoughtful, more commonly attach themselves to the latter. To conclude, as something may be learned of characters from the invectives of enemies, as well as from the encomiums of friends, those who have not judgment to discern the good qualities of the first-born, accuse her of dulness, pedantry, and stiffness, those who have not taste to relish the charms of the second, charge her with folly, levity, and falseness. Meantime, it appears to be the universal opinion of the impartial, and such as have been best acquainted with both, that though the attractives of the younger be more

irresistible

irresistible at sight, the virtues of the elder will be longer remembered.

So much for the two qualities, probability and plausibility, on which I have expatiated the more, as they are the principal, and in some respect, indispensable. The others are not compatible with every subject; but as they are of real moment, it is necessary to attend to them, that so they may not be overlooked in cases wherein the subject requires that they be urged.

Part III. *Importance.*

The third circumstance I took notice of was *importance*, the appearance of which always tends by fixing attention more closely to add brightness and strength to the ideas. The importance in moral subjects is analogous to the quantity of matter in physical subjects, as on quantity the moment of moving bodies in a great measure depends. An action may derive importance from its own nature, from those concerned in it as acting or suffering, or from its consequences. It derives importance from its own nature, if it be stupendous in its kind, if the result of what is uncommonly great, whether good or bad, passion or invention, virtue or vice, as what in respect

respect of generosity is godlike, what in respect of atrocity is diabolical. it derives importance from those concerned in it, when the actors or the sufferers are considerable, on account either of their dignity or of their number, or of both: it derives importance from its consequences, when these are remarkable in regard to their greatness, their multitude, their extent, and that either as to the many and distant places affected by them, or as to the future and remote periods to which they may reach, or as to both.

All the four remaining circumstances derive their efficacy purely from one and the same cause, the connexion of the subject with those occupied, as speaker or hearers, in the discourse. *Self* is the centre here, which hath a similar power in the ideal world, to that of the sun in the material world, in communicating both light and heat to whatever is within the sphere of its activity, and in a greater or a less degree, according to the nearness or remoteness.

Part IV. *Proximity of time.*

First, as to proximity of time, every one knows, that any melancholy incident is the more affecting that it is recent. Hence it is become

come common with story-tellers, that they may make a deeper impression on their hearers, to introduce remarks like these, that the tale which they relate is not old, that it happened but lately, or in their own time, or that they are yet living who had a part in it, or were witnesses of it. Proximity of time regards not only the past but the future. An event that will probably soon happen, hath greater influence upon us than what will probably happen a long time hence. I have hitherto proceeded on the hypothesis, that the orator rouses the passions of his hearers, by exhibiting some past transaction; but we must acknowledge that passion may be as strongly excited by his reasonings concerning an event yet to come. In the judiciary orations there is greater scope for the former, in the deliberative for the latter, though in each kind there may occasionally be scope for both. All the seven circumstances enumerated are applicable, and have equal weight, whether they relate to the future or to the past. The only exception that I know of is, that probability and plausibility are scarce distinguishable, when used in reference to events in futurity. As in these there is no access for testimony, what constitutes the principal distinction is quite excluded. In comparing the influence

of

of the past upon our minds, with that of the future, it appears in general, that if the evidence, the importance, and the distance of the objects be equal, the latter will be greater than the former. The reason, I imagine, is, we are conscious, that as every moment, the future, which seems placed before us, is approaching; and the past, which lies, as it were, behind, is retiring, our nearness or relation to the one constantly increaseth as the other decreaseth. There is something like attraction in the first case, and repulsion in the second. This tends to interest us more in the future than in the past, and consequently to the present view aggrandizes the one and diminishes the other.

What, nevertheless, gives the past a very considerable advantage, is its being generally susceptible of much stronger evidence than the future. The lights of the mind are, if I may so express myself, in an opposite situation to the lights of the body. These discover clearly the prospect lying before us, but not the ground we have already passed. By the memory, on the contrary, that great luminary of the mind, things past are exhibited in retrospect; we have no correspondent faculty to irradiate the future: and even

even in matters which fall not within the reach of our memory, past events are often clearly discoverable by testimony, and by effects at present existing; whereas, we have nothing equivalent to found our arguments upon in reasoning about things to come. It is for this reason, that the future is considered as the province of conjecture and uncertainty.

PART V. *Connexion of Place.*

LOCAL *connexion*, the fifth in the above enumeration, hath a more powerful effect than proximity of time. Duration and space are two things, (call them entities, or attributes, or what you please) in some respects the most like, and in some respects the most unlike to one another. They resemble in continuity, divisibility, infinity, in their being deemed essential to the existence of other things, and in the doubts that have been raised as to their having a real or independent existence of their own. They differ in that the latter is permanent, whereas the very essence of the former consisteth in transitoriness; the parts of the one are all successive, of the other all co-existent. The greater portions of time are all distinguished by the memorable things which have been transacted in them, the smaller portions

tions by the revolutions of the heavenly bodies: the portions of place, great and small, (for we do not here consider the regions of the fixed stars and planets) are distinguished by the various tracts of land and water, into which the earth is divided, and subdivided; the one distinction intelligible, the other sensible; the one chiefly known to the inquisitive, the other in a great measure obvious to all.

HENCE perhaps it arises, that the latter is considered as a firmer ground of relation, than the former. Who is not more curious to know the notable transactions which have happened in his own country from the earliest antiquity, than to be acquainted with those which have happened in the remotest regions of the globe, during the century wherein he lives? It must be owned, however, that the former circumstance is more frequently aided by that of personal relation than the latter. Connexion of place not only includes vicinage, but every other local relation, such as being in a province under the same government with us, in a state that is in alliance with us, in a country well known to us, and the like. Of the influence of this connexion in operating on our passions, we have daily proofs. With how much

much indifference, at least with how slight and transient emotion, do we read in news-papers the accounts of the most deplorable accidents in countries distant and unknown? How much, on the contrary, are we alarmed and agitated on being informed, that any such accident hath happened in our neighbourhood, and that even though we be totally unacquainted with the persons concerned?

PART VI. *Relation to the persons concerned.*

STILL greater is the power of *relation* to the persons concerned, which was the sixth circumstance mentioned, as this tie is more direct than that which attacheth us to the scene of action. It is the persons, not the place, that are the immediate objects of the passions love or hatred, pity or anger, envy or contempt. Relation to the actors commonly produces an effect contrary to that produced by relation to the sufferers, the first in extenuation, the second in aggravation of the crime alleged. The first makes for the apologist, the second for the accuser. This, I say, is commonly the case, not always. A remote relation to the actors, when the offence is heinous, especially if the sufferers be more nearly related, will sometimes rather aggravate than extenuate

the

the guilt in our estimation. But it is impossible with any precision to reduce these effects to rules, so much depending on the different tempers and sentiments of different audiences. Personal relations are of various kinds. Some have generally greater influence than others; some again have greater influence with one person, others with another. They are consanguinity, affinity, friendship, acquaintance, being fellow-citizens, countrymen, of the same surname, language, religion, occupation, and innumerable others.

PART VII. *Interest in the consequences.*

BUT of all the connexive circumstances, the most powerful is *interest*, which is the last. Of all relations, personal relation, by bringing the object very near, most enlivens that sympathy which attacheth us to the concerns of others, interest in the effects brings the object, if I may say so, into contact with us, and makes the mind cling to it, as a concern of its own. Sympathy is but a reflected feeling, and therefore, in ordinary cases, must be weaker than the original. Though the mirror be ever so true, a lover will not be obliged to it for presenting him with the figure of his mistress, when he hath an opportunity of gazing on her person. Nor will the orator place his chief confidence in the affiftance of the focial and fympathetic affections, when he hath it in his power to arm the felfifh.

MEN univerfally, from a juft conception of the difference, have, when felf is concerned, given a different name to what feems originally the fame paffion in a higher degree. Injury, to whomfoever offered, is to every man that obferves it, and whofe fenfe of right is not debauched by vicious practice, the natural object of *indignation*. Indignation always implies *refentment*, or a defire of retaliating on the injurious perfon, fo far at leaft as to make him repent the wrong he hath committed. This indignation in the perfon injured, is, from our knowledge of mankind, fuppofed to be, not indeed univerfally, but generally, fo much ftronger, that it ought to be diftinguifhed by another appellation, and is accordingly denominated *revenge*. In like manner, beneficence, on whomfoever exercifed, is the natural object of our *love*, love always implies *benevolence*, or a defire of promoting the happinefs of the beneficent perfon; but this paffion in the perfon benefited, is conceived to be fo much greater, and to infer fo ftrong an obligation to a return of good offices to his benefactor, that it

merits

merits to be distinguished by the title *gratitude*. Now by this circumstance of *interest* in the effects, the speaker, from engaging *pity* in his favour, can proceed to operate on a more powerful principle *self-preservation*. The *benevolence* of his hearers he can work up into *gratitude*, their *indignation* into *revenge*.

The two last mentioned circumstances, personal relation and interest, are not without influence, as was hinted in the enumeration, though they regard the speaker only and not the hearers. The reason is, a person present with us, whom we see and hear, and who by words, and looks, and gestures, gives the liveliest signs of his feelings, has the surest and most immediate claim upon our sympathy. We become infected with his passions. We are hurried along by them, and not allowed leisure to distinguish between his relation and our relation, his interest and our interest.

Section VI.

Other passions, as well as moral sentiments, useful auxiliaries.

So much for those circumstances in the object presented by the speaker, which serve to awaken and inflame the passions of the hearers*. But when

---

* To illustrate most of the preceding circumstances, and show the manner of applying them, I shall take an example from Cicero's last oration against Verres, where, after relating the crucifixion of Gavius a Roman citizen, he exclaims, 1. " O nomen
" dulce libertatis ! o jus eximium nostræ civitatis ! o lex Porcia
" legesque Semproniæ ! o graviter desiderata et aliquando reddi-
" ta plebi Romanæ tribunitia potestas 2. Huccine tandem om-
" nia reciderunt, ut civis Romanus in provincia populi Romani,
" in oppido fœderatorum, ab eo qui beneficio populi Romani
" fasceis et secureis haberet, deligatus in foro virgis cæderetur ?"
" ——3. Sed quid ego plura de Gavio ? quasi tu Gavio tum fu-
" eris infestus, ac non nomini, generi, juri civium hostis, non
" illi inquam homini, sed causæ communi libertatis inimicus
" fuisti 4. Quid enim attinuit, cum Mamertini more atque insti-
" tuto suo, crucem fixissent post urbem, in via Pompeia, te
" jubere in ea parte figere, quæ ad fretum spectat, et hoc ad-
" dere, quod negare nullo modo potes, quod omnibus audi-
" entibus dixisti palam, te idcirco illum locum deligere, ut ille
" qui se civem Romanum esse diceret, ex cruce Italiam cer-
" nere, ac domum suam prospicere posset ? 5. Itaque illa crux
" sola, judices, post conditam Messanam, illo in loco fixa est.
" 6. Italiæ conspectus ad eam rem ab isto delectus est, ut ille in
" dolore cruciatuque moriens, perangusto freto divisa servitutis
" ac libertatis jura cognosceret. Italia autem alumnum suum,
" servitutis extremo summoque supplicio affectum videret 7.
" Facinus

when a passion is once raised, there are also other means by which it may be kept alive, and even aug-

"Facinus est vincire civem Romanum, scelus verberare, prope "parricidium necare, quid dicam, in crucem tollere? verbo sa- "tis digno tam nefaria res appellari nullo modo potest. 8. Non "fuit his omnibus iste contentus Spectet, inquit, patriam, in "conspectu legum libertatisque moriatur. 9. Non tu hoc loco "Gavium, non unum hominem, nescio quem, civem Romanum, "sed communem libertatis et civitatis causam in illum crucia- "tum et crucem egisti. 10. Jam vero videte hominis auda- "ciam Nonne enim graviter tulisse arbitramini, quod illam "civibus Romanis crucem non posset in foro, non in comitio, "non in rostris defigere. 11 Quod enim his locis in provincia "sua celebritate simillimum, regione proximum potuit, elegit. "12 Monumentum sceleris—audaciæque suæ voluit esse in "conspectu Italiæ, prætervectione omnium qui ultro citroque "navigarent."———" 13 Paulo ante, judices, lacrymas in "morte miserâ atque indignissimâ navarchorum non tenebamus: "et recte ac merito sociorum innocentium miseriâ commoveba- "mur. 14 Quid nunc in nostro sanguine tandem facere de- "bemus? nam civium Romanorum sanguis conjunctus existi- "mandus est."———" 15. Omnes hoc loco cives Romani, et "qui adsunt et qui ubicunque sunt, vestram severitatem deside- "rant, vestram fidem implorant, vestrum auxilium requirunt. "16. Omnia sua jura, commoda, auxilia, totam denique liberta- "tem in vestris sententiis versari arbitrantur."———I shall point out the pathetic circumstances exemplified in this passage, ob serving the order wherein they were enumerated. I have num bered the sentences in the quotation to prevent repetition in re ferring to them. It must be remarked first of all, that in judi ciary oration, such as this, the proper place for plausibility is the narration, for probability, the confirmation or proof the other five, though generally admissible into either of those places, shine principally in the peroration. I shall show how the orator hath availed himself of these in the passage now cited. First, *import* augmented. Other passions or dispositions may be called in as auxiliaries. Nothing is more efficacious

ance, and that first in respect of the enormity of the action, N°. 7; of the disposition of the actor, N°. 3. 9, 10, and to render probable what might otherwise appear merely conjectural, N°. 4, 5. 8. 11, 12., in respect of consequences, their greatness, N°. 1, 2., where the crime is most artfully, though implicitly, represented as subversive of all that was dear to them, liberty, the right of citizens, their most valuable laws, and that idol of the people, the tribunitian power, their extent, N°. 15, 16. Secondly, *proximity of time*, there is but an insinuation of this circumstance in the word *tandem*, N°. 2. There are two reasons which probably induced the orator in this particular to be so sparing. One 1st, the recency of the crime, as of the criminal's pretorship was notorious; the other and the weightier is, that of all relations this is the weakest, and even what influence it hath, reflection serves rather to correct than to confirm. In appearing to lay stress on so slight a circumstance, a speaker displays rather penury of matter than abundance. It is better therefore, in most cases, to suggest it, as it were, by accident, than to insist on it as of design. It deserves also to be remarked, that the word here employed is very emphatical, as it conveys at the same time a tacit comparison of their so recent degeneracy with the freedom, security, and glory which they had long enjoyed. The same word is again introduced, N°. 14. to the same intent. Thirdly, *local connexion*, in respect of vicinage, how affectingly, though indirectly, is it touched, N°. 4. 6. 8. 11, 12.? indirectly, for reasons similar to those mentioned on the circumstance of time, as to other local connexions, N°. 2. " in provincia populi Romani, in oppido fœderatorum." Fourthly, *personal relation*, first of the perpetrator, N°. 2. " ab " eo qui beneficio, &c." his crime therefore more atrocious and ungrateful, the most sacred rights violated by one who ought to have protected them; next of the sufferer, N°. 2. " civis " Romanus." This is most pathetically urged, and by a comparison

ficacious in this respect than a sense of justice, a sense of public utility, a sense of glory; and nothing conduceth more to operate on these, than the sentiments of sages whose wisdom we venerate, the example of heroes whose exploits we admire. I shall conclude what relates to the exciting of passion, when I have remarked, that pleading the importance and the other pathetic circumstances,

parison introduced, greatly heightened, N°. 13, 14. Fifthly, the *interest*; which, not the hearers only, but all who bear the Roman name, have, in the consequences, N°. 15, 16. We see in the above example, with what uncommon address and delicacy those circumstances ought to be sometimes blended, sometimes but insinuated, sometimes, on the contrary, warmly urged, sometimes shaded a little, that the art may be concealed, and in brief, the whole conducted so as that nothing material may be omitted, that every sentiment may easily follow that which precedes, and usher that which follows it, and that every thing said may appear to be the language of pure nature. The art of the rhetorician, like that of the philosopher, is analytical; the art of the orator is synthetical. The former acts the part of the skilful anatomist, who, by removing the teguments, and nicely separating the parts, presents us with views at once naked, distinct, and hideous, now of the structure of the bones, now of the muscles and tendons, now of the arteries and veins, now of the bowels, now of the brain and nervous system. The latter imitates Nature in the constructing of her work, who, with wonderful symmetry, unites the various organs, adapts them to their respective uses, and covers all with a decent veil, the skin. Thus, though she hide entirely the more minute and the interior parts, and show not to equal advantage even the articulations of the limbs, and the adjustment of the larger members, adds inexpressible beauty, and strength, and energy to the whole.

cumstances, or pleading the authority of opinions or precedents, is usually considered, and aptly enough, as being likewise a species of reasoning.

This concession, however, doth not imply, that by any reasoning we are ever taught that such an object ought to awaken such a passion. This we must learn originally from feeling, not from argument. No speaker attempts to prove it; though he sometimes introduceth moral considerations, in order to justify the passion when raised, and to prevent the hearers from attempting to suppress it. Even when he is enforcing their regard to the pathetic circumstances abovementioned, it is not so much his aim to show that these circumstances ought to augment the passion, as that these circumstances are in the object. The effect upon their minds he commonly leaves to nature; and is not afraid of the conclusion, if he can make every aggravating circumstance be, as it were, both perceived and felt by them. In the enthymeme, (the syllogism of orators, as Quintilian* terms it) employed in such cases, the sentiment that such a quality or circumstance ought to rouse such a passion, though the foundation of all, is generally as-

* Inſtit. l. 1. c. 9.

sumed

sumed without proof, or even without mention. This forms the major propofition, which is fuppreffed as obvious. His whole art is exerted in evincing the minor, which is the antecedent in his argument, and which maintains the reality of thofe attendant circumftances in the cafe in hand. A careful attention to the examples of vehemence in the Firft Chapter, and the quotation in the foregoing note, will fufficiently illuftrate this remark.

SECTION VII.

How an unfavourable paffion muft be calmed.

I COME now to the fecond queftion on the fubject of paffion. How is an unfavourable paffion, or difpofition, to be calmed? The anfwer is, either, firft, by annihilating, or at leaft diminifhing the object which raifed it; or fecondly, by exciting fome other paffion which may counterwork it.

By proving the falfity of the narration, or the utter incredibility of the future event, on the fuppofed truth of which the paffion was founded, the object is annihilated. It is diminifhed by all fuch circumftances as are contrary to thofe by which

which it is increased. These are, improbability, implausibility, insignificance, distance of time, remoteness of place, the persons concerned such as we have no connexion with, the consequences such as we have no interest in. The method recommended by Gorgias, and approved by Aristotle, though peculiar in its manner, is, in those cases wherein it may properly be attempted, coincident in effect with that now mentioned. "It was a just opinion of Gorgias, that the se-"rious argument of an adversary, should be "confounded by ridicule, and his ridicule by "serious argument*." For this is only endeavouring, by the aid of laughter and contempt, to diminish, or even quite undo, the unfriendly emotions that have been raised in the minds of the hearers; or, on the contrary, by satisfying them of the seriousness of the subject, and of the importance of its consequences, to extinguish the contempt, and make the laughter which the antagonist wanted to excite, appear, when examined, no better than madness.

The second way of silencing an unfavourable passion or disposition, is, by conjuring up some

---

* Διὸ ἔφη Γοργίας τὴν μὲν σπουδὴν διαφθείρειν τῶν ἐναντίων γέλωτι, τὸν δ. γέλωτα σπουδῇ· ὀρθῶς λέγων. Rhet. l. iii. c. 18.

other paſſion or diſpoſition which may overcome it. With regard to conduct, whenever the mind deliberates, it is conſcious of contrary motives impelling it in oppoſite directions; in other words, it finds that acting thus would gratify one paſſion; not acting, or acting otherwiſe, would gratify another. To take ſuch a ſtep, I perceive, would promote my intereſt but derogate from my honour. Such another will gratify my reſentment, but hurt my intereſt. When this is the caſe, as the ſpeaker can be at no loſs to diſcover the conflicting paſſions, he muſt be ſenſible, that whatever force he adds to the diſpoſition that favours his deſign, is in fact ſo much ſubtracted from the diſpoſition that oppoſeth it, and converſely; as in the two ſcales of a balance, it is equal in regard to the effect, whether you add ſo much weight to one ſcale, or take it from the other.

Thus we have ſeen in what manner paſſion to an abſent object may be excited by eloquence, which, by enlivening and invigorating the ideas of imagination, makes them reſemble the impreſſions of ſenſe and the traces of memory; and in this reſpect hath an effect on the mind ſimilar to that produced by a teleſcope on the ſight;
things

things remote are brought near, things obscure rendered conspicuous. We have seen also in what manner a passion already excited may be calmed; how by the oratorical magic, as by inverting the telescope, the object may be again removed and diminished.

It were endless to enumerate all the rhetorical figures that are adapted to the pathetic: Let it suffice to say, that most of those already named may be successfully employed here. Of others the principal are these, correction, climax, vision, exclamation, apostrophé, and interrogation. The three first, correction, climax, and vision, tend greatly to enliven the ideas, by the implicit, but animated comparison, and opposition, conveyed in them. Implicit and indirect comparison is more suitable to the disturbed state of mind required by the pathetic, than that which is explicit and direct. The latter implies leisure and tranquillity, the former rapidity and fire. Exclamation and apostrophé operate chiefly by sympathy, as they are the most ardent expressions of perturbation in the speaker. That first sight appears more difficult to account for the effect of interrogation, which, being an appeal to the hearers, though it might awaken a

closer

closer attention, yet could not, one would imagine, excite in their minds any new emotion that was not there before. This, neverhelefs, it doth excite, through an oblique operation of the fame principle. Such an appeal implies in the orator the ftrongeft confidence in the rectitude of his fentiments, and in the concurrence of every reasonable being. The auditors, by sympathizing with this frame of fpirit, find it impracticable to withhold an affent which is fo confidently depended on. But there will be occafion afterwards for difcuffing more particularly the rhetorical tropes and figures, when we come to treat of elocution.

Thus I have finifhed the confideration which the fpeaker ought to have of his hearers as men in general; that is, as thinking beings endowed with underftanding, imagination, memory, and paffions, fuch as we are confcious of in ourfelves, and learn from the experience of their effects to be in others. I have pointed out the arts to be employed by him in engaging all thofe faculties in his fervice, that what he advanceth may not only be underftood, not only command attention, not only be remembered, but, which is the chief point of all, may intereft the heart.

CHAP.

CHAP. VIII.

Of the confideration which the fpeaker ought to have of the hearers, as fuch men in particular.

IT was remarked in the beginning of the preceding chapter, that the hearers ought to be confidered in a twofold view, as men in general, and as fuch men in particular. The firft confideration I have difpatched, I now enter on the second.

WHEN it is affirmed that the hearers are to be confidered as fuch men in particular, no more is meant, than that regard ought to be had by the fpeaker, to the fpecial character of the audience, as compofed of fuch individuals; that he may fuit himfelf to them, both in his ftyle and in his arguments[*]. Now the difference between one audience and another is very great, not only in intellectual, but in moral attainments. It may be clearly intelligible to a Houfe of Commons, which would appear as if fpoken in an unknown tongue to a conventicle of enthufiafts. It may kindle fury in the latter, which would create

[*] He muft be " Orpheus in fylvis, inter delphinas Arion." VIRG.

no emotion in the former, but laughter and contempt. The most obvious difference that appears in different auditories, results from the different cultivation of the understanding; and the influence which this, and their manner of life, have both upon the imagination and upon the memory.

But even in cases wherein the difference in education and moral culture hath not been considerable, different habits afterwards contracted, and different occupations in life, give different propensities, and make one incline more to one passion, another to another. They consequently afford the intelligent speaker an easier passage to the heart, through the channel of the favourite passion. Thus liberty and independence will ever be prevalent motives with republicans, pomp and splendour with those attached to monarchy. In mercantile states, such as Carthage among the ancients, or Holland among the moderns, interest will always prove the most cogent argument; in states solely or chiefly composed of soldiers, such as Sparta and ancient Rome, no inducement will be found a counterpoise to glory. Similar differences are also to be made in addressing different classes of men. With men of genius the most successful topic will be fame, with men of industry, riches; with men of fortune, pleasure.

But as the characters of audiences may be infinitely diversified, and as the influence they ought to have respectively upon the speaker, must be obvious to a person of discernment, it is sufficient here to have observed thus much in the general concerning them.

CHAP. IX.

Of the consideration which the speaker ought to have of himself.

THE last consideration I mentioned, is that which the speaker ought to have of himself. By this we are to understand, not that estimate of himself which is derived directly from consciousness or self-acquaintance, but that which is obtained reflexively from the opinion entertained of him by the hearers, or the character which he bears with them. Sympathy is one main engine by which the orator operates on the passions.

With them who laugh, our social joy appears,
With them who mourn, we sympathize in tears.

If you would have me weep, begin the strain,
Then I shall feel your sorrows, feel your pain *. Francis.

Whatever therefore weakens that principle of sympathy, must do the speaker unutterable prejudice in respect of his power over the passions of his audience, but not in this respect only. One source at least of the primary influence of testimony on faith, is doubtless to be attributed to the same communicative principle. At the same time it is certain, as was remarked above, that every testimony doth not equally attach this principle; that in this particular the reputation of the attester hath a considerable power. Now the speaker's apparent conviction of the truth of what he advanceth, adds to all his other arguments an evidence, though not precisely the same, yet near a-kin to that of his own testimony †. This hath some weight even with the wisest hearers, but is every thing with the vulgar. Whatever therefore lessens sympathy, must also impair belief.

---

* Ut ridentibus arrident, ita flentibus adflent
Humani vultus. Si vis me flere, dolendum est
Primum ipsi tibi. tunc tua me infortunia lædent.
Hor. De Arte Poet.

† Ne illud quidem prætenbo, quantam afferat fidem expositioni, narrantis auctoritas. Quint. lib. iv. cap. 2.

SYMPATHY in the hearers to the speaker may be lessened several ways, chiefly by these two; by a low opinion of his intellectual abilities, and by a bad opinion of his morals. The latter is the more prejudicial of the two. Men generally will think themselves in less danger of being seduced by a man of weak understanding but of distinguished probity, than by a man of the best understanding who is of a profligate life. So much more powerfully do the qualities of the heart attach us, than those of the head. This preference, though it may be justly called untaught and instinctive, arising purely from the original frame of the mind, reason, or the knowledge of mankind acquired by experience, instead of weakening, seems afterwards to corroborate. Hence it hath become a common topic with rhetoricians, that, in order to be a successful orator, one must be a good man; for to be good is the only sure way of being long esteemed good, and to be esteemed good is previously necessary to one's being heard with due attention and regard. Consequently, the topic hath a foundation in human nature. There are indeed other things in the character of the speaker, which, in a less degree, will hurt his influence, youth, inexperience of affairs, former want of success, and the like.

BUT

But of all the prepoffeffions in the minds of the hearers which tend to impede or counteract the defign of the fpeaker, party-fpirit, where it happens to prevail, is the moft pernicious, being at once the moft inflexible and the moft unjuft. This prejudice I mention by itfelf, as thofe above recited may have place at any time, and in any national circumftances. This hath place only when a people is fo unfortunate as to be torn by faction. In that cafe, if the fpeaker and the hearers, or the bulk of the hearers, be of contrary parties, their minds will be more prepoffeffed againft him, though his life were ever fo blamelefs, than if he were a man of the moft flagitious manners, but of the fame party. This holds but too much alike of all parties, religious and political. Violent party-men not only lofe all fympathy with thofe of the oppofite fide, but contract an antipathy to them. This, on fome occafions, even the divineft eloquence will not furmount.

As to perfonal prejudices in general, I fhall conclude with two remarks. The firft is, the more grofs the hearers are, fo much the more fufceptible they are of fuch prejudices. Nothing expofes the mind more to all their baneful influences

ences than ignorance and rudeness; the rabble chiefly consider who speaks, men of sense and education what is spoken. Nor are the multitude, to do them justice, less excessive in their love than in their hatred, in their attachments than in their aversions. From a consciousness, it would seem, of their own incapacity to guide themselves, they are ever prone blindly to submit to the guidance of some popular orator, who hath had the address first, either to gain their approbation by his real or pretended virtues, or, which is the easier way, to recommend himself to their esteem by a flaming zeal for their favourite distinctions, and afterwards by his eloquence to work upon their passions. At the same time it must be acknowledged, on the other hand, that even men of the most improved intellects, and most refined sentiments, are not altogether beyond the reach of preconceived opinion, either in the speaker's favour or to his prejudice.

The second remark is, that when the opinion of the audience is unfavourable, the speaker hath need to be much more cautious in every step he takes, to show more modesty, and greater deference to the judgment of his hearers, perhaps, in order to win them, he may find it neceſſary to make ſome conceſſions in relation to his former principles or conduct, and to entreat their attention from pure regard to the ſubject, that, like men of judgment and candour, they would impartially conſider what is ſaid, and give a welcome reception to truth, from what quarter ſoever it proceed. Thus he muſt attempt, if poſſible, to mollify them, gradually to inſinuate himſelf into their favour, and thereby imperceptibly to transfuſe his ſentiments and paſſions into their minds.

The man who enjoys the advantage of popularity needs not this caution. The minds of his auditors are perfectly attuned to his. They are prepared for adopting implicitly his opinions, and accompanying him in all his moſt paſſionate excurſions. When the people are willing to run with you, you may run as faſt as you can, eſpecially when the caſe requires impetuoſity and diſpatch. But if you find in them no ſuch ardour, if it is not even without reluctance that they are induced to walk with you, you muſt ſlacken your pace and keep them company, leſt they either ſtand ſtill or turn back. Different rules are given by rhetoricians as adapted to different circumstances. Differences in this respect are numberless. It is enough here to have observed those principles in the mind, on which the rules are founded.

CHAP. X.

The different kinds of public speaking in use among the moderns, compared, with a view to their different advantages in respect of eloquence.

THE principal sorts of discourses which here demand our notice, and on which I intend to make some observations, are the three following, the orations delivered at the bar, those pronounced in the senate, and those spoken from the pulpit. I do not make a separate article of the speeches delivered by judges to their colleagues on the bench, because, though there be something peculiar here, arising from the difference in character that subsists between the judge and the pleader, in all the other material circumstances, the persons addressed, the subject, the occasion, and the purpose in speaking, there is in these two sorts a perfect coincidence. In like manner, I forbear to mention the theatre, because so entirely dissimilar, both in form and in kind,

kind, as hardly to be capable of a place in the comparison. Besides, it is only a cursory view of the chief differences, and not a critical examination of them all, that is here proposed; my design being solely to assist the mind both in apprehending rightly, and in applying properly, the principles above laid down. In this respect, the present discussion will serve to exemplify and illustrate those principles. Under these five particulars therefore, the speaker, the hearers or persons addressed, the subject, the occasion, and the end in view, or the effect intended to be produced by the discourse, I shall range, for order's sake, the remarks I intend to lay before the reader.

Section I.

In regard to the speaker.

THE first consideration is that of the character to be sustained by the speaker. It was remarked in general, in the preceding chapter, that for promoting the success of the orator, (whatever be the kind of public speaking in which he is concerned) it is a matter of some consequence, that, in the opinion of those whom he addresseth, he is both a wise and a good man. But though this in some measure holds universally,

sally, nothing is more certain than that the degree of consequence which lies in their opinion, is exceedingly different in the different kinds. In each it depends chiefly on two circumstances, the nature of his profession as a public speaker, and the character of those to whom his discourses are addressed. As to the first, arising from the nature of the profession, it will not admit a question, that the preacher hath in this respect the most difficult task, inasmuch as he hath a character to support, which is much more easily injured than that either of the senator, or of the speaker at the bar. No doubt the reputation of capacity, experience in affairs, and as much integrity as is thought attainable by those called men of the world, will add weight to the words of the senator, that of skill in his profession, and fidelity in his representations, will serve to recommend what is spoken by the lawyer at the bar, but if these characters in general remain unimpeached, the public will be sufficiently indulgent to both in every other respect. On the contrary, there is little or no indulgence, in regard to his own failings, to be expected by the man who is professedly a sort of authorized censor, who hath it in charge to mark, and reprehend the faults of others. And even in the execution of this so ticklish

ticklish a part of his office, the least excess on either hand exposeth him to censure and dislike. Too much lenity is enough to stigmatize him as lukewarm in the cause of virtue, and too much severity as a stranger to the spirit of the gospel.

But let us consider more directly what is implied in the character, that we may better judge of the effect it will have on the expectations and demands of the people, and consequently on his public teaching. First then, it is a character of some authority, as it is of one educated for a purpose so important as that of a teacher of religion. This authority, however, from the nature of the function, must be tempered with moderation, candour, and benevolence. The preacher of the gospel, as the very terms import, is the minister of grace, the herald of divine mercy to ignorant, sinful, and erring men. The magistrate, on the contrary, (under which term may be included secular judges and counsellors of every denomination) is the minister of divine justice and of wrath. *He beareth not the sword in vain**. He is on the part of heaven the avenger of the society with whose protection he is intrusted, against all who invade its rights. The

* Rom. xiii 4.

first operates chiefly on our love, the second on our fear. *Minister of religion*, like angel of God, is a name that ought to convey the idea of something endearing and attractive: whereas the title *minister of justice* invariably suggests the notion of something awful and unrelenting. In the former, even his indignation against sin ought to be surmounted by his pity of the condition, and concern for the recovery, of the sinner. Though firm in declaring the will of God, though steady in maintaining the cause of truth, yet mild in his addresses to the people, condescending to the weak, using rather entreaty than command, beseeching them by the lowliness and gentleness of Christ, knowing that *the servant of the Lord must not strive, but be gentle to all men, apt to teach patience, in meekness instructing those that oppose themselves* *. He must be grave without moroseness, cheerful without levity. And even in setting before his people the terrors of the Lord, affection ought manifestly to predominate in the warning which he is compelled to give. From these few hints it plainly appears, that there is a certain delicacy in the character of a preacher, which he is never at liberty totally to overlook, and to which, if there appear any thing incongruous,

* 2 Tim. ii. 24, 25.

either

either in his conduct or in his public performances, it will never fail to injure their effect. On the contrary, it is well known, that as, in the other professions, the speaker's private life is but very little minded, so there are many things which, though they would be accounted nowise unsuitable from the bar or in the senate, would be deemed altogether unbefitting the pulpit.

It was affirmed that the consequence of the speaker's own character in furthering or hindering his success, depends in some measure on the character of those whom he addresseth. Here also it will be found, on inquiry, that the preacher labours under a manifest disadvantage. Most congregations are of that kind, as will appear from the article immediately succeeding, which, agreeably to an observation made in the former chapter, very much considers who speaks; those addressed from the bar, or in the senate, almost solely consider what is spoken.

Section II.

In regard to the persons addressed.

The second particular mentioned as a ground of comparison, is the consideration of the character of the hearers, or more properly the persons

sons addressed. The necessity which a speaker is under of suiting himself to his audience, both that he may be understood by them, and that his words may have influence upon them, is a maxim so evident as to need neither proof nor illustration.

Now the first remark that claims our attention here is, that the more mixed the auditory is, the greater is the difficulty of speaking to them with effect. The reason is obvious, what will tend to favour your success with one, may tend to obstruct it with another. The more various therefore the individuals are, in respect of age, rank, fortune, education, prejudices, the more delicate must be the art of preserving propriety in an address to the whole. The pleader has, in this respect, the simplest and the easiest task of all, the judges to whom his oration is addressed, being commonly men of the same rank, of similar education, and not differing greatly in respect of studies or attainments. The difference in these respects is much more considerable when he addresses the jury. A speaker in the house of peers hath not so mixt an auditory as one who harangues in the house of commons. And even here, as all the members may be supposed to have

have been educated as gentlemen, the audience is not nearly so promiscuous as were the popular assemblies of Athens and of Rome, to which their demagogues declaimed with so much vehemence, and so wonderful success. Yet, even of these, women, minors, and servants, made no part.

We may therefore justly reckon a christian congregation in a populous and flourishing city, where there is great variety in rank and education, to be of all audiences the most promiscuous. And though it is impossible, that, in so mixed a multitude, every thing that is advanced by the speaker should, both in sentiment and in expression, be adapted to the apprehension of every individual hearer, and fall in with his particular prepossessions, yet it may be expected, that whatever is advanced shall be within the reach of every class of hearers, and shall not unnecessarily shock the innocent prejudices of any. This is still, however, to be understood with the exception of mere children, fools, and a few others, who, through the total neglect of parents or guardians in their education, are grossly ignorant. Such, though in the audience, are not to be considered as constituting a part of it.

But

But how great is the attention requisite in the speaker in such an assembly, that, whilst on the one hand he avoids, either in style or in sentiment, soaring above the capacity of the lower class, he may not, on the other, sink below the regard of the higher. To attain simplicity without flatness, delicacy without refinement, perspicuity without recurring to low idioms and similitudes, will require his utmost care

Another remark on this article that deserves our notice, is, that the less improved in knowledge and discernment the hearers are, the easier it is for the speaker to work upon their passions, and by working on their passions, to obtain his end. This, it must be owned, appears, on the other hand, to give a considerable advantage to the preacher, as in no congregation can the bulk of the people be regarded as on a footing, in point of improvement, with either house of parliament, or with the judges in a court of judicature. It is certain, that the more gross the hearers are, the more avowedly may you address yourself to their passions, and the less occasion there is for argument, whereas, the more intelligent they are, the more covertly must you operate on their passions, and the more attentive

attentive muſt you be in regard to the juſtneſs, or at leaſt the ſpeciouſneſs of your reaſoning. Hence ſome have ſtrangely concluded, that the only ſcope for eloquence is in haranguing the multitude; that in gaining over to your purpoſe men of knowledge and breeding, the exertion of oratorical talents hath no influence. This is preciſely as if one ſhould argue, becauſe a mob is much eaſier ſubdued than regular troops, there is no occaſion for the art of war, nor is there a proper field for the exertion of military ſkill, unleſs when you are quelling an undiſciplined rabble. Every body ſees in this caſe, not only how abſurd ſuch a way of arguing would be, but that the very reverſe ought to be the concluſion. The reaſon why people do not ſo quickly perceive the abſurdity in the other caſe, is, that they affix no diſtinct meaning to the word eloquence, often denoting no more by that term than ſimply the power of moving the paſſions. But even in this improper acceptation, their notion is far from being juſt; for wherever there are men, learned or ignorant, civilized or barbarous, there are paſſions, and the greater the difficulty is in affecting theſe, the more art is requiſite. The truth is, eloquence, like every other art, propoſeth the accompliſhment of a certain

certain end. Paffion is for the moft part but the means employed for effecting the end, and therefore, like all other means, will no further be regarded in any cafe, than it can be rendered conducible to the end.

Now the preacher's advantage even here, in point of facility, at leaft in feveral fituations, will not appear, on reflection, to be fo great, as on a fuperficial view it may be thought. Let it be obferved, that in fuch congregations as was fuppofed, there is a mixture of fuperior and inferior ranks. It is therefore the bufinefs of the fpeaker, fo far only to accommodate himfelf to one clafs, as not wantonly to difguft another. Befides, it will fcarcely be denied, that thofe in the fuperior walks of life, however much by reading and converfation improved in all genteel accomplifhments, often have as much need of religious inftruction and moral improvement, as thofe who in every other particular are acknowledged to be their inferiors. And doubtlefs the reformation of fuch will be allowed to be, in one refpect, of greater importance, (and therefore never to be overlooked) that, in confequence of fuch an event, more good may redound to others, from the more extenfive influence of their authority and example.

SECTION III.

In regard to the Subject.

The third particular mentioned was the subject of discourse. This may be considered in a twofold view, first, as implying the topics of argument, motives, and principles, which are suited to each of the different kinds, and must be employed in order to produce the intended effect on the hearers; secondly, as implying the persons or things in whose favour, or to whose prejudice, the speaker purposes to excite the passions of the audience, and thereby to influence their determinations.

On the first of these articles, I acknowledge the preacher hath incomparably the advantage of every other public orator. At the bar, critical explications of dark and ambiguous statutes, quotations of precedents sometimes contradictory, and comments on jarring decisions and reports, often necessarily consume the greater part of the speaker's time. Hence the mixture of a sort of metaphysics and verbal criticism, employed by lawyers in their pleadings, hath come to be distinguished by the name *chicane*, a species of reasoning too abstruse to command attention of any continuance even from the studious, and consequently not very favourable to the powers of rhetoric. When the argument doth not turn on the common law, or on nice and hypercritical explications of the statute, but on the great principles of natural right and justice, as sometimes happens, particularly in criminal cases, the speaker is much more advantageously situated for exhibiting his rhetorical talents, than in the former case. When, in consequence of the imperfection of the evidence, the question happens to be more a question of fact, than either of municipal law, or of natural equity, the pleader hath more advantages than in the first case, and fewer than in the second.

Again, in the deliberations in the senate, the utility or the disadvantages that will probably follow on a measure proposed, if it should receive the sanction of the legislature, constitute the principal topics of debate. This, though it sometimes leads to a kind of reasoning rather too complex and involved for ordinary apprehension, is in the main more favourable to the display of pathos, vehemence, and sublimity, than the much greater part of forensic causes can be said to be. That these qualities have been sometimes found in a very high degree in the orations pronounced in the British senate, is a fact uncontrovertible.

But

But beyond all question, the preacher's subject of argument, considered in itself, is infinitely more lofty and more affecting. The doctrines of religion are such as relate to God, the adorable Creator and Ruler of the world, his attributes, government, and laws. What science to be compared with it in sublimity! It teaches also the origin of man, his primitive dignity, the source of his degeneracy, the means of his recovery, the eternal happiness that awaits the good, and the future misery of the impenitent. Is there any kind of knowledge, in which human creatures are so deeply interested! In a word, whether we consider the doctrines of religion or its documents, the examples it holds forth to our imitation, or its motives, promises, and threatenings, we see on every hand a subject that gives scope for the exertion of all the highest powers of rhetoric. What are the sanctions of any human laws, compared with the sanctions of the divine law, with which we are brought acquainted by the gospel? Or where shall we find instructions, similitudes, and examples, that speak so directly to the heart, as the parables and other divine lessons of our blessed Lord?

In regard to the second thing which I took notice of as included under the general term *subject*, namely,

namely, the persons or things in whose favour, or to whose prejudice the speaker intends to excite the passions of the audience, and thereby to influence their determinations, the other two have commonly the advantage of the preacher. The reason is, that his subject is generally things, theirs, on the contrary, is persons. In what regards the painful passions, indignation, hatred, contempt, abhorrence, this difference invariably obtains. The preacher's business is solely to excite your detestation of the crime, the pleader's business is principally to make you detest the criminal. The former paints vice to you in all its odious colours, the latter paints the vicious. There is a degree of abstraction, and consequently a much greater degree of attention requisite, to enable us to form just conceptions of the ideas and sentiments of the former, whereas, those of the latter, referring to an actual, perhaps a living, present, and well-known subject, are much more level to common capacity, and therefore not only are more easily apprehended by the understanding, but take a stronger hold of the imagination. It would have been impossible even for Cicero, to inflame the minds of the people to so high a pitch against *oppression* considered in the abstract, as he actually did inflame them

against

against Verres *the oppressor*. Nor could he have incensed them so much against *treason* and *conspiracy*, as he did incense them against Catiline the *traitor* and *conspirator*. The like may be observed of the effects of his orations against Antony, and in a thousand other instances.

Though the occasions in this way are more frequent at the bar, yet, as the deliberations in the senate often proceed on the reputation and past conduct of individuals, there is commonly here also a much better handle for rousing the passions, than that enjoyed by the preacher. How much advantage Demosthenes drew from the known character and insidious arts of Philip king of Macedon, for influencing the resolves of the Athenians, and other Grecian states, those who are acquainted with the Philippics of the orator, and the history of that period, will be very sensible. In what concerns the pleasing affections, the preacher may sometimes, not often, avail himself of real human characters, as in funeral sermons, and in discourses on the patterns of virtue given us by our Saviour, and by those saints of whom we have the history in the sacred code. But such examples are comparatively few.

Section IV.

In regard to the Occasion.

The fourth circumstance mentioned as a ground of comparison, is the particular occasion of speaking. And in this I think it evident, that both the pleader and the senator have the advantage of the preacher. When any important cause comes to be tried before a civil judicatory, or when any important question comes to be agitated in either house of parliament, as the point to be discussed hath generally, for some time before, been a topic of conversation in most companies, perhaps throughout the kingdom, (which of itself is sufficient to give consequence to any thing) people are apprized before-hand of the particular day fixed for the discussion. Accordingly, they come prepared with some knowledge of the case, a persuasion of its importance, and a curiosity which sharpens their attention, and assists both their understanding and their memory.

Men go to church without any of these advantages. The subject of the sermon is not known to the congregation, till the minister announce it just as he begins, by reading the text.

Now, from our experience of human nature, we may be fenfible, that whatever be the comparative importance of the things themfelves, the generality of men cannot here be wrought up in an inftant, to the like anxious curiofity about what is to be faid, nor can they be fo well prepared for hearing it. It may indeed be urged, in regard to thofe fubjects which come regularly to be difcuffed at ftated times, as on public feftivals, as well as in regard to affize-fermons, charity-fermons, and other occafional difcourfes, that thefe muft be admitted as exceptions. Perhaps in fome degree they are, but not altogether: for firft, the precife point to be argued, or propofition to be evinced, is very rarely known. The moft that we can fay is, that the fubject will have a relation (fometimes remote enough) to fuch an article of faith, or to the obligations we lie under to the practice of fuch a duty. But further, if the topic were ever fo well known, the frequent recurrence of fuch occafions, once a-year at leaft, hath long familiarifed us to them, and by deftroying their novelty, hath abated exceedingly of that ardour which arifeth in the mind for hearing a difcuffion, conceived to be of importance, which one never had accefs to hear before, and probably never will have accefs to hear again.

I SHALL

I shall here take notice of another circumstance, which, without great stretch, may be classed under this article, and which likewise gives some advantage to the counsellor and the senator. It is the opposition and contradiction which they expect to meet with. Opponents sharpen one another, as iron sharpeneth iron. There is not the same spur either to exertion in the speaker, or to attention in the hearer, where there is no conflict, where you have no adversary to encounter on equal terms. Mr. Bickerstaff would have made but small progress in the science of defence, by pushing at the human figure which he had chalked upon the wall*, in comparison of what he might have made by the help of a fellow-combatant of flesh and blood. I do not, however, pretend, that these cases are entirely parallel. The whole of an adversary's plea may be perfectly known, and may, to the satisfaction of every reasonable person, be perfectly confuted, though he hath not been heard by counsel at the bar.

Section V.

In regard to the End in view.

The fifth and last particular mentioned, and indeed the most important of them all, is the effect

---

* Tatler.

effect in each species intended to be produced. The primary intention of preaching is the reformation of mankind. " The grace of God, " that bringeth salvation, hath appeared to all " men, teaching us, that denying ungodliness " and worldly lusts, we should live soberly, " righteously, and godly, in this present " world*." Reformation of life and manners —of all things that which it is the most difficult by any means whatever to effectuate, I may add, of all tasks ever attempted by persuasion, that which has the most frequently baffled its power.

WHAT is the task of any other orator compared with this? It is really as nothing at all, and hardly deserves to be named. An unjust judge, gradually worked on by the resistless force of human eloquence, may be persuaded, against his inclination, perhaps against a previous resolution, to pronounce an equitable sentence. All the effect on him, intended by the pleader, was merely momentary. The orator hath had the address to employ the time allowed him, in such a manner as to secure the happy moment. Notwithstanding this, there may be no real change wrought upon the judge. He may continue the same obdurate wretch he was before. Nay, if

* Tit. ii. 11, 12.

the sentence had been delayed but a single day after hearing the cause, he would perhaps have given a very different award.

Is it to be wondered at, that when the passions of the people were agitated by the persuasive powers of a Demosthenes, whilst the thunder of his eloquence was yet sounding in their ears, the orator should be absolute master of their resolves? But an apostle or evangelist, (for there is no anachronism in a bare supposition) might have thus addressed the celebrated Athenian, ' You
' do, indeed, succeed to admiration, and the ad-
' dress and genius which you display in speak-
' ing, justly entitle you to our praise. But,
' however great the consequences may be of the
' measures to which, by your eloquence, they
' are determined, the change produced in the
' people is nothing, or next to nothing. If you
' would be ascertained of the truth of this, allow
' the assembly to disperse immediately after
' hearing you, give them time to cool, and then
' collect their votes, and it is a thousand to one,
' you shall find that the charm is dissolved. But
' very different is the purpose of the Christian
' orator. It is not a momentary, but a perma-
' nent effect at which he aims. It is not an im-
' mediate

'mediate and favourable suffrage, but a tho-
'rough change of heart and disposition, that
'will satisfy his view. That man would need to
'be possessed of oratory superior to human, who
'would effectually persuade him that stole, to
'steal no more, the sensualist to forego his plea-
'sures, and the miser his hoards, the insolent and
'haughty to become meek and humble, the vin-
'dictive forgiving, the cruel and unfeeling mer-
'ciful and humane.'

I MAY add to these considerations, that the difficulty lies not only in the permanency, but in the very nature of the change to be effected. It is wonderful, but is too well vouched to admit a doubt, that by the powers of rhetoric you may produce in mankind, almost any change more easily than this. It is not unprecedented, that one should persuade a multitude, from mistaken motives of religion, to act the part of ruffians, fools, or madmen; to perpetrate the most extravagant, nay, the most flagitious actions, to steel their hearts against humanity, and the loudest calls of natural affection but where is the eloquence that will gain such an ascendant over a multitude, as to persuade them, for the love of God, to be wise, and just, and good? Happy

the

the preacher, whose sermons, by the blessing of Heaven, have been instrumental in producing even a few such instances! Do but look into the annals of church-history, and you will soon be convinced of the surprising difference there is in the two cases mentioned, the amazing facility of the one, and the almost impossibility of the other.

As to the foolish or mad extravagancies hurtful only to themselves, to which numbers may be excited by the powers of persuasion, the history of the flagellants, and even the history of monachism, afford many unquestionable examples. But what is much worse, at one time you see Europe nearly depopulated, at the persuasion of a fanatical monk, its inhabitants rushing armed into Asia, in order to fight for Jesus Christ, as they termed it, but as it proved in fact, to disgrace, as far as lay in them, the name of Christ and of Christian amongst infidels, to butcher those who never injured them, and to whose lands they had at least no better title, than those whom they intended, by all possible means, to dispossess; and to give the world a melancholy proof, that there is no pitch of brutality and rapacity, to which the passions of avarice and ambition, consecrated and inflamed by religious enthu-

enthusiasm, will not drive mankind. At another time you see multitudes, by the like methods, worked up into a fury against their innocent countrymen, neighbours, friends, and kinsmen, glorying in being the most active in cutting the throats of those who were formerly held dear to them.

Such were the crusades preached up but too effectually, first against the Mahometans in the East, and next against Christians whom they called heretics, in the heart of Europe. And even in our own time, have we not seen new factions raised by popular declaimers, whose only merit was impudence, whose only engine of influence was calumny and self-praise, whose only moral lesson was malevolence? As to the dogmas whereby such have at any time affected to discriminate themselves, these are commonly no other than the *shibboleth*, the watch-word of the party, worn, for distinction's sake, as a badge, a jargon unintelligible alike to the teacher and to the learner. Such apostles never fail to make proselytes. For who would not purchase heaven at so cheap a rate? There is nothing that people can more easily afford. It is only to think very well of their leader and of themselves, to think very ill of their neighbour, to calumniate him freely, and to hate him heartily.

I am sensible that some will imagine, that this account itself throws an insuperable obstacle in our way, as from it one will naturally infer, that oratory must be one of the most dangerous things in the world, and much more capable of doing ill than good. It needs but some reflection to make this mighty obstacle entirely vanish. Very little eloquence is necessary for persuading people to a conduct, to which their own depravity hath previously given them a bias. How soothing is it to them not only to have their minds made easy under the indulged malignity of their disposition, but to have that very malignity sanctified with a good name. So little of the oratorical talents is required here, that those who court popular applause, and look upon it as the pinnacle of human glory to be blindly followed by the multitude, commonly recur to defamation, especially of superiors and brethren, not so much for a subject on which they may display their eloquence, as for a succedaneum to supply their want of eloquence, a succedaneum which never yet was found to fail. I knew a preacher who, by this expedient alone, from being long the aversion of the populace, on account of his dulness, awkwardness, and coldness, all of a sudden became their idol. Little force is necessary to push down heavy bodies placed on the verge of a declivity, but much force is requisite, to stop them in their progress, and push them up.

If a man should say, that because the first is more frequently effected than the last, it is the best trial of strength, and the only suitable use to which it can be applied, we should at least not think him remarkable for distinctness in his ideas. Popularity alone, therefore, is no test at all of the eloquence of the speaker, no more than velocity alone would be, of the force of the external impulse originally given to the body moving. As in this, the direction of the body, and other circumstances, must be taken into the account, so in that, you must consider the tendency of the teaching, whether it favours or opposes the vices of the hearers. To head a sect, to infuse party-spirit, to make men arrogant, uncharitable, and malevolent, is the easiest task imaginable, and to which almost any blockhead is fully equal. But to produce the contrary effect, to subdue the spirit of faction, and that monster spiritual pride, with which it is invariably accompanied, to inspire equity, moderation, and charity into men's sentiments and conduct with regard to others, is the genuine test of eloquence. Here its triumph is truly glorious, and in its application to this end lies its great utility:

> The gates of hell are open night and day,
> Smooth the descent, and easy is the way:
> But to return and view the cheerful skies,
> In this the task and mighty labour lies*. DRYDEN.

Now in regard to the comparison, from which I fear I shall be thought to have digressed, between the forensic and senatorian eloquence, and that of the pulpit, I must not omit to observe, that in what I say of the difference of the effect to be produced by the last mentioned species, I am to be understood as speaking of the effect intended by preaching in general, and even of that which, in whole or in part, is, or ought to be, either more immediately or more remotely, the scope of all discourses proceeding from the pulpit. I am, at the same time, sensible, that in some of these, besides the ultimate view, there is an immediate and outward effect which the sermon is intended to produce. This is the case particularly in charity-sermons, and perhaps some other occasional discourses. Now of these

---

* ——— Facilis descensus Averni
Noctes atque dies patet atri janua Ditis
Sed revocare gradum, superasque evadere ad auras
Hic labor, hoc opus est. VIRG. lib. vi.

few, in respect of such immediate purpose, we must admit, that they bear a pretty close analogy to the pleadings of the advocate, and the orations of the senator.

Upon the whole of the comparison I have stated, it appears manifest, that, in most of the particulars above enumerated, the preacher labours under a very great disadvantage. He hath himself a more delicate part to perform than either the pleader or the senator, and a character to maintain, which is much more easily injured. The auditors, though rarely so accomplished as to require the same accuracy of composition, or acuteness in reasoning, as may be expected in the other two, are more various in age, rank, taste, inclinations, sentiments, prejudices, to which he must accommodate himself. And if he derives some advantages from the richness, the variety, and the nobleness of the principles, motives, and arguments, with which his subject furnishes him, he derives also some inconveniencies from this circumstance, that almost the only engine by which he can operate on the passions of his hearers, is the exhibition of abstract qualities, virtues, and vices, whereas that chiefly employed by other orators, is the exhibition of real persons, the virtuous and the vicious. Nor are the occasions of his addresses to the people equally fitted with those of the senator and of the pleader, for exciting their curiosity and riveting their attention. And finally, the task assigned him, the effect which he ought ever to have in view, is so great, so important, so durable, as seems to bid defiance to the strongest efforts of oratorical genius.

Nothing is more common than for people, I suppose without reflecting, to express their wonder, that there is so little eloquence amongst our preachers, and that so little success attends their preaching. As to the last, their success, it is a matter not to be ascertained with so much precision, as some appear fondly to imagine. The evil prevented, as well as the good promoted, ought here, in all justice, to come into the reckoning. And what that may be, it is impossible in any supposed circumstances to determine. As to the first, their eloquence, I acknowledge, that, for my own part, considering how rare the talent is among men in general, considering all the disadvantages preachers labour under, not only those above enumerated, but others, arising from their different situations, particularly considering the frequency of this exercise, together with the other duties of their office, to which the fixed pastors are obliged, I have been of a long time more disposed to wonder, that we hear so many instructive and even eloquent sermons, than that we hear so few.

CHAP. XI.

Of the cause of that pleasure which we receive from objects or representations that excite pity and other painful feelings.

IT hath been observed already*, that without some gratification in hearing, the attention must inevitably flag. And it is manifest from experience, that nothing tends more effectually to prevent this consequence, and keep our attention alive and vigorous, than the pathetic, which consists chiefly in exhibitions of human misery. Yet that such exhibitions should so highly gratify us, appears somewhat mysterious. Every body is sensible, that of all qualities in a work of genius, this is that which endears it most to the generality of readers. One would imagine, on

* Chapter IV.

the first mention of this, that it were impossible to account for it otherwise than from an innate principle of malice, which teacheth us to extract delight to ourselves from the sufferings of others, and as it were to enjoy their calamities. A very little reflection, however, would suffice for correcting this error, nay, without any reflection, we may truly say, that the common sense of mankind prevents them effectually from falling into it. Bad as we are, and prone as we are, to be hurried into the worst of passions by self-love, partiality, and pride, malice is a disposition, which, either in the abstract, or as it discovers itself in the actions of an indifferent person, we never contemplate without feeling a just detestation and abhorrence, being ready to pronounce it the ugliest of objects. Yet this sentiment is not more universal, than is the approbation and even love that we bestow on the tender-hearted, or those who are most exquisitely susceptible of all the influence of the pathetic. Nor are there any two dispositions of which human nature is capable, that have ever been considered as farther removed from each other, than the malicious and the compassionate are. The fact itself, that the mind derives pleasure from representations of anguish, is undeniable, the question about the

cause

cause is curious, and hath a manifest relation to my subject.

I PURPOSED indeed, at first, to discuss this point in that part of the sixth chapter which relates to the means of operating on the passions, with which the present inquiry is intimately connected. Finding afterwards that the discussion would prove rather too long an interruption, and that the other points which came naturally to be treated in that place, could be explained with sufficient clearness, independently of this, I judged it better to reserve this question for a separate chapter. Various hypotheses have been devised by the ingenious, in order to solve the difficulty. These I shall first briefly examine, and then lay before the reader what appears to me to be the true solution. Of all that have entered into the subject, those who seem most to merit our regard, are two French critics, and one of our own country.

Section I.

The different solutions hitherto given by philosophers, examined.

Part I. *The first hypothesis.*

Abbé du Bos begins his excellent Reflections on Poetry and Painting, with that very question which is the subject of this chapter, and in answer to it supports at some length* a theory, the substance of which I shall endeavour to comprise in a few words. Few things, according to him, are more disagreeable to the mind, than that listlessness into which it falls, when it has nothing to occupy it, or to awake the passions. In order to get rid of this most painful situation, it seeks with avidity every amusement and pursuit; business, gaming, news, shows, public executions, romances; in short, whatever will rouse the passions, and take off the mind's attention from itself. It matters not what the emotion be, only the stronger it is, so much the better. And for this reason, those passions which, considered in themselves, are the most afflicting and disagreeable, are preferable to the pleasant, inasmuch

---

* Reflexions critiques sur la Poesie et sur la Peinture, Sect. I. II. III.

as they most effectually relieve the soul from that oppressive languor which preys upon it in a state of inactivity. They afford it ample occupation, and by giving play to its latent movements and springs of action, convey a pleasure which more than counterbalances the pain.

I ADMIT, with Mr. Hume*, that there is some weight in these observations, which may sufficiently account for the pleasure taken in gaming, hunting, and several other diversions and sports. But they are not quite satisfactory, as they do not assign a sufficient reason why poets, painters, and orators, exercise themselves more in actuating the painful passions, than in exciting the pleasant. These, one would think, ought in every respect to have the advantage, because, at the same time that they preserve the mind from a state of inaction, they convey a feeling that is allowed to be agreeable. And though it were granted, that passions of the former kind are stronger than those of the latter (which doth not hold invariably, there being perhaps more examples of persons who have been killed with joy, than of those who have died of grief), strength alone will not account for the

* Essay on Tragedy.

preference. It by no means holds here, that the stronger the emotion is, so much the fitter for this purpose. On the contrary, if you exceed but ever so little a certain measure, instead of that sympathetic delightful sorrow, which makes affliction itself wear a lovely aspect, and engages the mind to hug it, not only with tenderness, but with transport, you only excite horror and aversion. " It is certain," says the author last quoted, very justly *, " that the same object of " distress which pleases in a tragedy, were it " really set before us, would give the most un- " feigned uneasiness, though it be then the most " effectual cure of languor and indolence." And it is more than barely possible, even in the representations of the tragedian, or in the descriptions of the orator or the poet, to exceed that measure. I acknowledge, indeed, that this measure or degree is not the same to every temper. Some are much sooner shocked with mournful representations than others. Our mental, like our bodily appetites and capacities, are exceedingly various. It is, however, the business of both the speaker and the writer, to accommodate himself to what may be styled the common standard, for there is a common standard in

* Essay on Tragedy.

what regards the faculties of the mind, as well as in what concerns the powers of the body. Now if there be any quality in the afflictive passions, besides their strength, that renders them peculiarly adapted to rescue the mind from that torpid, but corrosive rest which is considered as the greatest of evils, that quality ought to have been pointed out. for till then, the phenomenon under examination is not accounted for. The most that can be concluded from the Abbé's premises, is the utility of exciting passion of some kind or other, but nothing that can evince the superior fitness of the distressful affections.

PART II. *The second hypothesis.*

THE next hypothesis is Fontenelle's*. Not having the original at hand at present, I shall give Mr. Hume's translation of the passage, in his Essay on Tragedy above quoted "Pleasure "and pain, which are two sentiments so differ- "ent in themselves, differ not so much in their "cause. From the instance of tickling it ap- "pears, that the movement of pleasure pushed "a little too far, becomes pain, and that the "movement of pain, a little moderated, becomes "pleasure. Hence it proceeds, that there is

* Reflexions sur la Poetique, Sect. xxxvi.

"such

" such a thing as a sorrow, soft and agreeable.
" It is a pain weakened and diminished. The
" heart likes naturally to be moved and affected.
" Melancholy objects suit it, and even disastrous
" and sorrowful, provided they are softened by
" some circumstance. It is certain that, on the
" theatre, the representation has almost the ef-
" fect of reality; but yet it has not altogether
" that effect. However we may be hurried
" away by the spectacle, whatever dominion the
" senses and imagination may usurp over the
" reason, there still lurks at the bottom, a cer-
" tain idea of falsehood in the whole of what we
" see. This idea, though weak and disguised,
" suffices to diminish the pain which we suffer
" from the misfortunes of those whom we love,
" and to reduce that affliction to such a pitch
" as converts it into a pleasure. We weep for
" the misfortunes of a hero to whom we are at-
" tached. In the same instant we comfort our-
" selves by reflecting, that it is nothing but a
" fiction: and it is precisely that mixture of
" sentiments, which composes an agreeable sor-
" row, and tears, that delight us. But as that
" affliction which is caused by exterior and sen-
" sible objects, is stronger than the consolation
" which arises from an internal reflection, they
" are

" are the effects and symptoms of sorrow, which
" ought to prevail in the composition."

I CANNOT affirm that this solution appears to me so just and convincing, as it seems it did to Mr. Hume. If this English version, like a faithful mirror, reflect the true image of the French original, I think the author in some degree chargeable, with what in that language is emphatically enough styled *verbiage*, a manner of writing very common with those of his nation, and with their imitators in ours. The only truth that I can discover in his hypothesis, lies in one small circumstance, which is so far from being applicable to the whole case under consideration, that it can properly be applied but to a very few particular instances, and is therefore no solution at all. That there are at least many cases to which it cannot be applied, the author last mentioned declares himself to be perfectly sensible.

BUT let us examine the passage more narrowly. He begins with laying it down as a general principle, that however different the feelings of pleasure and of pain are in themselves, they differ not much in their cause, that the movement of pleasure pushed a little too far, becomes pain;

and that the movement of pain a little moderated, becomes pleasure. For an illustration of this he gives an example in tickling. I will admit that there are several other similar instances, in which the observation to appearance holds. The warmth received from sitting near the fire by one who hath been almost chilled with cold, is very pleasing, yet you may increase this warmth, first to a disagreeable heat, and then to burning, which is one of the greatest torments. It is nevertheless extremely hazardous, on a few instances, and those not perfectly parallel to the case in hand, to found a general theory. Let us make the experiment, how the application of this doctrine to the passions of the mind will answer. And for our greater security against mistake, let us begin with the simplest cases in the direct, and not in the reflex or sympathetic passions, in which hardly ever any feeling or affection comes alone. A merchant loseth all his fortune by a shipwreck, and is reduced at one stroke from opulence to indigence. His grief, we may suppose, will be very violent. If he had lost half his stock only, it is natural to think he would have born the loss more easily; though still he would have been affected: perhaps the loss of fifty pounds he would have scarcely felt. but I should be glad to know how much the movement or passion must be moderated, or, in other words, as the difference ariseth solely from the different degrees of the cause, how small the loss must be, when the sentiment or feeling of it begins to be converted into a real pleasure: for to me it doth not appear natural that any the most trifling loss, were it of a single shilling, should be the subject of positive delight.

But to try another instance, a gross and public insult commonly provokes a very high degree of resentment, and gives a most pungent vexation to a person of sensibility. I would gladly know, whether a smaller affront, or some slight instance of neglect or contempt, gives such a person any pleasure. Try the experiment also on friendship and hatred, and you will find the same success. As the warmest friendship is highly agreeable to the mind, the slightest liking is also agreeable, though in a less degree. Perfect hatred is a kind of torture to the breast that harbours it, which will not be found capable of being mitigated into pleasure, for there is no degree of ill-will without pain. The gradation in the cause and in the effect, are entirely correspondent.

and that the movement of pain a little moderated, becomes pleasure. For an illustration of this he gives an example in tickling. I will admit that there are several other similar instances, in which the observation to appearance holds. The warmth received from sitting near the fire by one who hath been almost chilled with cold, is very pleasing, yet you may increase this warmth, first to a disagreeable heat, and then to burning, which is one of the greatest torments. It is nevertheless extremely hazardous, on a few instances, and those not perfectly parallel to the case in hand, to found a general theory. Let us make the experiment, how the application of this doctrine to the passions of the mind will answer. And for our greater security against mistake, let us begin with the simplest cases in the direct, and not in the reflex or sympathetic passions, in which hardly ever any feeling or affection comes alone. A merchant loseth all his fortune by a shipwreck, and is reduced at one stroke from opulence to indigence. His grief, we may suppose, will be very violent. If he had lost half his stock only, it is natural to think he would have born the loss more easily, though still he would have been affected perhaps the loss of fifty pounds he would have scarcely felt. but I should be glad to to know how much the movement or paſſion muſt be moderated, or, in other words, as the difference ariſeth ſolely from the different degrees of the cauſe, how ſmall the loſs muſt be, when the ſentiment or feeling of it begins to be converted into a real pleaſure: for to me it doth not appear natural that any the moſt trifling loſs, were it of a ſingle ſhilling, ſhould be the ſubject of poſitive delight.

But to try another inſtance, a groſs and public inſult commonly provokes a very high degree of reſentment, and gives a moſt pungent vexation to a perſon of ſenſibility. I would gladly know, whether a ſmaller affront, or ſome ſlight inſtance of neglect or contempt, gives ſuch a perſon any pleaſure. Try the experiment alſo on friendſhip and hatred, and you will find the ſame ſucceſs. As the warmeſt friendſhip is highly agreeable to the mind, the ſlighteſt liking is alſo agreeable, though in a leſs degree. Perfect hatred is a kind of torture to the breaſt that harbours it, which will not be found capable of being mitigated into pleaſure, for there is no degree of ill-will without pain. The gradation in the cauſe and in the effect, are entirely correſpondent.

Nor can any juſt concluſion be drawn from the affections of the body, as in theſe the conſequence is often ſolely imputable to a certain proportion of ſtrength, in the cauſe that operates, to the preſent diſpoſition of the organs. But though I cannot find that in any uncompounded paſſion the moſt remote degrees are productive of ſuch contrary effects, I do not deny that when different paſſions are blended, ſome of them pleaſing and ſome painful, the pleaſure or the pain of thoſe which predominate, may, through the wonderful mechaniſm* of our mental frame, be conſiderably augmented by the mixture.

The only truth which, as I hinted already, I can diſcover in the preceding hypotheſis, is, that the mind in certain caſes avails itſelf of the notion of falſehood, in order to prevent the repreſentation or narrative from producing too ſtrong an effect upon the imagination, and conſequently to relieve itſelf from ſuch an exceſs of paſſion, as could not otherwiſe fail to be painful. But

---

* The word *mechaniſm* applied to the mind, ought not reaſonably to give offence to any. I only uſe the term metaphorically for thoſe effects in the operation of the mental faculties, produced in conſequence of ſuch fixed laws as are independent of the will. It hath here therefore no reference to the doctrine of the materialiſt, a ſyſtem which, in my opinion, is not only untenable, but abſurd.

let it be observed, that this notion is not a necessary concomitant of the pleasure that results from pity and other such affections, but is merely accidental. It was remarked above, that if the pathetic exceeds a certain measure, from being very pleasant it becomes very painful. Then the mind recurs to every expedient, and to disbelief amongst others, by which it may be enabled to disburden itself of what distresseth it. And indeed, whenever this recourse is had by any, it is a sure indication that, with regard to such, the poet, orator, or historian, hath exceeded the proper measure.

But that this only holds when we are too deeply interested by the sympathetic sorrow, will appear from the following considerations: first, from the great pains often taken by writers (whose design is certainly not to shock, but to please their readers) to make the most moving stories they relate, be firmly believed: secondly, from the tendency, nay fondness of the generality of mankind, to believe what moves them, and their averseness, to be convinced that it is a fiction. This can result only from the consciousness that, in ordinary cases, disbelief, by weakening their pity, would diminish, instead of increasing,

creasing, their pleasure. They must be very far then from entertaining Fontenelle's notion, that it is necessary to the producing of that pleasure; for we cannot well suspect them of a plot against their own enjoyment: thirdly, and lastly, from the delight which we take in reading or hearing the most tragical narrations, of orators and historians, of the reality of which we entertain no doubt; I might add, in revolving in our own minds, and in relating to others, disastrous incidents, which have fallen within the compass of our own knowledge, and as to which, consequently, we have an absolute assurance of the fact.

PART III. *The third hypothesis.*

THE third hypothesis which I shall produce on this subject, is Mr. Hume's. Only it ought to be remarked previously, that he doth not propose it as a full solution of the question, but rather as a supplement to the former two, in the doctrine of both which, he, in a great measure, acquiesces. Take his theory in his own words. He begins with putting the question, " What is " it then, which, in this case," that is, when the sorrow is not softened by fiction, " raises a plea-
" sure from the bosom of uneasiness, so to speak;
" and

"and a pleasure, which still retains all the fea-
"tures and outward symptoms of distress and
"sorrow? I answer: This extraordinary effect
"proceeds from that very eloquence, with which
"the melancholy scene is represented. The ge-
"nius required to paint objects in a lively man-
"ner, the art employed in collecting all the pa-
"thetic circumstances, the judgment displayed
"in disposing them; the exercise, I say, of these
"noble talents, together with the force of ex-
"pression, and beauty of oratorial numbers,
"diffuse the highest satisfaction on the audience,
"and excite the most delightful movements.
"By this means, the uneasiness of the melancholy
"passions is not only overpowered and effaced
"by something stronger of an opposite kind,
"but the whole movement of those passions is
"converted into pleasure, and swells the delight
"which the eloquence raises in us. The same
"force of oratory employed on an uninteresting
"subject, would not please half so much, or ra-
"ther would appear altogether ridiculous; and
"the mind being left in absolute calmness and
"indifference, would relish none of those beau-
"ties of imagination or expression, which, if
"joined to passion, give it such exquisite enter-
"tainment. The impulse or vehemence arising
"from

"from sorrow, compassion, indignation, re-
"ceives a new direction from the sentiments of
"beauty. The latter, being the predominant
"emotion, seize the whole mind, and convert
"the former into themselves, or at least tincture
"them so strongly, as totally to alter their na-
"ture: and the soul being, at the same time,
"roused by passion, and charmed by eloquence,
"feels on the whole a strong movement, which
"is altogether delightful."

I am sorry to say, but truth compells me to acknowledge, that I have reaped no more satisfaction from this account of the matter, than from those which preceded it. I could have wished indeed, that the author had been a little more explicit in his manner of expressing himself; for I am not certain that I perfectly comprehend his meaning. At one time he seems only to intend to say, that it is the purpose of eloquence, to the promoting of which, its tropes and figures are wonderfully adapted, to infuse into the mind of the hearer, such compassion, sorrow, indignation, and other passions, as are, notwithstanding their original character when abstractly considered, accompanied with pleasure. At another time it appears rather his design to signify,

signify, though he doth not plainly speak it out, that the discovery made by the hearer, of the admirable art and ingenuity of the speaker, and of the elegance and harmony of what is spoken, gives that peculiar pleasure to the mind, which makes even the painful passions become delightful.

If the first of these be all that he intended to affirm, he hath told us indeed a certain truth, but nothing new or uncommon, nay more, he hath told us nothing that can serve in the smallest degree for a solution of the difficulty. Who ever doubted, that it is the design and work of eloquence to move the passions, and to please? The question which this naturally gives rise to, is, How doth eloquence produce this effect? This, I believe, it will be acknowledged to do principally, if not solely, agreeably to the doctrine explained above*, by communicating lively, distinct, and strong ideas of the distress which it exhibits. By a judicious, yet natural arrangement of the most affecting circumstances, by a proper selection of the most suitable tropes and figures, it enlivens the ideas raised in the imagination to such a pitch, as makes them strongly

* Chap. VI.

resemble the perceptions of the senses, or the transcripts of the memory. The question then, with which we are immediately concerned, doth obviously recur, and seems, if possible, more mysterious than before: for how can the aggravating of all the circumstances of misery in the representation, make it be contemplated with pleasure? One would naturally imagine, that this must be the most effectual method for making it give still greater pain. How can the heightening of grief, fear, anxiety, and other uneasy sensations, render them agreeable?

BESIDES, this ingenious author has not adverted, that his hypothesis, instead of being supplementary to Fontenelle's, as he appears to have intended, is subversive of the principles on which the French critic's theory is founded. The effect, according to the latter, results from moderating, weakening, softening, and diminishing the passion: according to the former, it results from what is directly opposite, from the arts employed by the orator for the purpose of exaggerating, strengthening, heightening, and inflaming the passion. Indeed, neither of these writers seems to have attended sufficiently to one particular, which of itself might have shown the insufficiency of their systems. The particular alluded to is, that pity, if it exceed not a certain degree, gives pleasure to the mind, when excited by the original objects in distress, as well as by the representations made by poets, painters, and orators. and, on the contrary, if it exceed a certain degree, it is on the whole painful, whether awakened by the real objects of pity, or roused by the exhibitions of the historian or of the poet. Indeed, as sense operates much more strongly on the mind than imagination does, the excess is much more frequent in the former case than in the latter.

Now in attempting to give a solution of the difficulty, it is plain, that all our theorists ought regularly and properly to begin with the former case. If in that, which is the original and the simplest, the matter is sufficiently accounted for, it is accounted for in every case, it being the manifest design both of painting and of oratory, as nearly as possible, to produce the same affections which the very objects represented would have produced in our minds: whereas, though Mr. Hume should be admitted to have accounted fully for the impression made by the poet and the orator, we are as far as ever from the discovery of the cause why pity excited by the objects themselves, when it hath no eloquence to recommend it, is on the whole, if not excessive, a pleasant emotion.

But if this celebrated writer intended to assert, that the discovery of the oratory, that is, of the address and talents of the speaker; is what gives the hearer a pleasure, which, mingling itself with pity, fear, indignation, converts the whole, as he expresseth it, into one strong movement, which is altogether delightful: if this be his sentiment, he hath indeed advanced something extraordinary, and entirely new. And that this is his opinion, appears, I think, obliquely, from the expressions which he useth. " The genius re-
" quired, the art employed, the judgment dis-
" played, along with the force of expression,
" and beauty of oratorial numbers, diffuse the
" highest satisfaction on the audience."——
Again, " The impulse or vehemence arising from
" sorrow, compassion, indignation, receives a
" new direction from the sentiments of beauty."
If this then be a just solution of the difficulty, and the detection of the speaker's talents and address be necessary to render the hearer susceptible of this charming sorrow, this delightful anguish,

guish, how grossly have all critics and rhetoricians been deceived hitherto? These, in direct opposition to this curious theory, have laid it down in their rhetorics as a fundamental maxim, that " it is essential to the art to conceal the art *;" a maxim too, which, in their estimation, the orator, in no part of his province, is obliged to such a scrupulous observance of, as in the pathetic §. In this the speaker, if he would prove successful, must make his subject totally engross the attention of the hearers; insomuch that he himself, his genius, his art, his judgment, his richness of language, his harmony of numbers, are not minded in the least †.

Never does the orator obtain a nobler triumph by his eloquence, than when his sentiments and style and order appear so naturally to

---

* Artis est celare artem

§ Effugienda igitur in hac præcipuè parte omnis calliditatis suspicio: nihil videatur fictum, nihil solicitum omnia potius a causa, quam ab oratore profecta credantur. Sed hoc pati non possumus, et perire artem putamus, nisi appareat cùm desinat ars esse, si apparet. QUINT. Inst. lib. iv. cap. 2.

† Ubi res agitur, et vera dimicatio est, ultimus sit famæ locus. Propterea non debet quisquam, ubi maxima rerum momenta versantur, de verbis esse solicitus Neque hoc eò pertinet, ut in his nullus sit ornatus, sed uti pressior et severior, minus confessus, præcipuè ad materiam accommodatus. QUINT. Inst. lib. viii. cap. 3.

arise out of the subject, that every hearer is inclined to think, he could not have either thought or spoken otherwise himself, when every thing, in short, is exhibited in such a manner,

> As all might hope to imitate with ease,
> Yet while they strive the same success to gain,
> Should find their labour and their hopes are vain ‡ FRANCIS.

As to the harmony of numbers, it ought no further to be the speaker's care, than that he may avoid an offensive dissonance or halting in his periods, which, by hurting the ear, abstracts the attention from the subject, and must by consequence serve to obstruct the effect. Yet, even this, it may be safely averred, will not tend half so much to counteract the end, as an elaborate harmony, or a flowing elocution, which carries along with it the evident marks of address and study *.

Our author proceeds all along on the supposition that there are two distinct effects produced

---

‡ ――――――――Ut sibi quivis
  Speret idem, sudet multum, frustraque laboret,
  Ausus idem. HOR. De Arte Poet.

* Commoveaturne quisquam ejus fortuna, quem tumidum ac sui jactantem, et ambitiosum institorem eloquentiæ in ancipiti forte videat? Non imo oderit reum verba aucupantem, et anxium de fama ingenii, et cui esse diserto vacet. QUINT. l. xi. cap. 1.

by the eloquence on the hearers; one the sentiment of beauty, or (as he explains it more particularly) of the harmony of oratorial numbers, of the exercise of these noble talents, genius, art, and judgment, the other, the passion which the speaker purposeth to raise in their minds. He maintains, that when the first predominates, the mixture of the two effects becomes exceedingly pleasant, and the reverse when the second is superior. At least, if this is not what he means to assert and vindicate, I despair of being able to assign a meaning to the following expressions: " The genius required to paint—, the art em-
" ployed in collecting—, the judgment display-
" ed in disposing—diffuse the highest satisfaction
" on the audience, and excite the most delight-
" ful movements. By this means the uneasiness
" of the melancholy passions is not only over-
" powered and effaced by something stronger
" of an opposite kind, but the whole movement
" of those passions is converted into pleasure, and
" swells the delight which the eloquence raises
" in us." Again, " The impulse or vehemence
" arising from sorrow—receives a new direction
" from the sentiments of beauty. The latter be-
" ing the predominant emotion, seize the whole
" mind, and convert the former——." Again,
" The

" The soul being at the same time roused with
" passion, and charmed by eloquence, feels on
" the whole——." And in the paragraph immediately succeeding, " It is thus the fiction of
" tragedy softens the passion, by an infusion of
" a new feeling, not merely by weakening or
" diminishing the sorrow."——Now to me it is manifest, that this notion of two distinguishable, and even opposite effects, as he terms them, produced in the hearer by the eloquence, is perfectly imaginary, that, on the contrary, whatever charm or fascination, if you please to call it so, there is in the pity excited by the orator, it ariseth not from any extrinsic sentiment of beauty blended with it, but intimately from its own nature, from those passions which pity necessarily associates, or, I should rather say, includes.

But do we not often hear people speak of eloquence as moving them greatly, and pleasing them highly at the same time? Nothing more common. But these are never understood by them, as two original, separate, and independent effects, but as essentially connected. Push your inquiries but ever so little, and you will find all agree in affirming, that it is by being moved, and by that solely, that they are pleased. in philosophical
strictness,

strictness, therefore, the pleasure is the immediate effect of the passion, and the passion the immediate effect of the eloquence.

But is there then no pleasure in contemplating the beauty of composition, the richness of fancy, the power of numbers, and the energy of expression? There is undoubtedly. But so far is this pleasure from commixing with the pathos, and giving a direction to it, that, on the contrary, they seem to be in a great measure incompatible. Such indeed is the pleasure which the artist or the critic enjoys, who can coolly and deliberately survey the whole, upon whose passions the art of the speaker hath little or no influence, and that purely for this reason, because he discovers that art. The bulk of hearers know no further than to approve the man who affects them, who speaks to their heart, as they very properly and emphatically term it, and to commend the performance by which this is accomplished. But how it is accomplished, they neither give themselves the trouble to consider, nor attempt to explain*.

---

* The inquiry contained in this chapter was written long before I had an opportunity of perusing a very ingenious English Commentary and Notes on Horace's Epistles to the Pisos and to Augustus,

PART IV. *The fourth hypothesis.*

LASTLY, to mention only one other hypothesis, there are who maintain that compassion is " an example of unmixed selfishness and ma-
" lignity," and may be " resolved into that
" power of imagination, by which we apply the
" misfortunes of others to ourselves," that we are said " to pity no longer than we fancy our-
" selves to suffer, and to be pleased only by re-
" flecting that our sufferings are not real; thus
" indulging a dream of distress, from which we

Augustus, in which Mr. Hume's sentiments on this subject are occasionally criticised. The opinions of that commentator, in regard to Mr. Hume's theory, coincide in every thing material with mine. This author considers the question no farther than it relates to the representations of tragedy, and hath, by confining his view to this single point, been led to lay greater stress on Fontenelle's hypothesis, than, for the solution of the general phenomenon, it is entitled to. It is very true that our theatrical entertainments commonly exhibit a degree of distress which we could not bear to witness in the objects represented. Consequently the consideration that it is but a picture, and not the original, a fictitious exhibition, and not the reality, which we contemplate, is essential for rendering the whole, I may say, supportable as well as pleasant. But even in this case, when it is necessary to our repose, to consider the scenical misery before us as mere illusion, we are generally better pleased to consider the things represented as genuine fact. It requires, indeed, but a further degree of affliction to make us even pleased to think that the copy never had any archetype in nature. But when this is the case we may truly say, that the poet hath exceeded and wrought up pity to a kind of horror.

" can

" can awake whenever we please, to exult in our
" security, and enjoy the comparison of the
" fiction with truth *."

This is no other than the antiquated doctrine of the philosopher of Malmesbury, rescued from oblivion, to which it had been fast descending, and re-published with improvements. Hobbes indeed thought it a sufficient stretch, in order to render the sympathetic sorrow purely selfish, to define it " imagination or fiction of future " calamity to ourselves, proceeding from the " sense of another man's calamity †." But in the first quotation we have another kind of fiction; namely, that we are at present the very sufferers ourselves, the identical persons whose cases are exhibited as being so deplorable, and whose calamities we so sincerely lament. There were some things hinted in the beginning of the chapter, in relation to this paradoxical conceit, which I should not have thought it necessary to resume, had it not been adopted by a late author, whose periodical essays seemed to entitle him to the character of an ingenious, moral, and instructive writer ‡. For though he hath declined entering

* Adventurer, N° 110.
† Hum. Nat. chap. ix. sect. 10   ‡ Hawkesworth.

formally

formally into the debate, he hath sufficiently shown his sentiments on this article, and hath endeavoured indirectly to support them.

I DOUBT not that it will appear to many of my readers as equally silly to refute this hypothesis and to defend it. Nothing could betray reasonable men into such extravagancies, but the dotage with which one is affected towards every appendage of a favourite system. And this is an appendage of that system which derives all the affections and springs of action in the human mind from self-love. In almost all system-builders of every denomination, there is a vehement desire of simplifying their principles, and reducing all to one. Hence in medicine, the passion for finding a catholicon, or cure of all diseases; and in chymistry, for discovering the true alcahest, or universal dissolvent. Nor have our moralists entirely escaped the contagion. One reduceth all the virtues to *prudence*, and is ready to make it clear as sun-shine, that there neither is nor can be another source of moral good, but a right conducted self-love: another is equally confident, that all the virtues are but different modifications of disinterested *benevolence*. a third will demonstrate to you that *veracity* is the whole duty

duty of man: a fourth, with more ingenuity, and much greater appearance of reason, assures you, that the true system of ethics is comprised in one word *sympathy*.

But to the point in hand; it appears a great objection to the selfish system, that in pity we are affected with a real sorrow for the sufferings of others, or at least that men have universally understood this to be the case, as appears from the very words and phrases expressive of this emotion to be found in all known languages. But to one who has thoroughly imbibed the principles and spirit of a philosophic sect, which hath commonly as violent an appetite for mystery (though under a different name, for with the philosopher it is paradox) as any religious sect whatever; how paltry must an objection appear, which hath nothing to support it but the conviction of all mankind, those only excepted whose minds have been perverted by scholastic sophistry?

It is remarkable, that though so many have contended that some fiction of the imagination is absolutely necessary to the production of pity, and though the examples of this emotion are so frequent (I hope, in the theorists themselves no less than in others) as to give ample scope for examination, they are so little agreed what this fiction is. Some contend only, that in witnessing tragedy, one is under a sort of momentary deception, which a very little reflection can correct, and imagines that he is actually witnessing those distresses and miseries which are only represented in borrowed characters, and that the actors are the very persons whom they exhibit. This supposition, I acknowledge, is the most admissible of all. That children and simple people, who are utter strangers to theatrical amusements, are apt at first to be deceived in this manner, is undeniable. That therefore, through the magical power (if I may call it so) of natural and animated action, a transient illusion somewhat similar may be produced in persons of knowledge and experience, I will not take upon me to contravert. But this hypothesis is not necessarily connected with any particular theory of the passions. The persons for whom we grieve, whether the real objects or only their representatives mistaken for them, are still other persons, and not ourselves. Besides, this was never intended to account but for the degree of emotion in one particular case only.

OTHERS,

OTHERS, therefore, who refer every thing to self, will have it, that, by a fiction of the mind, we instantly conceive some future and similar calamity as coming upon ourselves, and that it is solely this conception, and this dread, which call forth all our sorrow and our tears. Others, not satisfied with this, maintain boldly, that we conceive ourselves to be the persons suffering the miseries related or represented, at the very instant that our pity is raised. When nature is deserted by us, it is no wonder that we should lose our way in the devious tracks of imagination, and not know where to settle.

THE first would say, 'When I see Garrick in
'the character of King Lear in the utmost ago-
'ny of distress, I am so transported with the
'passions raised in my breast, that I quite forget
'the tragedian, and imagine that my eyes are
'fixed on that much injured and most miserable
'monarch.' Says the second, 'I am not in the
'least liable to so gross a blunder; but I cannot
'help, in consequence of the representation, be-
'ing struck with the impression, that I am soon
'to be in the same situation, and to be used with
'the like ingratitude and barbarity.' Says the third, 'The case is still worse with me, for I
'conceive

less than in others) as to give ample scope for examination, they are so little agreed what this fiction is. Some contend only, that in witnessing tragedy, one is under a sort of momentary deception, which a very little reflection can correct, and imagines that he is actually witnessing those distresses and miseries which are only represented in borrowed characters, and that the actors are the very persons whom they exhibit. This supposition, I acknowledge, is the most admissible of all. That children and simple people, who are utter strangers to theatrical amusements, are apt at first to be deceived in this manner, is undeniable. That therefore, through the magical power (if I may call it so) of natural and animated action, a transient illusion somewhat similar may be produced in persons of knowledge and experience, I will not take upon me to contravert. But this hypothesis is not necessarily connected with any particular theory of the passions. The persons for whom we grieve, whether the real objects or only their representatives mistaken for them, are still other persons, and not ourselves. Besides, this was never intended to account but for the degree of emotion in one particular case only.

OTHERS,

OTHERS, therefore, who refer every thing to self, will have it, that, by a fiction of the mind, we instantly conceive some future and similar calamity as coming upon ourselves; and that it is solely this conception, and this dread, which call forth all our sorrow and our tears. Others, not satisfied with this, maintain boldly, that we conceive ourselves to be the persons suffering the miseries related or represented, at the very instant that our pity is raised. When nature is deserted by us, it is no wonder that we should lose our way in the devious tracks of imagination, and not know where to settle.

THE first would say, ' When I see Garrick in
' the character of King Lear in the utmost ago-
' ny of distress, I am so transported with the
' passions raised in my breast, that I quite forget
' the tragedian, and imagine that my eyes are
' fixed on that much injured and most miserable
' monarch.' Says the second, ' I am not in the
' least liable to so gross a blunder; but I cannot
' help, in consequence of the representation, be-
' ing struck with the impression, that I am soon
' to be in the same situation, and to be used with
' the like ingratitude and barbarity.' Says the third, ' The case is still worse with me, for I
' conceive

'conceive myself, and not the player, to be that
'wretched man at the very time that he is acted.
'I fancy that I am actually in the midst of
'the storm, suffering all his anguish, that my
'daughters have turned me out of doors, and
'treated me with such unheard-of cruelty and
'injustice.' It is exceedingly lucky that there
do not oftener follow terrible consequences from
these misconceptions. It will be said, 'they
'are transient, and quickly cured by recollec-
'tion.' But however transient, if they really
exist, they must exist for some time. Now if un-
happily a man had two of his daughters sitting
near him at the very instant he were under this
delusion, and if, by a very natural and consequential fiction, he fancied them to be Goneril
and Regan, the effects might be fatal to the ladies,
though they were the most dutiful children in the
world.

It hath never yet been denied (for it is impossible to say what will be denied) that pity influences a person to contribute to relieve the object when it is in his power. But if there is a
mistake in the object, there must of necessity be
a mistake in the direction of the relief. For instance, you see a man perishing with hunger,
and

and your compassion is raised; now you will pity no longer, say these acute reasoners, than you fancy yourself to suffer. You yourself properly are the sole object of your own pity, and as you desire to relieve the person only whom you pity; if there be any food within your reach, you will no doubt devour it voraciously, in order to allay the famine which you fancy you are enduring; but you will not give one morsel to the wretch who really needs your aid, but who is by no means the object of your regret, for whom you can feel no compunction, and with whose distress (which is quite a foreign matter to you) it is impossible you should be affected, especially when under the power of a passion consisting of unmixed selfishness and malignity. For though, if you did not pity him, you would, on cool reflection, give him some aid, perhaps from principle, perhaps from example, or perhaps from habit, unluckily this accursed pity, this unmixed malignant selfishness, interposeth, to shut your heart against him, and to obstruct the pious purpose.

I know no way of eluding this objection but one, which is indeed a very easy way. It is to introduce another fiction of the imagination, and to say, that when this emotion is raised, I lose all consciousness of my own existence and identity, and fancy that the pitiable object before me, is my very self, and that the real I, or what I formerly mistook for myself, is some other body, a mere spectator of my misery, or perhaps nobody at all. Thus unknowingly I may contribute to his relief, when under the strange illusion which makes me fancy, that, instead of giving to another, I am taking to myself. But if the man be scrupulously honest, he will certainly restore to me when I am awake, what I gave him unintentionally in my sleep.

That such fictions may sometimes take place in madness, which almost totally unhinges our mental faculties, I will not dispute, but that such are the natural operations of the passions in a sound state, when the intellectual powers are unimpaired, is what no man would have ever either conceived or advanced, that had not a darling hypothesis to support. And by such arguments, it is certain, that every hypothesis whatever, may equally be supported. Suppose I have taken it into my head to write a theory of the mind; and, in order to give unity and simplicity to my system, as well as to recommend it by by the grace of novelty, I have resolved to deduce all the actions, all the pursuits, and all the passions of men from self-hatred, as the common fountain. If to degrade human nature be so great a recommendation, as we find it is to many speculators, as well as to all atheists and fanatics, who happen, on this point, I know not how, to be most cordially united, the theory now suggested is by no means deficient in that sort of merit from which one might expect to it the very best reception. Self-love is certainly no vice, however justly the want of love to our neighbour be accounted one, but if any thing can be called vicious, self-hatred is undoubtedly so.

LET it not be imagined, that nothing specious can be urged in favour of this hypothesis, What else, it may be pleaded, could induce the miser to deny himself not only the comforts, but even almost the necessaries of life, to pine for want in the midst of plenty, to live in unintermitted anxiety and terror? All the world sees that it is not to procure his own enjoyment, which he invariably and to the last repudiates. And can any reasonable person be so simple as to believe that it is for the purpose of leaving a fortune

tune to his heir, a man whom he despises, for whose deliverance from perdition he would not part with half a crown, and whom of all mankind next to himself he hates the most? What else could induce the sensualist to squander his all in dissipation and debauchery; to rush on ruin certain and foreseen? You call it pleasure. But is he ignorant, that his pleasures are more than ten times counterbalanced by the plagues and even torments which they bring? Does the conviction, or even the experience of this, deter him? On the contrary, with what steady perseverance, with what determined resolution, doth he proceed in his career, not intimidated by the haggard forms which stare him in the face, poverty and infamy, disease and death? What else could induce the man who is reputed covetous, not of money, but of fame, that is of wind, to sacrifice his tranquillity, and almost all the enjoyments of life, to spend his days and nights in fruitless disquietude and endless care? Has a bare name, think you, an empty sound, such inconceivable charms? Can a mere nothing serve as a counterpoise to solid and substantial good? Are we not rather imposed on by appearances, when we conclude this to be his motive? Can we be senseless enough to imagine,

that

that it is the bubble reputation (which, were it any thing, a dead man surely cannot enjoy) that the soldier is so infatuated as to seek even in the cannon's mouth? Are not these, therefore, but the various ways of self-destroying, to which, according to their various tastes, men are prompted, by the same universal principle of self-hatred?

If you should insist on certain phenomena, which appear to be irreconcilable to my hypothesis, I think I am provided with an answer. You urge our readiness to resent an affront or injury, real or imagined, which we receive, and which ought to gratify instead of provoking us, on the supposition that we hate ourselves. But may it not be retorted, that its being a gratification is that which excites our resentment, inasmuch as we are enemies to every kind of self-indulgence? If this answer will not suffice, I have another which is excellent. It lies in the definition of the word revenge. Revenge, I pronounce, may be justly ' deemed an example
' of unmixed self-abhorrence and benignity, and
' may be resolved into that power of imagina-
' tion, by which we apply the sufferings that
' we inflict on others to ourselves; we are said
' to wreak our vengeance no longer than we
' fancy

'fancy ourselves to suffer, and to be satiated by
'reflecting, that the sufferings of others are not
'really ours, that we have been but indulging
'a dream of self-punishment, from which, when
'we awake and discover the fiction, our anger
'instantly subsides, and we are meek as lambs.'
Is this extravagant? Compare it, I pray you, with the preceding explication of compassion, to which it is a perfect counterpart. Consider seriously, and you will find that it is not in the smallest degree more manifest, that another and not ourselves is the object of our resentment when we are angry, than it is that another and not ourselves is the object of our compassion, when we are moved with pity. Both indeed have a self-evidence in them, which, whilst our minds remain unsophisticated by the dogmatism of system, extorts from us an unlimited assent.

Section II.

The Author's hypothesis on this subject.

WHERE so many have failed of success, it may be thought presumptuous to attempt a decision. But despondency in regard to a question which seems to fall within the reach of our faculties, and is entirely subjected to our observation and expe-

experience, must appear to the inquisitive and philosophic mind, a still greater fault than even presumption. The latter may occasion the introduction of a false theory, which must necessarily come under the review and correction of succeeding philosophers. And the detection of error proves often instrumental to the discovery of truth. Whereas the former quashes curiosity altogether, and influences one implicitly to abandon an inquiry as utterly undeterminable. I shall therefore now offer a few observations concerning the passions, which, if rightly apprehended and weighed, will, I hope, contribute to the solution of the present question.

My first observation shall be, that almost all the simple passions of which the mind is susceptible, may be divided into two classes; the *pleasant*, and the *painful*. It is at the same time acknowledged, that the pleasures and the pains created by the different passions, differ considerably from one another, both in kind and degree. Of the former class are love, joy, hope, pride, gratitude; of the latter, hatred, grief, fear, shame, anger. Let it be remarked, that by the name *pride* in the first class, (which I own admits a variety of acceptations) no more is meant here than the feeling which we have on obtaining the merited approbation of other men, in which sense it stands in direct opposition to *shame* in the second class, or the feeling which we have when conscious of incurring the deserved blame of others. In like manner, *gratitude*, or the resentment of favour, is opposed to *anger*, or the resentment of injury. To the second class I might have added *desire* and *aversion*, which give the mind some uneasiness or dissatisfaction with its present state, but these are often the occasion of pleasure, as they are the principal spurs to action, and perhaps more than any other passion, relieve the mind from that languor, which, according to the just remark of Abbé du Bos, is perfectly oppressive. Besides, as they are perpetually accompanied with some degree of either *hope* or *fear*, generally with both, they are either pleasant or painful, as the one or the other preponderates. For these reasons, they may be considered as in themselves of an indifferent or intermediate kind.

The second observation is, that there is an attraction or association among the passions, as well as among the ideas of the mind. Rarely any passion comes alone. To investigate the laws of this

this attraction, would be indeed a matter of curious inquiry, but it doth not fall within the limits of the prefent queftion. Almoft all the other affections attract or excite defire or averfion of fome fort or other. The paffions which feem to have the leaft influence on thefe, are joy and grief, and of the two, joy, I believe, will be acknowledged, to have lefs of the attractive power than grief. Joy is the end of defire, and the completion of hope: therefore when attained, it not only excludes occafion for the others, but feems, for a while at leaft, to repel them, as what would give an impertinent interruption to the pleafure refulting from the contemplation of prefent felicity, with which the mind, under the influence of joy, is engroffed. Grief hath a like tendency. When the mind is overwhelmed by this gloomy paffion, it refifts the inftigations of defire, as what would again, to no purpofe, roufe its activity; it difdains hope, it even loathes it as a vain and delufive dream. The firft fuggeftions of thefe paffions feem but as harbingers to the cutting recollection of former flattering profpects, once too fondly entertained, now utterly extinct, and fucceeded by an infupportable and irremediable difappointment, which every recollection ferves but to aggravate Nay, how unaccountable

accountable soever it may appear, the mind seems to have a mournful satisfaction in being allowed to indulge its anguish, and to immerse itself wholly in its own afflictions. But this can be affirmed of sorrow only in the extreme. When it begins to subside, or when originally, but in a weak degree, it leads the mind to seek relief from desire, and hope, and other passions. —Love naturally associates to it benevolence, which is one species of desire, for here no more is meant by it than a desire of the happiness of the person loved. Hatred as naturally associates malevolence or malice, which is the desire of evil to the person hated*.

My

---

* The ambiguity and even penury of all languages in relation to our internal feelings, make it very difficult in treating of them, to preserve at once perspicuity and accuracy. Benevolence is sometimes used, perhaps with little variation from its most common import, for charity or universal love; and love itself will be thought by some to be properly defined by the desire or wish of the happiness of its object. As to the first, it is enough that I have assigned the precise meaning in which I use the term, and in regard to the second, those who are duly attentive to what passes within their own breasts will be sensible, that by love, in the strictest acceptation, is meant a certain pleasurable emotion excited in the mind by a suitable object, to which the desire of the happiness of the object is generally consequent. The felicity of the object may however be such, as to leave no room for any desire or wish of ours in regard to it. This holds particularly in our love to God. Besides, there may be a desire of the happiness of others, arising from very different causes,

My third observation is, that pain of every kind generally makes a deeper impression on the imagination than pleasure does, and is longer retained by the memory. It is a common remark of every people and of every age, and consequently hath some foundation in human nature, that benefits are sooner forgotten than injuries, and favours than affronts. Those who are accustomed to attend the theatre will be sensible, that the plots of the best tragedies which they have witnessed, are better remembered by them, than those of the most celebrated comedies. And indeed every body that reflects may be satisfied, that no story takes a firmer hold of the memory than a tale of woe. In civil history, as well as in biography, it is the disastrous and not the joyous events, which are oftenest recollected and retailed.

causes, where there is nothing of that sentiment or feeling which is strictly called *love* I own at the same time, that the term love is also often used to denote simply benevolence or goodwill, as when we are commanded to love all men, known and unknown, good and bad, friendly and injurious. To that tender emotion which qualities supposed amiable alone can excite, the precept surely doth not extend. These things I thought it necessary to observe, in order to prevent mistake in a case which requires so much precision.

The fourth obfervation is, that from a group of paffions (if I may fo exprefs myfelf) affociated together, and having the fame object, fome of which are of the pleafant, others of the painful kind; if the pleafant predominate, there arifeth often a greater and a more durable pleafure to the mind, than would refult from thefe, if alone and unmixed. That the cafe is fo, will, I believe, on a careful inquiry, be found to be a matter of experience; how it happens to be fo, I am afraid, human fagacity will never be able to inveftigate.

This obfervation holds efpecially when the emotions and affections raifed in us are derived from fympathy, and have not directly felf for the object. Sympathy is not a paffion, but that quality of the foul which renders it fufceptible of almoft any paffion, by communication from the bofom of another. It is by fympathy we rejoice with them that rejoice, and weep with them that weep. This faculty, however, doth not act with equal ftrength in thefe oppofite cafes, but is much weaker in the firft than in the fecond. It would perhaps be eafier to affign the intention of nature in this difference, than the caufe of the difference. The miferable need the aid and fympathy

thy of others, the happy do not. I muſt further obſerve on this ſubject, what I believe was hinted once already, that ſympathy may be greatly ſtrengthened or weakened by the influence of connected paſſions. Thus love aſſociates to it benevolence, and both give double force to ſympathy. Hatred, on the contrary, aſſociates to it malice, and deſtroys ſympathy.

THERE are conſequently ſeveral reaſons why a ſcene of pure unmixed joy in any work of genius, cannot give a great or laſting pleaſure to the mind. Firſt, ſympathetic joy is much fainter and more tranſient than ſympathetic grief, and they are generally the ſympathetic paſſions, which are infuſed by poets, orators, painters, and hiſtorians: ſecondly, joy is the leaſt attractive of all the affections. It perhaps can never properly be ſaid to aſſociate to it deſire, the great ſpring of action. The moſt we can ſay is, that when it begins to ſubſide, it again gives place to deſire, this paſſion being of ſuch a nature, as that it can hardly for any time be baniſhed from the ſoul. Hence it is, that the joy which has no other foundation but ſympathy, quickly tires the mind, and runs into ſatiety. Hence it is alſo, that dramatic writers, and even romance writers, make a scene of pure joy always the last scene of the piece, and but a short one. It may just be mentioned, thirdly, not indeed as an argument, (for of its weakness in this respect I am very sensible) but as an illustration from analogy, that every thing in nature is heightened and set off by its contrary, which, by giving scope for comparison, enhances every excellence. The colours in painting acquire a double lustre from the shades; the harmony in music is greatly improved by a judicious mixture of discords. The whole conduct of life, were it necessary, might exemplify the position. A mixture of pain then seems to be of consequence to give strength and stability to pleasure.

The fifth observation is, that under the name *pity* may be included all the emotions excited by tragedy. In common speech all indeed are included under this name, that are excited by that species of eloquence which is denominated the pathetic. The passions moved by tragedy have been commonly said to be *pity* and *terror*. This enumeration is more popular than philosophical, even though adopted by the Stagyrite himself. For what is pity but a participation by sympathy in the woes of others, and the feelings naturally

naturally consequent upon them, of whatever kind they be, their fears as well as sorrows: whereas, this way of contradistinguishing terror from pity, would make one who knew nothing of tragedy but from the definition, imagine, that it were intended to make us compassionate others in trouble, and dread mischief to ourselves. If this were really the case, I believe there are few or none who would find any pleasure in this species of entertainment. Of this there is access to witness an example, when, as hath sometimes happened, in the midst of the performance, the audience are alarmed with the sudden report, that the house hath taken fire, or when they hear a noise which makes them suspect that the roof or walls are falling. Then, indeed, terror stares in every countenance, but such a terror as gives no degree of pleasure, and is so far from coalescing with the passions raised by the tragedy, that, on the contrary, it expells them altogether, and leaves not in the mind, for some time at least, another idea or reflection, but what concerns personal safety.

On the other hand, if all the sympathetic affections excited by the theatrical representation were to be severally enumerated, I cannot see, why hope, indignation, love and hatred, gratitude and refentment, fhould not be included as well as fear. To account then for the pleafure which we find in pity, is, in a great meafure, to give a folution of the queftion under review. I do not fay that this will fatisfy in every cafe. On the contrary, there are many cafes, in which Abbé du Bos' account above recited, of the pleafure arifing from the agitation and fluctuation of the paffions, is the only folution that can be given.

My fixth and laft obfervation on this head is, that pity is not a fimple paffion, but a group of paffions ftrictly united by affociation, and as it were blended, by centering in the fame object. Of thefe fome are pleafant, fome painful, commonly the pleafant preponderate. It hath been remarked already, that love attracts benevolence, benevolence quickens fympathy. The fame attraction takes place inverfely, though not, perhaps, with equal ftrength. Sympathy engages benevolence, and benevolence love. That benevolence, or the habit of wifhing happinefs to another, from whatever motive it hath originally fprung, will at length draw in love, might be proved from a thoufand inftances.

In the party-divisions which obtain in some countries, it often happens, that a man is at first induced to take a side, purely from a motive of interest; for some time, from this motive solely, he wishes the success of the party with which he is embarked. From a habit of wishing this, he will continue to wish it, when, by a change of circumstances, his own interest is no longer connected with it; nay, which is more strange, he will even contract such a love and attachment to the party, as to promote their interest in direct opposition to his own. That commiseration or sympathy in woe, hath still a stronger tendency to engage our love, is evident.

This is the only rational account that can be given why mothers of a humane disposition generally love most the sicklest child in the family, though perhaps far from being the loveliest in respect either of temper or of other qualities. The habit of commiseration habituates them to the feeling and exertion of benevolence. Benevolence habitually felt and exerted, confirms and augments their love. " Nothing," says Mr. Hume*, " endears so much a friend, as sorrow " for his death. The pleasure of his company

---

* Essay on Tragedy.

" has not so powerful an influence." Distress to the pitying eye, diminishes every fault, and sets off every good quality in the brightest colours. Nor is it a less powerful advocate for the mistress than for the friend: often does the single circumstance of misfortune subdue all resentment of former coldness and ill usage, and make a languid and dying passion revive and flame out with a violence which it is impossible any longer to withstand. Every body acknowledges, that beauty is never so irresistible as in tears. Distress is commonly sufficient with those who are not very hard-hearted or pityless, (for these words are nearly of the same import) to make even enmity itself relent.

There are then in *pity*, these three different emotions: first, *commiseration*, purely painful; secondly, *benevolence*, or a desire of the relief and happiness of the object pitied, a passion, as was already observed, of the intermediate kind; thirdly, *love*, in which is always implied one of the noblest and most exquisite pleasures, whereof the soul is susceptible, and which is itself, in most cases, sufficient to give a counterpoise of pleasure to the whole.

For

For the further confirmation of this theory, let it be remarked, that orators and poets, in order to strengthen this association and union, are at pains to adorn the character of him for whom they would engage our pity, with every amiable quality, which, in a consistency with probability, they can crowd into it. On the contrary, when the character is hateful, the person's misfortunes are unpitied. Sometimes they even occasion a pleasure of a very different kind; namely, that which the mind naturally takes in viewing the just punishment of demerit. When the character hath such a mixture of good and odious qualities, as that we can neither withhold our commiseration, nor bestow our love; the mind is then torn opposite ways at once, by passions which, instead of uniting, repel one another. Hence the piece becomes shocking and disgustful. Such, to a certain degree, in my judgment, the tragedy of *Venice Preserved*, wherein the hero, notwithstanding several good qualities, is a villain and a traitor, will appear to every well-disposed mind. All the above cases, if attended to, will be found exactly to tally with the hypothesis here suggested.

All the answer then which I am able to produce, upon the whole, and which results from the foregoing observations, is this: The principal pleasure in pity ariseth from its own nature, or from the nature of those passions of which it is compounded, and not from any thing extrinsic or adventitious. The tender emotions of love which enter into the composition, sweeten the commiseration or sympathetic sorrow, the commiseration gives a stability to those emotions, with which otherwise the mind would soon be cloyed, when directed towards a person, imaginary, unknown, or with whom we are totally unacquainted. The very benevolence or wish of contributing to his relief, affords an occupation to the thoughts, which agreeably rouses them. It impels the mind to devise expedients by which the unhappy person (if our pity is excited by some present calamitous incident) may be, or (if it is awaked by the art of the poet, the orator, or the historian) might have been, relieved from his distress. Yet the whole movement of the combined affections is not converted into pleasure, for though the uneasiness of the melancholy passions be overpowered, it is not effaced by something stronger of an opposite kind.

Mr.

Mr. Hume, indeed, in his manner of expressing himself on this article, hath not observed either an entire uniformity, or his usual precision. I should rather say, from some dubiousness in relation to the account he was giving, he seems to have, in part, retracted what he had been establishing, and thus leaves the reader with an alternative in the decision. First he tells us, that "the whole movement of those [melan-"choly] passions is converted into pleasure." Afterwards, "the latter [the sentiments of beau-"ty] being the predominant emotion, seize the "whole mind, and convert the former [the im-"pulse or vehemence arising from sorrow, com-"passion, indignation,] into themselves," he adds, by way of correction, "or at least tincture "them so strongly, as totally to alter their na-"ture." Again, "The soul feels, on the whole, "a strong movement, which is altogether de-"lightful." All this, I acknowledge, appears to me to be neither sufficiently definite, nor quite intelligible.

But passing that, I shall only subjoin, that the combination of the passions in the instance under our examination, is not like the blending of colours, two of which will produce a third,
where-

wherein you can difcern nothing of the original hues united in producing it, but it rather refembles a mixture of taftes, when you are quite fenfible of the different favours of the ingredients. Thus blue and yellow mingled make green, in which you difcover no tint of either, and all the colours of the rainbow blended, conftitute a white, which to the eye appears as fimple and original as any of them, and perfectly unlike to each. On the other hand, in eating meat with falt, for inftance, we tafte both diftinctly; and though the latter fingly would be difagreeable, the former is rendered more agreeable by the mixture than it would otherwife have been.

I own, indeed, that certain adventitious circumftances may contribute to heighten the effect. But thefe cannot be regarded as effential to the paffion. They occur occafionally. Some of them actually occur but feldom. Of this fort is the fatisfaction which arifeth from a fenfe of our own eafe and fecurity, compared with the calamity and the danger of another.

> 'Tis pleafant, fafely to behold from fhore
> The rowling fhip, and hear the tempeft roar:
> Not that another's pain is our delight,
> But pains unfelt produce the pleafing fight.

'Tis pleasant also to behold from far
The moving legions mingled in the war *.

The poet hath hit here on some of the very few circumstances, in which it would be natural to certain tempers, not surely the most humane, to draw comfort in the midst of sympathetic sorrow, from such a comparison. The reflection, in my opinion, occurs almost only when a very small change in external situation, as a change in place to the distance of a few furlongs, would put us into the same lamentable circumstances which we are commiserating in others. Even something of this kind will present itself to our thoughts, when there is no particular object to demand our pity. A man who, in tempestuous weather, sits snug in a close house, near a good fire, and hears the wind and rain beating upon the roof and windows, will naturally think of his own comfortable situation, compared with that of a traveller, who, perhaps, far from shelter, is exposed to all the violence of the tempest. But in such cases, a difference, as I said, in a

---

* Suave mari magno, turbantibus æquora ventis,
E terra magnum alterius spectare laborem.
Non quia vexari quemquam 'st jucunda voluptas,
Sed quibus ipse malis careas, quia cernere suave 'st.
Suave etiam belli certamina magna tueri
Per campos instructa, tua sine parte pericli. LUCRET. l. 2.

single accidental circumstance, which may happen at any time, is all that is necessary to put a man in the same disastrous situation, wherein he either sees or conceives others to be. And the very slightness of the circumstance which would have been sufficient to reverse the scene, makes him so ready to congratulate with himself on his better luck. Whereas, nothing is less natural, and I will venture to say, less common, than such a reflection, when the differences are many, and of a kind which cannot be reckoned merely accidental, as when the calamity is what the person pitying, must consider himself as not liable to, or in the remotest hazard of. A man who, with the most undissembled compassion, bewails the wretched and undeserved fate of Desdemona, is not apt to think of himself, how fortunate he is, in not being the wife of a credulous, jealous, and revengeful husband, though perhaps a girl who hath lately rejected a suitor of this character, will reflect with great complacency, on the escape that she hath made.

ANOTHER adventitious source of pleasure is, the satisfaction that results from the conscious exercise of the humane affections, which it is our duty to cherish and improve. I mention this as adventitious, becaufe, though not unnatural, I do not imagine that the fenfations of fympathetic forrow, either always or immediately, give rife to this reflection. Children, and even favages, are fufceptible of pity, who think no more of claiming any merit to themfelves on this fcore, than they think of claiming merit from their feeling the natural appetites of hunger and thirft. Nay, it is very poffible that perfons may know its power and fweetnefs to, when, through the influence of education and bad example, they confider it as a weaknefs or blemifh in their difpofition, and as fuch endeavour to conceal and ftifle it. A certain degree of civilization feems to be neceffary, to make us thoroughly fenfible of its beauty and utility, and confequently, that it ought to be cultivated. Bigotry may teach a man to think inhumanity, in certain circumftances, a virtue. Yet nature will reclaim, and may make him, in fpite of the dictates of a mifguided confcience, feel all the tendernefs of pity to the heretic, who, in his opinion, has more than merited the very worft that can be inflicted on him.

I acknowledge, that, on the other hand, when the fentiment comes generally to prevail, that

that compassion is in itself praiseworthy, it may be rendered a source of much more self-satisfaction to the vain-glorious, than reasonably it ought to yield. Such persons gladly lay hold of every handle which serves to raise them in their own esteem. And I make no doubt that several, from this very motive, have exalted this principle as immoderately as others have vilified it. Every good man will agree, that this is the case when people consider it as either a veil for their vices, or an atonement for the neglect of their duty. For my own part, I am inclined to think, that those who are most ready to abuse it thus, are not the most remarkable for any exercise of it, by which society can be profited. There is a species of deception in the case, which it is not beside the purpose briefly to unravel.

It hath been observed, that sense invariably makes a stronger impression than memory, and memory a stronger than imagination, yet there are particular circumstances which appear to form an exception, and to give an efficacy to the ideas of imagination, beyond what either memory or sense can boast. So great is the anomaly which sometimes displays itself in human characters, that it is not impossible to find persons who are

are quickly made to cry at seeing a tragedy, or reading a romance, which they know to be fictious, and yet are both inattentive and unfeeling in respect of the actual objects of compassion, who live in their neighbourhood, and are daily under their eye. Nevertheless, this is an exception from the rule, more in appearance than in reality. The cases are not parallel. there are certain circumstances which obtain in the one, and have no place in the other; and to these peculiarities the difference in the effect is solely imputable. What follows will serve fully to explain my meaning.

Men may be of a selfish, contracted, and even avaricious disposition, who are not what we should denominate hard-hearted, or insusceptible of sympathetic feeling. Such will gladly enjoy the luxury of pity (as Hawkesworth terms it) when it nowise interferes with their more powerful passions; that is, when it comes unaccompanied with a demand upon their pockets. With the tragic or the romantic hero or heroine, they most cordially sympathize, because the only tribute which wretches of their dignity exact from them, is sighs and tears. And of these their consciences inform them, to their inexpressible consolation,

solation, that they are no niggards. But the case is totally different with living objects. Barren tears and sighs will not satisfy these. Hence it is that people's avarice, a most formidable adversary to the unhappy, is interested to prevent their being moved by such, and to make them avoid, as much as possible, every opportunity of knowing or seeing them*. But as that cannot always be done, as commiseration is attended with benevolence, and as benevolence itself, if not gratified, by our giving relief when it is in our power,

* In the parable of the compassionate Samaritan, Luke x. 30. &c. this disposition, to shun the sight of misery, which one is resolved not to redress, is finely touched in the conduct of the priest and the Levite, who, when they espied a person naked, wounded, and almost expiring on the road, are said to have *passed by on the other side*. Indeed in the account given of the Levite in our version, there is something, which, to me, has a contradictory appearance. He *came and looked on him, and passed by on the other side*. There is not a vestige of this inconsistency in the original, which says simply, ἐλθὼν καὶ ἰδὼν ἀντιπαρῆλθεν, the meaning of which plainly is, " travelling that way, " and seeing one in this wretched plight, he kept on the other " side of the road, and passed on." In such a case, a man who is not quite obdurate, would avoid the cutting reflection, that he knows any thing of the matter. And though he must be conscious that he knew a little, and might have known more if he would, he is glad to gloss his inhumanity even to himself, with some pretext of hurry or thoughtlessness, or any thing that may conceal the naked truth, a truth which he is as averse to discover in himself, as he is to see in another the misery which he is determined not to relieve.

embitters

embitters the pleasure which would otherwise result from pity, as the refusal is also attended with self-reproach; a person of such a temper, strongly, and for the most part effectually resists his being moved. He puts his ingenuity to the rack, in order to satisfy himself that he ought not to be affected. He is certain, that the person is not a proper object of beneficence, he is convinced that his distress is more pretended than real, or, if that cannot be alleged, the man hath surely brought it on himself by his vices, therefore he deserves to suffer, and is nowise entitled to our pity; or at least he makes not a good use of what may charitably, but injudiciously, be bestowed upon him. Such are the common shifts by which selfishness eludes the calls of humanity, and chooses to reserve all its worthless stock of pity for fictitious objects, or for those who, in respect of time, or place, or eminence, are beyond its reach.

For these reasons, I am satisfied that compassion alone, especially that displayed on occasion of witnessing public spectacles, is at best but a very weak evidence of philanthropy. The only proof that is entirely unequivocal, is actual beneficence, when one seeks out the real objects of commiseration, not as a matter of self-indulgence, but in order to bring relief to those who need it, to give hope to the desponding, and comfort to the sorrowful, for the sake of which one endures the sight of wretchedness, when, instead of giving pleasure, it distresseth every feeling heart. Such, however, enjoy at length, a luxury far superior to that of pity, the godlike luxury of dispelling grief, communicating happiness, and doing good.

THE PHILOSOPHY OF RHETORIC.

BOOK II.

The Foundations and essential Properties of Elocution.

CHAP. I.

The Nature and Characters of the Use which gives Law to Language.

ELOQUENCE hath always been considered, and very justly, as having a particular connexion with language. It is the intention of eloquence, to convey our sentiments into the minds of others, in order to produce a certain effect upon them. Language is the only vehicle by which this conveyance can be made. The art of speaking then is not less necessary to the orator, than the art of thinking. Without the latter, the former could not have existed. Without the former, the latter would be ineffective. Every tongue whatever is founded in use or custom,

———————Whose arbitrary sway
Words and the forms of language must obey *. FRANCIS.

LANGUAGE is purely a species of fashion (for this holds equally of every tongue) in which, by the general, but tacit consent of the people of a particular state or country, certain sounds come to be appropriated to certain things, as their signs, and certain ways of inflecting and combining those sounds come to be established, as denoting the relations which subsist among the things signified.

IT is not the business of grammar, as some critics seem preposterously to imagine, to give law to the fashions which regulate our speech. On the contrary, from its conformity to these, and from that alone, it derives all its authority and value. For, what is the grammar of any language? It is no other than a collection of general observations methodically digested, and

---

* ———————Usus
Quem penes arbitrium est et jus et norma loquendi.
HOR. De Arte Poet.

comprising

comprising all the modes previously and independently established, by which the significations, derivations, and combinations of words in that language, are ascertained. It is of no consequence here to what causes originally these modes or fashions owe their existence, to imitation, to reflection, to affectation, or to caprice; they no sooner obtain and become general, than they are laws of the language, and the grammarian's only business is to note, collect, and methodise them. Nor does this truth concern only those more comprehensive analogies or rules, which affect whole classes of words, such as nouns, verbs, and the other parts of speech, but it concerns every individual word, in the inflecting or the combining of which, a particular mode hath prevailed. Every single anomaly, therefore, though departing from the rule assigned to the other words of the same class, and on that account called an exception, stands on the same basis, on which the rules of the tongue are founded, custom having prescribed for it a separate rule[*].

THE

---

[*] Thus in the two verbs *call* and *shall*, the second person singular of the former is *callest*, agreeably to the general rule, the second person singular of the latter is *shalt*, agreeably to a particular rule affecting that verb. To say *shallest* for *shalt*, would be

THE truth of this position hath never, for ought I can remember, been directly contraverted by any body, yet it is certain, that both critics and grammarians often argue in such a way as is altogether inconsistent with it. What, for example, shall we make of that complaint of Doctor Swift, "that our language, in many "instances, offends against every part of gram- "mar†?" Or what could the Doctor's notion of grammar be, when he expressed himself in this manner? Some notion, possibly, he had of grammar in the abstract, an universal archetype by which the particular grammars of all different tongues ought to be regulated. If this was his meaning, I cannot say whether he is in the right or in the wrong in this accusation. I acknowledge myself to be entirely ignorant of this ideal grammar, nor can I form a conjecture where its laws are to be learnt. One thing, indeed, every smatterer in philosophy will tell us, that there can be no natural connexion between the sounds of any language, and the things signified, or between the modes of inflection and combination, and the relations they are intended to express.

be as much a barbarism, though according to the general rule, as to say *calt* for *callest*, which is according to no rule.

† Letter to the Lord High Treasurer, &c.

Perhaps

Perhaps he meant the grammar of some other language, if so, the charge was certainly true, but not to the purpose, since we can say with equal truth, of every language, that it offends against the grammar of every other language whatsoever. If he meant the English grammar, I would ask, whence has that grammar derived its laws? If from general use, (and I cannot conceive another origin) then it must be owned, that there is a general use in that language as well as in others; and it were absurd to accuse the language which is purely what is conformable to general use in speaking and writing, as offending against general use. But if he meant to say, that there is no fixed, established, or general use in the language, that it is quite irregular, he hath been very unlucky in his manner of expressing himself. Nothing is more evident, than that where there is no law, there is no transgression. In that case, he ought to have said, that it is not susceptible of grammar, which, by the way, would not have be entrue of English, or indeed of any the most uncultivated language on the earth.

It is easy then to assign the reason, why the justness of the complaint, as Doctor Lowth observes,

serves*, has never yet been questioned; it is purely, because, not being understood, it hath never been minded. But if, according to this ingenious gentleman, the words *our language*, have, by a new kind of trope, been used to denote those who speak and write English, and no more hath been intended than to signify, that our best speakers, and most approved authors, frequently offend against the rules of grammar, that is, against the general use of the language, I shall not here enter on a discussion of the question. Only let us rest in these as fixed principles, that use, or the custom of speaking, is the sole original standard of conversation, as far as regards the expression, and the custom of writing is the sole standard of style, that the latter comprehends the former, and something more, that to the tribunal of use, as to the supreme authority, and consequently, in every grammatical controversy, the last resort, we are entitled to appeal from the laws and the decisions of grammarians, and that this order of subordination ought never, on any account, to be reversed. But if use be here a matter of such consequence, it will be necessary, before advancing any farther, to ascertain precisely what it is. We shall otherwise be in dan-

* Preface to his Introduction to English Grammar.

ger,

ger, though we agree about the name, of differing widely in the notion that we assign to it.

Section I.

Reputable use.

In what extent then must the word be understood? It is sometimes called *general use*; yet is it not manifest that the generality of people speak and write very badly? Nay, is not this a truth that will be even generally acknowledged? It will be so, and this very acknowledgment shows that many terms and idioms may be common, which, nevertheless, have not the general sanction, no, nor even the suffrage of those that use them. The use here spoken of, implies not only *currency*, but *vogue*. It is properly *reputable custom*.

This leads to a distinction between good use and bad use in language, the former of which will be found to have the approbation of those who have not themselves attained it. The far greater part of mankind, perhaps ninety-nine of a hundred, are, by reason of poverty and other circumstances, deprived of the advantages of education, and condemned to toil for bread, almost incessantly, in some narrow occupation.

They have neither the leisure nor the means of attaining any knowledge, except what lies within the contracted circle of their several professions. As the ideas which occupy their minds are few, the portion of the language known to them must be very scanty. It is impossible that our knowledge of words should outstrip our knowledge of things. It may, and often doth, come short of it. Words may be remembered as sounds, but cannot be understood as signs, whilst we remain unacquainted with the things signified.

Hence it will happen, that in the lower walks of life, from the intercourse which all ranks occasionally have with one another, the people will frequently have access to hear words of which they never had access to learn the meaning. These they will pick up and remember, produce and misapply. But there is rarely any uniformity in such blunders, or any thing determinate in the senses they give to words which are not within their sphere. Nay, they are not themselves altogether unconscious of this defect. It often ariseth from an admiration of the manner of their superiors, and from an ill-judged imitation of their way of speaking, that the greatest errors

errors of the illiterate, in respect of conversation, proceed. And were they sensible how widely different their use and application of such words is, from that of those whom they affect to imitate, they would renounce their own immediately.

But it may be said, and said with truth, that in such subjects as are within their reach, many words and idioms prevail among the populace, which, notwithstanding a use pretty uniform and extensive, are considered as corrupt, and like counterfeit money, though common, not valued. This is the case particularly with those terms and phrases which critics have denominated *vulgarisms*. Their use is not reputable. On the contrary, we always associate with it such notions of meanness, as suit those orders of men amongst whom chiefly the use is found. Hence it is, that many who have contracted a habit of employing such idioms, do not approve them, and though, through negligence, they frequently fall into them in conversation, they carefully avoid them in writing, or even in a solemn speech on any important occasion. Their currency, therefore, is without authority and weight. The tattle of children hath a currency, but, however universal their manner of corrupting words may be among themselves, it can never establish what is accounted use in language. Now, what children are to men, that precisely the ignorant are to the knowing.

From the practice of those who are conversant in any art, elegant or mechanical, we always take the sense of the terms and phrases belonging to that art, in like manner, from the practice of those who have had a liberal education, and are therefore presumed to be best acquainted with men and things, we judge of the general use in language. If in this particular there be any deference to the practice of the great and rich, it is not ultimately because they are greater and richer than others, but because, from their greatness and riches, they are imagined to be wiser and more knowing. The source, therefore, of that preference which distinguisheth good use from bad in language, is a natural propension of the human mind to believe, that those are the best judges of the proper signs, and of the proper application of them, who understand best the things which they represent.

But who are they that in the public estimation are possessed of this character? This question is of the greatest moment for ascertaining that use, which is entitled to the epithets reputable and good. Vaugelas makes them in France to be " the soundest part of the court, and the " soundest part of the authors of the age*." With us Britons, the first part at least of this description will not answer. In France, which is a pure monarchy, as the dependance of the inferior orders is much greater, their submission to their superiors, and the humble respect which in every instance they show them, seem, in our way of judging, to border even upon adoration. With us, on the contrary, who in our spirit, as well as in the constitution of our government, have more of the republican than of the monarchical, there is no remarkable partiality in favour of courtiers. At least their being such, rarely enhanceth our opinion, either of their abilities or of their virtues.

I would not by this be understood to signify, that the primary principle which gives rise to the distinction between good use and bad in language, is different in different countries. It is

---

* " Voicy comme on definit le bon usage. C'est la façon " de parler de la plus saine partie de la cour, conformément à " la façon d'ecrire de la plus saine partie des auteurs du tems.' Preface aux Remarques sur la Langue Françoise.

not originally, even in France, a deference to power, but to wisdom. Only it must be remarked, that the tendency of the imagination is to accumulate all great qualities into the same character. Wherever we find one or two of these, we naturally presume the rest. This is particularly true of those qualities, which, by their immediate consequences, strongly affect the external senses. We are in a manner dazzled by them.—Hence it happens, that it is difficult even for a man of discernment, till he be better instructed by experience, to restrain a veneration for the judgment of a person of uncommon splendour and magnificence, as if one who is more powerful and opulent than his neighbours, were of necessity wiser too. Now this original bias of the mind some political constitutions serve to strengthen, others to correct.

But without resting the matter entirely on the difference in respect of government between France and Britain, the British court is commonly too fluctuating an object. Use in language requires firmer ground to stand upon. No doubt, the conversation of men of rank and eminence, whether of the court or not, will have its influence. And in what concerns merely the pro-

pronunciation, it is the only rule to which we can refer the matter in every doubtful case; but in what concerns the words themselves, their construction and application, it is of importance to have some certain, steady, and well-known standard to recur to, a standard which every one hath access to canvass and examine. And this can be no other than authors of reputation. Accordingly we find that these are, by universal consent, in actual possession of this authority; as to this tribunal, when any doubt arises, the appeal is always made.

I choose to name them, authors of reputation, rather than good authors, for two reasons: first, because it is more strictly conformable to the truth of the case. It is solely the esteem of the public, and not their intrinsic merit (though these two go generally together), which raises them to this distinction, and stamps a value on their language. Secondly, this character is more definitive than the other, and therefore more extensively intelligible. Between two or more authors, different readers will differ exceedingly, as to the preference in point of merit, who agree perfectly as to the respective places they hold in the favour of the public. You may find persons of
a taste

a taste so particular as to prefer Prinel to Milton, but you will hardly find a person that will dispute the superiority of the latter in the article of fame. For this reason, I affirm, that Vaugelas' definition labours under an essential defect; inasmuch as it may be difficult to meet with two persons whose judgments entirely coincide in determining who are the sounder part of the court, or of the authors of the age. I need scarcely add, that when I speak of reputation, I mean not only in regard to knowledge, but in regard to the talent of communicating knowledge. I could name writers, who, in respect of the first, have been justly valued by the public, but who, on account of a supposed deficiency in respect of the second, are considered as of no authority in language.

Nor is there the least ground to fear, that we should be cramped here within too narrow limits. In the English tongue there is a plentiful supply of noted writings in all the various kinds of composition, in prose and verse, serious and ludicrous, grave and familiar. Agreeably then to this first qualification of the term, we must understand to be comprehended under general use, *whatever modes of speech are authorised as good by the*

the writings of a great number, if not the majority of celebrated authors.

SECTION II.

National use.

ANOTHER qualification of the term *use* which deserves our attention, is that it must be *national*. This I consider in a twofold view, as it stands opposed both to *provincial* and to *foreign*.

IN every province there are peculiarities of dialect, which affect not only the pronunciation and the accent, but even the inflection and the combination of words, whereby their idiom is distinguished both from that of the nation, and from that of every other province. The narrowness of the circle to which the currency of the words and phrases of such dialects is confined, sufficiently discriminates them from that which is properly styled the language, and which commands a circulation incomparably wider. This is one reason, I imagine, why the term *use*, on this subject, is commonly accompanied with the epithet *general*. In the use of provincial idioms, there is, it must be acknowledged, a pretty considerable concurrence both of the middle and of the lower ranks. But still this use is bounded by the province, county, or district, which gives name to the dialect, and beyond which its peculiarities are sometimes unintelligible, and always ridiculous. But the language, properly so called, is found current, especially in the upper and the middle ranks, over the whole British empire. Thus, though in every province they ridicule the idiom of every other province, they all vail to the English idiom, and scruple not to acknowledge its superiority over their own.

For example, in some parts of Wales, (if we may credit Shakespeare*,) the common people say *goot* for good, in the South of Scotland they say *gude*, and in the North, *gueed*. Wherever one of these pronunciations prevails, you will never hear from a native either of the other two, but the word *good* is to be heard every where from natives as well as strangers, nor do the people ever dream that there is any thing laughable in it, however much they are disposed to laugh at the county-accents and idioms which they discern in one another. Nay more, though the people of distant provinces do not understand one another, they mostly all understand one who

* Fluellen in Henry V.

speaks properly. It is a just and curious observation of Dr. Kenrick, that "the case of lan-
"guages, or rather speech, being quite contrary
"to that of science, in the former the ignorant
"understand the learned, better than the learn-
"ed do the ignorant; in the latter, it is other-
"wise *."

HENCE it will perhaps be found true, upon inquiry, notwithstanding its paradoxical appearance, that though it be very uncommon to speak or write pure English, yet, of all the idioms subsisting amongst us, that to which we give the character of purity, is the commonest. The faulty idioms do not jar more with true English, than they do with one another; so that, in order to our being satisfied of the truth of the apparent paradox, it is requisite only that we remember that these idioms are diverse one from another, though they come under the common denomination of *impure*. Those who wander from the road may be incomparably more than those who travel in it, and yet, if it be into a thousand different bypaths that they deviate, there may not in any one of these be found so

* Rhet. Gram. Chap. ii. Sect. 4.

many as those whom you will meet upon the king's highway.

What hath been now said of provincial dialects, may, with very little variation, be applied to professional dialects, or the cant which is sometimes observed to prevail among those of the same profession or way of life. The currency of the latter cannot be so exactly circumscribed as that of the former, whose distinction is purely local, but their use is not on that account either more extensive or more reputable. Let the following serve as instances of this kind. *Advice*, in the commercial idiom, means information or intelligence, *nervous*, in open defiance of analogy, doth in the medical cant, as Johnson expresseth it, denote, having weak nerves, and the word *turtle*, though pre-occupied time immemorial by a species of doves, is, as we learn from the same authority, employed by sailors and gluttons, to signify a tortoise*.

It was remarked, that national might also be opposed to foreign. I imagine it is too evident to need illustration, that the introduction of extraneous words and idioms, from other languages and foreign nations, cannot be a smaller trans-

* See those words in the English Dictionary

gression against the established custom of the English tongue, than the introduction of words and idioms peculiar to some precincts of England, or at least somewhere current within the British pale. The only material difference between them is, that the one is more commonly the error of the learned, the other of the vulgar. But if, in this view, the former is entitled to greater indulgence, from the respect paid to learning, in another view, it is entitled to less, as it is much more commonly the result of affectation. Thus two essential qualities of usage, in regard to language, have been settled, that it be both *reputable* and *national*.

Section III.

Present use.

But there will naturally arise here another question, "Is not use, even good and national
" use, in the same country, different in different
" periods? And if so, to the usage of what pe-
" riod shall we attach ourselves, as the proper
" rule? If you say *the present*, as it may reason-
" ably be expected that you will, the difficulty
" is not entirely removed. In what extent of
" signification must we understand the word
" present?

"*present?* How far may we safely range in "quest of authorities? or, at what distance "backwards from this moment are authors still "to be accounted as possessing a legislative voice "in language?" To this, I own, it is difficult to give an answer with all the precision that might be desired. Yet it is certain, that when we are in search of precedents for any word or idiom, there are certain mounds which we cannot overleap with safety. For instance, the authority of Hooker or of Raleigh, however great their merit and their fame be, will not now be admitted in support of a term or expression, not to be found in any good writer of a later date.

In truth, the boundary must not be fixed at the same distance in every subject. Poetry hath ever been allowed a wider range than prose, and it is but just that, by an indulgence of this kind, some compensation should be made for the peculiar restraints she is laid under by the measure. Nor is this only a matter of convenience to the poet, it is also a matter of gratification to the reader. Diversity in the style relieves the ear, and prevents its being tired with the too frequent recurrence of the rhymes, or sameness of the metre. But still there are limits to this diversity. The

The authority of Milton and of Waller, on this article, remains as yet unquestioned. I should not think it prudent often to introduce words or phrases, of which no example could be produced since the days of Spenser and of Shakespeare.

And even in prose, the bounds are not the same for every kind of composition. In matters of science, for instance, whose terms, from the nature of the thing, are not capable of such a currency as those which belong to ordinary subjects, and are within the reach of ordinary readers, there is no necessity of confining an author within a very narrow circle. But in composing pieces which come under this last denomination, as history, romance, travels, moral essays, familiar letters, and the like, it is safest for an author to consider those words and idioms as obsolete, which have been disused by all good authors, for a longer period than the age of man extends to. It is not by ancient, but by present use, that our style must be regulated. And that use can never be denominated present, which hath been laid aside time immemorial, or, which amounts to the same thing, falls not within the knowledge or remembrance of any now living.

THIS remark not only affects terms and phrases, but also the declension, combination, and construction of words. Is it not then surprising to find, that one of Lowth's penetration should think a single person entitled to revive a form of inflection in a particular word, which had been rejected by all good writers, of every denomination, for more than a hundred and fifty years*? But if present use is to be renounced for ancient, it will be necessary to determine at what precise period antiquity is to be regarded as a rule. One inclines to remove the standard to the distance of a century and a half, another may, with as good reason, fix it three centuries backwards, and another six. And if the language of any of these periods is to be judged by the use of any other, it will be found, no doubt, entirely bar-

---

* Introd. &c In a note on the irregular verb *sit*, he says, "Dr. Middleton hath, with great propriety, restored the true "participle *sitten*." Would he not have acted with as great propriety, had he restored the true participles *pight* for *pitched*, *raught* for *reached*, *blent* for *blended*, and *shright* for *shrieked*, on full as good authority, the authority of Spenser, one of the sweetest of our ancient bards? And why might not Dr. Lowth himself, have, with great propriety, restored the true participles *bitten*, *casten*, *letten*, *putten*, *setten*, *shutten*, *slitten*, *splitten*, *founden*, *grounden*, of the verbs *bit*, *cast*, *let*, *put*, *set*, *shut*, *slit*, *split*, *find*, *grind*, for it would not be impossible to produce antiquated authors in support of all these. Besides, they are all used to this day in some provincial dialect.

barous.

barous. To me it is so evident, either that the present use must be the standard of the present language, or that the language admits no standard whatsoever, that I cannot conceive a clearer or more indisputable principle, from which to bring an argument to support it.

Yet it is certain, that even some of our best critics and grammarians, talk occasionally, as if they had a notion of some other standard, though they never give us a single hint to direct us where to search for it. Doctor Johnson, for example, in the preface to his very valuable Dictionary, acknowledges properly the absolute dominion of custom over language, and yet, in the explanation of particular words, expresseth himself sometimes in a manner that is inconsistent with this doctrine, "This word," says he in one place, " though common, and used by the best writers, " is perhaps barbarous*." I have always understood a barbarism in speech to be a term or expression totally unsupported by the present usage of good writers in the language. A meaning very different is suggested here, but what that meaning is, it will not be easy to conjecture. Nor has this celebrated writer given us on the

* See the word *Nowadays*

word *barbarous*, any definition of the term which will throw light on his application of it in the passage quoted. I entirely agree with Doctor Priestley, that it will never be the arbitrary rules of any man, or body of men whatever, that will ascertain the language †, there being no other dictator here but use.

It is indeed easier to discover the aim of our critics in their observations on this subject, than the meaning of the terms which they employ. These are often employed without precision; their aim, however, is generally good. It is, as much as possible, to give a check to innovation. But the means which they use for this purpose, have sometimes even a contrary tendency. If you will replace what hath been long since expunged from the language, and extirpate what is firmly rooted, undoubtedly you yourself become an innovator. If you desert the present use, and by your example at least, establish it as a maxim, that every critic may revive at pleasure old-fashioned terms, inflections, and combinations, and make such alterations on words as will bring them nearer to what he supposeth to be the etymon, there can be nothing fixed or stable on

* Preface to his Rudiments of English Grammar.

the subject. Possibly you prefer the usage that prevailed in the reign of queen Elizabeth; another may, with as good reason, have a partiality for that which subsisted in the days of Chaucer. And with regard to etymology, about which grammarians make so much useless bustle; if every one hath a privilege of altering words, according to his own opinion of their origin, the opinions of the learned being on this subject so various, nothing but a general chaos can ensue.

On the other hand, it may be said, ' Are we ' to catch at every new-fashioned term and phrase ' which whim or affectation may invent, and ' folly circulate? Can this ever tend to give either ' dignity to our style, or permanency to our ' language?' It cannot, surely. This leads to a further explanation and limitation of the term *present use*, to prevent our being misled by a mere name. It is possible, nay, it is common, for men, in avoiding one error, to run into another and a worse*. There is a mean in every thing. I have purposely avoided the expressions *recent use* and *modern use*, as these seem to stand in direct opposition to what is *ancient*. But I

---

* In vitium ducit culpæ fuga, si caret arte.
HOR. De Arte Poet.

used the word *present*, which, in respect of place, is always opposed to *absent*, and in respect of time, to *past* or *future*, that now have no existence. When, therefore, the word is used of language, its proper contrary is not ancient but *obsolete*. Besides, though I have acknowledged language to be a species of *mode* or *fashion*, as doubtless it is, yet, being much more permanent than articles of apparel, furniture, and the like, that, in regard to their form, are under the dominion of that inconstant power, I have avoided also using the words *fashionable* and *modish*, which but too generally convey the ideas of novelty and levity. Words, therefore, are by no means to be accounted the worse for being old, if they are not obsolete, neither is any word the better for being new. On the contrary, some time is absolutely necessary to constitute that custom or use, on which the establishment of words depends.

If we recur to the standard already assigned, namely, the writings of a plurality of celebrated authors, there will be no scope for the comprehension of words and idioms which can be denominated novel and upstart. It must be owned, that we often meet with such terms and phrases,

in news-papers, periodical pieces, and political pamphlets. The writers to the times, rarely fail to have their performances ftudded with a competent number of thefe fantaftic ornaments. A popular orator in the Houfe of Commons, hath a fort of patent from the public, during the continuance of his popularity, for coining as many as he pleafes. And they are no fooner iffued, than they obtrude themfelves upon us from every quarter, in all the daily papers, letters, effays, addreffes, &c. But this is of no fignificancy. Such words and phrafes are but the infects of a feafon at the moft. The people, always fickle, are juft as prompt to drop them, as they were to take them up. And not one of a hundred furvives the particular occafion or party-ftruggle which gave it birth. We may juftly apply to them what Johnfon fays of a great number of the terms of the laborious and mercantile part of the people, "This fugitive cant cannot be regard-
"ed as any part of the durable materials of a
"language, and therefore muft be fuffered to
"perifh, with other things unworthy of prefer-
"vation*."

As ufe, therefore, implies duration, and as even a few years are not fufficient for afcertain-

* Preface to his Dictionary.

ing the characters of authors, I have, for the most part, in the following sheets, taken my prose examples, neither from living authors, nor from those who wrote before the Revolution; not from the first, because an author's fame is not so firmly established in his lifetime; nor from the last, that there may be no suspicion that the style is superannuated. The vulgar translation of the Bible I must indeed except from this restriction. The continuance and universality of its use throughout the British dominions, affords an obvious reason for the exception.

Thus I have attempted to explain what that *use* is, which is the sole mistress of language, and to ascertain the precise import and extent of these her essential attributes, *reputable*, *national*, and *present*, and to give the directions proper to be observed in searching for the laws of this empress. In truth, grammar and criticism are but her ministers, and though, like other ministers, they would sometimes impose the dictates of their own humour upon the people, as the commands of their sovereign, they are not so often successful in such attempts, as to encourage the frequent repetition of them.

CHAP.

CHAP. II.

The nature and use of verbal Criticism, with its principal canons.

THE first thing in elocution that claims our attention, is purity; all its other qualities have their foundation in this. The great standard of purity is use, whose essential properties, as regarding language, have been considered and explained in the preceding chapter. But before I proceed to illustrate and specify the various offences against purity, or the different ways in which it may be violated, it will be proper to inquire so much further into the nature of the subject, as will enable us to fix on some general rules or canons, by which, in all our particular decisions, we ought to be directed. This I have judged the more necessary, as many of the verbal criticisms which have been made on English authors, since the beginning of the present century (for in this island we had little or nothing of the kind before), seem to have preceded either from no settled principles at all, or from such as will not bear a near examination. There is this further advantage in beginning with establishing certain canons, that, if they shall be found reasonable, they will tend to make what remains of our road both shorter and clearer, than it would otherwise have been. Much in the way of illustration and eviction may be saved, on the particular remarks. And if, on the contrary, they should not be reasonable, and consequently the remarks raised on them should not be well founded, no way that I can think of, bids fairer for detecting the fallacy, and preventing every reader from being misled. A fluent and specious, but superficial manner of criticising, is very apt to take at first, even with readers whom a deliberate examination into the principles on which the whole is built, would quickly undeceive.

'But,' it may be said, 'if custom, which is 'so capricious and unaccountable, is every thing 'in language, of what significance is either the 'grammarian or the critic?' Of considerable significance notwithstanding, and of most then when they confine themselves to their legal departments, and do not usurp an authority that doth not belong to them. The man who, in a country like ours, should compile a succinct, perspicuous, and faithful digest of the laws, though no lawgiver, would be universally acknowledged to be a public benefactor. How easy

easy would that important branch of knowledge be rendered by such a work, in comparison of what it must be, when we have nothing to have recourse to, but a labyrinth of statutes, reports, and opinions. That man also would be of considerable use, though not in the same degree, who should vigilantly attend to every illegal practice that were beginning to prevail, and evince its danger, by exposing its contrariety to law Of similar benefit, though in a different sphere, are grammar and criticism. In language, the grammarian is properly the compiler of the digest, and the verbal critic, the man who seasonably notifies the abuses that are creeping in. Both tend to facilitate the study of the tongue to strangers, and to render natives more perfect in the knowledge of it, to advance general use into universal, and to give a greater stability at least, if not a permanency, to custom, the most mutable thing in nature. These are advantages which, with a moderate share of attention, may be discovered from what hath been already said on the subject. but they are not the only advantages. From what I shall have occasion to observe afterwards, it will probably appear, that these arts, by assisting to suppress every unlicenced term, and to stigmatize every improper idiom,

idiom, tend to give greater precision, and confequently more perfpicuity and beauty to our ftyle.

The obfervations made in the preceding chapter, might eafily be converted into fo many canons of criticifm, by which, whatever is repugnant to reputable, to national, or to prefent ufe, in the fenfe wherein thefe epithets have been explained, would be condemned as a tranfgreffion of the radical laws of the language. But on this fubject of ufe, there arife two eminent queftions, the determination of which may lead to the eftablifhment of other canons not lefs important. The firft queftion is this, Is reputable, national, and prefent ufe, which, for brevity's fake, I fhall hereafter fimply denominate good ufe, always uniform in her decifions? The fecond, is, As no term, idiom, or application, that is totally unfupported by her, can be admitted to be good, is every term, idiom, and application that is countenanced by her, to be efteemed good, and therefore worthy to be retained?

SECTION I.

Good use not always uniform in her decisions.

In answer to the former of these questions, I acknowledge, that in every case there is not a perfect uniformity in the determinations even of such use as may justly be denominated good. Wherever a considerable number of authorities can be produced in support of two different, though resembling modes of expression for the same thing, there is always a divided use, and one cannot be said to speak barbarously, or to oppose the usage of the language, who conforms to either side†. This divided use hath place sometimes in single words, sometimes in construction, and sometimes in arrangement. In all

---

† The words *nowise*, *noway*, and *noways*, afford a proper instance of this divided use. Yet our learned and ingenious lexicographer hath denominated all those who either write or pronounce the word *noways*, ignorant barbarians. These ignorant barbarians (but he hath surely not adverted to this circumstance) are only Pope, and Swift, and Addison, and Locke, and several others of our most celebrated writers. This censure is the more astonishing, that even in the form which he has thought fit to repudiate, the meaning assigned to it, is strictly conformable to that which etymology, according to his own explication, would suggest. See Johnson's Dictionary on the words *nowise* and *way*, particularly the senses of *way*, marked with these numbers, 15, 16, 18, and 19.

such cases there is scope for choice, and it belongs, without question, to the critical art, to lay down the principles, by which, in doubtful cases, our choice should be directed.

There are, indeed, some differences in single words, which ought still to be retained. They are a kind of synonymas, and afford a little variety, without occasioning any inconvenience whatever‡. In arrangement too, it certainly holds, that various manners suit various styles, as various styles suit various subjects, and various sorts of composition. For this reason, unless when some obscurity, ambiguity, or inelegance is created, no disposition of words which hath obtained the public approbation, ought to be altogether rejected. In construction the case is somewhat different. Purity, perspicuity, and elegance generally require, that in this there be the strictest uniformity. Yet differences here are not only allowable, but even convenient when attended with correspondent differences in the

‡ Such are, *subterranean* and *subterraneous*, *homogeneal* and *homogeneous*, *authentic* and *authentical*, *isle* and *island*, *mount* and *mountain*, *clime* and *climate*, *near* and *nigh*, *betwixt* and *between*, *amongst* and *among*, *amidst* and *amid*. Nor do I see any hurt that would ensue from adding *nowise* and *noway* to the number.

application. Thus the verb *to found*, when used literally, is more properly followed by the prepofition *on*, as, 'The house was *founded on* a rock,' in the metaphorical application, it is often better with *in*, as in this sentence, 'They maintained, 'that dominion is *founded in* grace.' Both sentences would be badly expressed, if these prepofitions were transposed, though there are perhaps cases wherein either would be good. In those instances, therefore, of divided use, which give scope for option, the following canons are humbly proposed, in order to assist us in assigning the preference. Let it, in the mean time, be remembered, as a point always presupposed, that the authorities on the opposite sides are equal, or nearly so. When those of one side greatly preponderate, it is in vain to oppose the prevailing usage. Custom, when wavering, may be swayed, but when reluctant, will not be forced. And in this department a person never effects so little, as when he attempts too much *.

Canon

---

* For this reason it is to no purpose with Johnson to pronounce the word *news* a plural, (whatever it might have been in the days of Sidney and Raleigh) since custom hath evidently determined otherwise. Nor is the observation on the letter [ ] in his Dictionary well founded, that 'it seems to be established 'as a rule, that no noun singular should end with [s] single,' the words *amends, summons, fous genus, species, genius, chorus,*

Canon the first.

The first canon, then, shall be, When use is divided as to any particular word or phrase, and the expression used by one part hath been pre-occupied, or is in any instance susceptible of a different signification, and the expression employed by the other part never admits a different sense, both perspicuity and variety require, that the form of expression which is in every instance strictly univocal, be preferred.

For this reason *aught*, signifying any thing, is preferable to *ought*, which is one of our defective verbs: *by consequence*, meaning consequently, is preferable to *of consequence*; as this expression is often employed to denote momentous or important. In the preposition *toward* and *towards*, and the adverbs *forward* and *forwards*, and several others, show the contrary. For the same reason the words *averse* and *aversion*, are more properly construed with *to* than with *from*. The examples in favour of the latter preposition, are beyond comparison outnumbered by those in favour of the former. The argument from etymology is here of no value, being taken from the use of another language. If by the same rule we were to regulate all nouns and verbs of Latin original, our present syntax would be overturned. It is more conformable to English analogy with *to*; the words *dislike* and *hatred*, nearly synonymous, are thus construed.

back-

backward and *backwards*, the two forms are used indiscriminately. But as the first form in all these is also an adjective, it is better to confine the particles to the second. Custom, too, seems at present to lean this way. This principle likewise leads me to prefer *extemporary* as an adjective to *extempore*, which is properly an adverb, and ought, for the sake of precision, to be restrained to that use. It is only of late that this last term begins to be employed adjectively. Thus we say, with equal propriety, an *extemporary prayer*, an *extemporary sermon*, and, he *prays extempore*, he *preaches extempore*. I know not how Dr. Priestley hath happened to mention the term *extemporary*, in a way which would make one think he considered it as a word peculiar to Mr. Hume. The word hath evidently been in good use for a longer time than one thinks of searching back in quest of authorities, and remains in good use to this day. By the same rule we ought to prefer *scarcely*, as an adverb, to *scarce*, which is an adjective, and *exceedingly*, as an adverb, to *exceeding*, which is a participle. For the same reason also I am inclined to prefer that use, which makes *ye* invariably the nominative plural of the personal pronoun *thou*, and *you* the accusative, when applied to an actual plurality. When used for the singular number, custom hath determined that it shall be *you* in both cases. This renders the distinction rather more important, as for the most part it would show directly whether one or more were addressed, a point in which we are often liable to mistake in all modern languages. From the like principle, in those verbs which have for the participle passive both the preterit form and one peculiar, the peculiar form ought to have the preference. Thus, I have *gotten*, I have *hidden*, I have *spoken*, are better than I have *got*, I have *hid*, I have *spoke* †. From the same principle I think *ate* is preferable in the preterit tense, and *eaten* in the participle, to *eat*, which is the constant form of the present, though sometimes also used for both the others.

But though in this judgment concerning the participles, I agree entirely with all our approved modern grammarians, I can by no means concur with some of them in their manner of supporting it. " We should be immediately shock-" ed," says one of the best of them ‡, " at *I have* " *knew, I have saw, I have gave*, &c. but our ears

† Yet I should prefer ' I have *held, helped, melted*,' to ' I have *holden, holpen, molten*, these last participles being now obsolete.

‡ Lowth's Introduction to English Grammar.

" are

" are grown familiar with *I have wrote, I have*
" *drank, I have bore*, &c. which are altogether
" as barbarous." Nothing can be more inconsistent, in my opinion, with the very first principles of grammar, than what is here advanced. This ingenious gentleman surely will not pretend, that there is a barbarism in every word which serves for preterit and participle both, else the far greater part of the preterits and participles of our tongue are barbarous. If not, what renders many of them, such as *loved, hated, sent, brought*, good English when employed either way? I know no answer that can be given, but custom; that is, in other words, our ears are familiarised to them by frequent use. And what was ever meant by a barbarism in speech, but that which shocks us by violating the constant usage in speaking or in writing? If so, to be equally barbarous, and to be equally shocking, are synonymous, whereas to be barbarous, and to be in familiar use, are a contradiction in terms. Yet in this manner does our author often express himself. " No authority," says he in another place, " is
" sufficient to justify so manifest a solecism." No man needed less to be informed, that authority is every thing in language, and that it is the

want

want of it alone that constitutes both the barbarism and the solecism.

Canon the second.

THE second canon is, In doubtful cases regard ought to be had in our decisions to the analogy of the language.

FOR this reason I prefer *contemporary* to *cotemporary*. The general use in words compounded with the inseparable preposition *con*, is to retain the [n] before a consonant, and to expunge it before a vowel or an [h] mute. Thus we say *condisciple, conjuncture, concomitant*; but *co-equal, co-eternal, co-incide, co-heir*. I know but one exception, which is *co-partner*. But in dubious cases we ought to follow the rule, and not the exception. If by the former canon the adverbs *backwards* and *forwards* are preferable to *backward* and *forward*, by this canon, from the principle of analogy, *afterwards* and *homewards* should be preferred to *afterward* and *homeward*. Of the two adverbs *thereabout* and *thereabouts*, compounded of the particle *there* and the preposition, the former alone is analogical, there being no such word in the language as *abouts*. The same holds
of

of *hereabout* and *whereabout*. In the verbs *to dare* and *to need*, many say, in the third person present singular, *dare* and *need*, as ' he *need* not go; he *dare* not do it.' Others say, *dares* and *needs*. As the first usage is exceedingly irregular, hardly any thing less than uniform practice could authorise it. This rule supplies us with another reason for preferring *scarcely* and *exceedingly* as adverbs, to *scarce* and *exceeding*. The phrases *Would to God*, and *Would God*, can both plead the authority of custom; but the latter is strictly analogical, the former is not. It is an established idiom in the English tongue, that any of the auxiliaries *might, could, would, should, did*, and *had*, with the nominative subjoined, should express sometimes a supposition, sometimes a wish: which of the two it expresses in any instance, is easily discovered from the context. Thus the expression ' *Would he* but ask it of me,' denotes either ' *If he would*, or *I wish that he would* but ask it of me.' *Would God* then, is properly, *I wish that God would*, or *O that God would*. The other expression it is impossible to reconcile to analogy in any way*. For a like reason the

* What has given rise to it is evidently the French *Plût à Dieu*, of the same import. But it has not been adverted to (so servile commonly are imitators), that the verb *plaire* is impersonal, and regularly construed with the preposition *a*, neither of which is the case with the English *will* and *would*

phrase

phrase *ever so*, as when we say, 'though he were 'ever so good,' is preferable to *never so*. In both these decisions I subscribe to the judgment of Dr. Johnson. Of the two phrases, *in no wise* in three words, and *nowise* in one, the last only is conformable to the present genius of the tongue. The noun *wise*, signifying manner, is quite obsolete. It remains now only in composition, in which, along with an adjective or other substantive, it forms an adverb or conjunction. Such are *sidewise, lengthwise, coastwise, contrariwise, likewise, otherwise*. These always preserve the compound form, and never admit a preposition; consequently *nowise*, which is an adverb of the same order, ought analogically to be written in one word, and not to be preceded by *in*. In very ancient style all these words were uncompounded, and had the preposition. They said *in like wise*, and *in other wise* †. And even if custom at present

---

† In proof of this I shall produce a passage taken from the Prologue of the English translation of the Legenda Aurea, which seems to have been made towards the end of the fifteenth century. "I haue submysed my selfe to translate into Engylsshe "the legende of sayntes whyche is called legenda aurea in la-
" tyn; that is to saye, the golden legende. For in lyke wyse "as golde is moost noble aboue all other metallis, in lyke "wyse is thys legende holden moost noble aboue all other "werkes." About the time that our present version of the
scriptures

present were uniform, as it is divided, in admitting *in* before *nowise*, it ought to be followed, though anomalous. In these matters it is foolish to attempt to struggle against the stream. All that I here plead for is, that when custom varies, analogy should decide the question. In the determination of this particular instance I differ from Dr. Priestley. Sometimes *whether* is followed by *no*, sometimes by *not*. For instance, some would say, 'Whether he will or *no*,' others, 'Whether he will or *not*.' Of these it is the latter only that is analogical. There is an ellipsis of the verb in the last clause, which when you supply, you find it necessary to use the adverb *not*, 'Whether he will *or* will *not*.' I shall only add, that by both the preceding canons we ought always to say *rend* in the present of the indicative and of the infinitive, and never *rent*, as is sometimes done. The latter term hath been pre-occupied by the preterit and the participle passive, besides that it is only in this application that it can be said to be used analogically. For this reason,

scriptures was made, the old usage was wearing out. The phrase *in like wise* occurs but once, (Matt xx' 24) whereas the compound term *likewise* occurs frequently. We find in several places, *on this wise*, *in any wise*, and *in no wise*. The two first phrases are now obsolete, and the third seems to be in the state which Dr. Johnson calls *obsolescent*

the

the active participle ought always to be *rending*, and not *renting*.

Canon the third.

THE third canon is, When the terms or expressions are in other respects equal, that ought to be preferred which is most agreeable to the ear.

THIS rule hath perhaps a greater chance of being observed than any other, it having been the general bent for some time to avoid harsh sounds and unmusical periods. Of this we have many examples. *Delicateness* hath very properly given way to *delicacy*; and for a like reason *authenticity* will probably soon displace *authenticalness*, and *vindictive* dispossess *vindicative* altogether. Nay, a regard to sound hath, in some instances, had an influence on the public choice, to the prejudice of both the former canons, which one would think ought to be regarded as of more importance. Thus the term *ingenuity* hath obtained, in preference to *ingeniousness*, though the former cannot be deduced analogically from *ingenious*, and had besides been preoccupied, and consequently would be equivocal, being a regular derivative from the term *ingenuous,*

ous, if the newer acceptation had not before now supplanted the other altogether.

Canon the fourth.

THE fourth canon is, In cases wherein none of the foregoing rules gives either side a ground of preference, a regard to simplicity (in which I include etymology when manifest) ought to determine our choice.

UNDER the name simplicity I must be understood to comprehend also brevity, for that expression is always the simplest which, with equal purity and perspicuity, is the briefest. We have, for instance, several active verbs, which are used either with or without a preposition indiscriminately. Thus we say either *accept* or *accept of*, *admit* or *admit of*, *approve* or *approve of*; in like manner *address* or *address to*, *attain* or *attain to*. In such instances it will hold, I suppose, pretty generally, that the simple form is preferable. This appears particularly in the passive voice, in which every one must see the difference. ' His 'present was *accepted of* by his friend.' ' His 'excuse was *admitted of* by his master.' ' The 'magistrates were *addressed to* by the townsmen,' are evidently much worse than, ' His present was
' *accepted*

'*accepted* by his friend.' 'His excuse was *admitted* by his master.' 'The magistrates were *addressed* by the townsmen.' We have but too many of this awkward, disjointed sort of compounds, and therefore ought not to multiply them without necessity. Now if once the preposition should obtain in the active voice, the rules of syntax will absolutely require it in the passive. Sometimes indeed the verb hath two regimens, and then the preposition is necessary to one of them, as 'I address myself to my judges.' 'They addressed their vows to Apollo.' But of such cases I am not here speaking.

Both etymology and analogy, as well as euphony and simplicity, determine us in preferring *subtract* to *substract*, and consequently *subtraction* to *substraction*[*].

Canon

---

[*] *Subtract* is regularly deduced from the supine *subtractum* of the Latin verb *subtraho*, in the same way as *act* from *actum*, the supine of *ago*, and *translate* from *translatum*, the supine of *transfero*. But it would be quite unexampled to derive the English verb from the French *soustraire*. Besides, there is not another instance in the language of a word beginning with the Latin preposition *sub*, where the *sub* is followed by an *s*, unless when the original word compounded with the preposition, begins with an *s*. Thus we say *subscribe* from *sub* and *scribo*, *subsist* from *sub* and *sisto*, *substitute* from *sub* and *statuo*. But we cannot say *substract* from *sub* and *straho*, there being no such word

Canon the fifth.

THE fifth and only other canon that occurs to me on the subject of divided use is, In the few cases wherein neither perspicuity nor analogy, neither sound nor simplicity, assists us in fixing our choice, it is safest to prefer that manner which is most conformable to ancient usage.

THIS is founded on a very plain maxim, that in language, as in several other things, change itself, unless when it is clearly advantageous, is ineligible. This affords another reason for preferring that usage which distinguishes *ye* as the nominative plural of *thou*, when more than one are addressed, from *you* the accusative. For it may be remarked, that this distinction is very regularly observed in our translation of the Bible, as well as in all our best ancient authors. Milton too is particularly attentive to it. The words *causey* and *causeway* are at present used promiscuously, though I do not know whether there be any difference but in the spelling. The old way is *causey*, which, as there appears no good reason for

word There can be no doubt, therefore, that a mistaken etymology, arising from an affinity to the French term, not in the verb, but in the verbal noun, has given rise to this harsh anomaly.

altering it, ought to be held the best. The alteration, I suppose, hath sprung from some mistaken notion about the etymology, but if the notion had been just, the reason would not have been sufficient. It tends, besides, either to introduce a viciated pronunciation, or to add to the anomalies in orthography (by far too numerous already), with which the language is encumbered. Much the same may be said of *jail* and *gaol*, *jailer* and *gaoler*. That *jail* and *jailer* have been first used is probable, from the vulgar translation of the Bible †. The quotations on the other side from Shakespeare, are not much to be minded, as it is well known that his editors have taken a good deal of freedom with his orthography. The argument, from its derivation from the French *geole*, is very puerile. For the same reason we ought to write *jarter*, and not garter, and plead the spelling of the French primitive *jartiere*. Nor would it violate the laws of pronunciation in English, more to sound the [ja] as though it were written [ga], than to sound the [ga] as though it were written [ja].

† Acts xvi. 23.

Sec-

SECTION II.

Every thing favoured by good use, not on that account worthy to be retained.

I COME now to the second question for ascertaining both the extent of the authority claimed by custom, and the rightful prerogatives of criticism. As no term, idiom, or application that is totally unsupported by use, can be admitted to be good, is every term, idiom, and application, that is countenanced by use, to be esteemed good, and therefore worthy to be retained? I answer, that though nothing in language can be good from which use withholds her approbation, there may be many things to which she gives it, that are not in all respects good, or such as are worthy to be retained and imitated. In some instances *custom* may very properly be checked by *criticism*, which hath a sort of negative, and though not the censorian power of instant degradation, the privilege of remonstrating, and by means of this, when used discreetly, of bringing what is bad into disrepute, and so cancelling it gradually, but which hath no positive right to establish any thing. Her power too is like that of eloquence, she operates on us purely by perfuafion, depending for fuccefs on the folidity, or at leaft the fpecioufnefs of her arguments; whereas cuftom hath an unaccountable and irrefiftible influence over us, an influence which is prior to perfuafion, and independent of it, nay fometimes even in contradiction to it. Of different modes of expreffion, that which comes to be favoured by general practice may be denominated beft, becaufe eftablifhed; but it cannot always be faid with truth, that it is eftablifhed becaufe beft. And therefore, though I agree in the general principles maintained by Prieftley ‡ on this fubject, I do not concur in this fentiment as holding univerfally, that " the " beft forms of fpeech will in time eftablifh " themfelves by their own fuperior excellence." Time and chance have an influence on all things human, and on nothing more remarkably than on language; infomuch that we often fee that, of various forms, thofe will recommend themfelves, and come into general ufe, which, if abftractly confidered, are neither the fimpleft nor the moft agreeable to the ear, nor the moft conformable to analogy. And though we cannot fay properly of any expreffion which has the fanction of

‡ Preface to the Rudiments of Englifh Grammar.

good

good use, that it is barbarous, we must admit that, in other respects, it may be faulty.

It is therefore, I acknowledge, not without meaning, that Swift, in the proposal above quoted*, affirms, that, " there are many gross im-" proprieties, which, though authorised by prac-" tice, ought to be discarded." Now, in order to discard them, nothing more is necessary than to disuse them. And to bring us to disuse them, both the example and the arguments of the critic will have their weight. A very little attention will satisfy every reasonable person of the difference there is between the bare omission, or rather the not employing of what is used, and the introduction of what is unusual. The former, provided what you substitute in its stead be proper, and have the authority of custom, can never come under the observation, or at least the reprehension of a reader; whereas the latter shocks our ears immediately. Here, therefore, lies one principal province of criticism, to point out the characters of those words and idioms which deserve to be disfranchised, and consigned to perpetual oblivion. It is by carefully filing off all roughnesses and inequalities, that lan-

§ For ascertaining the English tongue; see the Letter to the Lord High Treasurer.

guages, like metals, muſt be poliſhed. This indeed is an effect of taſte. And hence it happens, that the firſt rudiments of taſte no ſooner appear in any people, than the language begins, as it were of itſelf, to emerge out of that ſtate of rudeneſs, in which it will ever be found in uncivilized nations. As they improve in arts and ſciences, their ſpeech refines; it not only becomes richer and more comprehenſive, but acquires greater preciſion, perſpicuity, and harmony. This effect taſte inſenſibly produces among the people long before the language becomes the object of their attention. But when criticiſm hath called forth their attention to this object, there is a probability that the effect will be accelerated.

It is, however, no leſs certain, on the other hand, that in the declenſion of taſte and ſcience, language will unavoidably degenerate, and though the critical art may retard a little, it will never be able to prevent this degeneracy. I ſhall therefore ſubjoin a few remarks under the form of canons, in relation to thoſe words or expreſſions, which may be thought to merit degradation from the rank they have hitherto maintained, ſubmitting theſe remarks entirely, as every thing of the kind muſt be ſubmitted, to the final determination of the impartial public.

Canon

Canon the sixth.

THE first canon on this subject is, All words and phrases which are remarkably harsh and unharmonious, and not absolutely necessary, may justly be judged worthy of this fate.

I CALL a word or phrase absolutely necessary, when we have no synonymous words, in the event of a dismission, to supply its place, or no way of conveying properly the same idea without the aid of circumlocution. The rule, with this limitation, will, I believe, be generally assented to. The only difficulty is, to fix the criteria by which we may discriminate the obnoxious words from all others.

IT may well be reckoned that we have lighted on one criterion, when we have found a decompound or term composed of words already compounded, whereof the several parts are not easily, and therefore not closely united. Such are the words *bare-faced-ness, shame-faced-ness, un-success-ful-ness, dis-interest-ed-ness, wrong-headed-ness, tender-hearted-ness*. They are so heavy and drawling, and withal so ill compacted, that they have not more vivacity than a periphrasis, to compensate for the defect of harmony.

Another criterion is, when a word is so formed and accented as to render it of difficult utterance to the speaker, and consequently disagreeable in sound to the hearer. This happens in two cases; first, when the syllables which immediately follow the accented syllable, are so crowded with consonants, as of necessity to retard the pronunciation. The words *quéstionless, chrónicters, convénticlers, concúpiscence, remémbrancer*, are examples of this. The accent in all these is on the antepenultimate, for which reason the two last syllables ought to be pronounced quick; a thing scarcely practicable, on account of the number of consonants which occur in these syllables. The attempt to quicken the pronunciation, though familiar to Englishmen, exhibits to strangers the appearance of awkward hurry, instead of that easy fluency to be found in those words wherein the unaccented syllables are naturally short. Such are *lévity, vánity, avídity*, all accented in like manner on the antepenultimate. The second case in which a similar dissonance is found, is when too many syllables follow the accented syllable. For though these be naturally short, their number, if they exceed two, makes a disagreeable pronunciation. Examples of this are the words *primarily, cúrsorily, súmmarily, perémptorily,*

perémptorily, perémptoriness, vindicative; all of which are accented on the fourth syllable from the end. It were to be wished, that the use which now prevails in regard to the manner of accenting some words, would alter, as we cannot afford to part with every term that is liable to exception in this respect. Nor is a change here to be despaired of, since we find it hath happened to several words already, as the places which they occupy in ancient poetry sufficiently evince.

A THIRD criterion is when a short or unaccented syllable is repeated, or followed by another short or unaccented syllable very much resembling. This always gives the appearance of stammering to the pronunciation. Such are the words *hólily, fárriering, sillily*. We have not many words chargeable with this fault: nay, so early have the people been sensible of the disagreeable sound occasioned by such recurrences, that it would appear they have added the adverbial termination to very few of our adjectives ending in *ly*. I believe there are no examples extant of *heavenlily, godlily, timelily, daily*. Johnson hath given us in his Dictionary, the word *lowlily*, which is as bad as any of them, but without
quoting

quoting authorities. In these and suchlike, the simple forms, as *heavenly, godly, timely, daily, homely, courtly, comely*, seem always to have served both for adjective and adverb; though this too hath its inconvenience. It deserves our notice, that the repetition of a syllable is never offensive, when either one or both are long, as in *papa, mamma, murmur, tartar, barbarous, lily*.

Besides the cases aforesaid, I know of none that ought to dispose us to the total disuse of words really significant. A little harshness by the collision of consonants, which, nevertheless, our organs find no difficulty in articulating, and which do not suggest to the hearer the disagreeable idea either of precipitation or of stammering, are by no means a sufficient reason for the suppression of an useful term. The monosyllables *judg'd, drudg'd, grudg'd*, which some have thought very offensive, appear not in the least exceptionable, compared with the words abovementioned. It would not do well to introduce such hard and strong sounds too frequently; but when they are used sparingly and properly, they have even a good effect. Variety in sound is advantageous to a language; and it is convenient that we should have some sounds that are rough and masculine, as well as some that are liquid and feminine.

I OBSERVE this the rather, because I think there is at present a greater risk of going too far in refining, than of not going far enough. The ears of some critics are immoderately delicate. A late essayist*, one who seems to possess a considerable share of ingenuity and taste, proposes the utter extirpation of *encroach, encroachment, inculcate, purport, methinks,* and some others, the precise meaning of which, we have no single words in English that perfectly express. An ear so nice as to be hurt by these, appears to me in the same light as a stomach so squeamish as to nauseate our beef and beer, the ordinary food of the country. Such ears, I should say, are not adapted to our speech, nor such stomachs to our climate. This humour, were it to become general, would have a very unfavourable aspect to the language; and it might admit a question, whether, on such principles, if an expurgation of the vocabulary were attempted, there would remain one third of the whole stock, that would

---

* Sketches by Launcelot Temple, Esq,—of late republished and owned by Dr Armstrong.

not be deemed worthy of excision. This would be particularly inconvenient, if every body were as much an enemy as this gentleman seems to be, to all new-fashioned terms and phrases. We should hardly have words enow left for necessary purposes[*].

Canon

---

[*] I shall only observe here by the way, that those languages which are allowed to be the most susceptible of all the graces of harmony, have admitted many ill-sounding words. Such are in Greek σπλαγχνιζεσθαι, προσφθεγξασθαι, κακακακα, μεμιμημενοι. In the two last one finds a dissonant recurrence of the same letter to a degree quite unexampled with us. There is, however, such a mixture of long and short syllables, as prevents that difficulty of utterance which was remarked in some English words. Such are also in Latin, *dixisses, spississimus, percrebrescebantque*. The last of these words is very rough, and the two first have as much of the hissing letters as any English word whatever. The Italian is considered, and I believe justly, as the most musical of all languages, yet there are in it some sounds which even to us, accustomed to a dialect boisterous like our weather, appear harsh and jarring. Such are *incrocicchiare, sdrucciolosi, sprogiatrice*. There is a great difference between words which sound harshly, but are of easy pronunciation to the natives, and those words which even to natives occasion difficulty in the utterance, and consequently convey some idea of awkwardness to the hearer, which is prejudicial to the design. There are in the languages of all countries, many words which foreigners will find a difficulty in pronouncing, that the natives have no conception of. The Greeks could not easily articulate the Latin terminations in *ans* and *ens*. On the other hand, there were many sounds in Greek which appeared intolerable to the Latins, such as words beginning with φθ, ψ, πτ, κτ, and many others. No people have so studiously avoided the collision of consonants as the Italians. To their delicate ears *ps*, *ct*, and *cs*, or *x*, though

belong-

Canon the seventh.

THE second canon on this subject is, When etymology plainly points to a signification different from that which the word commonly bears, propriety and simplicity both require its dismission.

I use the word *plainly*, because, when the etymology is from an ancient or foreign language, or from obsolete roots in our own language, or when it is obscure or doubtful, no regard should be had to it. The case is different, when the roots either are, or strongly appear to be, English, are in present use, and clearly suggest another meaning. Of this kind is the word *beholden*, for obliged or indebted. It should regularly be the passive participle of the verb to *behold*, which would convey a sense totally different. Not that I consider the term as equivocal, for in the last

belonging to different syllables, and interposed between vowels, are offensive, nor can they easily pronounce them. Instead of *apto*, and *lecto*, and *Alexandro*, they must say *atto*, and *letto*, and *Allessandro*. Yet these very people begin some of their words with the three consonants *sdr*, which to our ears are perfectly shocking. It is not therefore so much harshness of sound, as difficulty of utterance, that should make some words be rejected altogether. The latter tends to divert our attention, and consequently to obstruct the effect. The former hath not this tendency, unless they be obtruded on us too frequently

acceptation it hath long since been disused, having been supplanted by *beheld*. But the formation of the word is so analogical, as to make it have at least the appearance of impropriety, when used in a sense that seems naturally so foreign to it. The word *beholding*, to express the same thing, is still more exceptionable than the other, and includes a real impropriety, being an active form with a passive signification. *To vouchsafe*, as denoting *to condescend*, is liable to a similar exception, and for that reason, more than for its harshness, may be dispensed with. The verb *to unloose*, should analogically signify *to tie*, in like manner as *to untie* signifies *to loose*. To what purpose is it then, to retain a term, without any necessity, in a signification the reverse of that which its etymology manifestly suggests? The verb *to unravel*, commonly indeed, as well as analogically, signifies to disentangle, to extricate, sometimes, however, it is absurdly employed to denote the contrary, to disorder, to entangle, as in these lines in the address to the goddess of Dulness,

> Or quite unravel all the reasoning thread,
> And hang some curious cobweb in its stead[*].

---

[*] Dunciad, B. 1.

All considerations of analogy, propriety, perspicuity, unite in persuading us to repudiate this preposterous application altogether.

Canon the eighth.

THE third canon is, When any words become obsolete, or at least are never used, except as constituting part of particular phrases, it is better to dispense with their service entirely, and give up the phrases.

THE reasons are, first, because the disuse in ordinary cases renders the term somewhat indefinite, and occasions a degree of obscurity: secondly, because the introduction of words which never appear but with the same attendants, gives the style an air of vulgarity and cant. Examples of this we have in the words *lief, dint, whit, moot, pro,* and *con,* as ' I had as *lief* go myself,' for ' I ' should like as well to go myself.' ' He con-' vinced his antagonist *by dint of argument,*' that is, ' by strength of argument.' ' He made them ' yield *by dint of arms,*'—' by force of arms.' ' He is *not a whit better,*'—' no better.' ' The ' case you mention is *a moot point,*'—' a disput-' able point.' ' The question was strenuously ' debated *pro and con,*'—' on both sides.'

THE

Canon the ninth.

THE fourth and laſt canon I propoſe, is, All thoſe phraſes, which, when analyſed grammatically, include a ſoleciſm, and all thoſe to which uſe hath affixed a particular ſenſe, but which, when explained by the general and eſtabliſhed rules of the language, are ſuſceptible either of a different ſenſe or of no ſenſe, ought to be diſcarded altogether.

IT is this kind of phraſeology which is diſtinguiſhed by the epithet *idiomatical*, and hath been originally the ſpawn, partly of ignorance, and partly of affectation. Of the firſt ſort, which includes a ſoleciſm, is the phraſe, ' I *had* rather ' *do* ſuch a thing,' for ' I would rather do it.' The auxiliary *had*, joined to the infinitive active *do*, is a groſs violation of the rules of conjugation in our language, and though good uſe may be conſidered as protecting this expreſſion from being branded with the name of a blunder, yet as it is both irregular and unneceſſary, I can foreſee no inconvenience that will ariſe from dropping it altogether. I have ſeen this idiom criticiſed in ſome eſſay, whoſe name I cannot now remember, and its origin very naturally accounted for, by supposing it to have sprung from the contraction *I'd*, which supplies the place both of *I had*, and of *I would*, and which hath been at first ignorantly resolved into *I had*, when it ought to have been *I would*. The phrase thus frequently mistaken, hath come at length to establish itself, and to stand on its own foot*.

Of the second sort, which, when explained grammatically, leads to a different sense from what the words in conjunction commonly bear, is, ' He sings a good song,' for ' he sings well.' The plain meaning of the words as they stand connected is very different, for who sees not that a good song may be ill sung? Of the same stamp is, ' He plays a good fiddle,' for ' he ' plays well on the fiddle.' This seems also to

* Whether with Johnson and Lowth we should consider the phrases *by this means, by that means, it is a means*, as liable to the same exception, is perhaps more doubtful Priestley considers the word *means* as of both numbers, and of such nouns we have several examples in the language. But it may be objected, that as the singular form *mean* is still frequently to be met with, this must inevitably give to the above phrases an appearance of solecism, in the judgment of those who are accustomed to attend to the rules of syntax. But however this may induce such critics to avoid the expressions in question, no person of taste, I presume, will venture so far to violate the present usage, and consequently to shock the ears of the generality of readers, as to say, ' By ' this mean,' or ' By that mean.'

involve a solecism. We speak indeed of playing a tune, but it is always on the instrument.

UNDER the third sort, which can scarcely be considered as literally conveying any sense, may be ranked a number of vile, but common phrases, sometimes to be found in good authors, like *shooting at rovers, having a month's mind, currying favour, dancing attendance,* and many others. Of the same kind also, though not reprehensible in the same degree, is the idiomatical use that is sometimes made of certain verbs, as *stand* for insist, ' *he stands* upon security,' *take* for understand, in such phrases as these, ' You *take* me,' and ' as I *take* it,' *hold* for continue, as ' he ' does not *hold* long in one mind.' But of all kinds, the worst is that wherein the words, when construed, are susceptible of no meaning at all. Such an expression is the following, ' There ' were seven ladies in the company, every one ' prettier than another,' by which it is intended, I suppose, to denote that they were all very pretty. One prettier, implies that there is another less pretty, but where every one is prettier, there can be none less, and consequently none more pretty. Such trash is the disgrace of any tongue. Ambitiously to display nonsensical

phrases

phrases of this sort, as some writers have affected to do, under the ridiculous notion of a familiar and easy manner, is not to set off the riches of a language, but to expose its rags. As such idioms, therefore, err alike against purity, simplicity, perspicuity, and elegance, they are entitled to no quarter from the critic. A few of these in the writings of good authors, I shall have occasion to point out, when I come to speak of the solecism and the impropriety.

So much for the canons of verbal criticism, which properly succeed the characters of good use, proposed in the preceding chapter for the detection of the most flagrant errors in the choice, the construction, and the application of words. The first five of these canons are intended to suggest the principles by which our choice ought to be directed, in cases wherein use itself is wavering, and the four last to point out those farther improvements which the critical art, without exceeding her legal powers, may assist in producing. There are, indeed, who seem disposed to extend her authority much further. But we ought always to remember, that as the principal mode of improving a language, which she is empowered to employ, is by condemning and exploding, there is a confiderable danger, left fhe carry her improvements this way too far. Our mother-tongue, by being too much impaired, may be impoverifhed, and fo more injured in copioufnefs and nerves, than all our refinements will ever be able to compenfate. For this reafon there ought, in fupport of every fentence of profcription, to be an evident plea from the principles of perfpicuity, elegance, or harmony.

IF fo, the want of etymology, whatever be the opinion of fome grammarians, cannot be reckoned a fufficient ground for the fuppreffion of a fignificant term, which hath come into good ufe. For my part, I fhould think it as unreafonable to reject, on this account, the affiftance of an expreffive word, which opportunely offers its fervice, when perhaps no other could fo exactly anfwer my purpofe, as to refufe the needful aid of a proper perfon, becaufe he could give no account of his family or pedigree. Though what is called *cant* is generally, not neceffarily, nor always, without etymology, it is not this defect, but the bafenefs of the ufe which fixeth on it that difgraceful appellation. No abfolute monarch hath it more in his power to nobilitate a perfon of obfcure birth, than it is in the power of good use to ennoble words of low or dubious extraction; such, for instance, as have either arisen, nobody knows how, like *fib, banter, bigot, fop, flippant,* among the rabble, or like *flimsy* sprung from the cant of manufacturers. It is never from an attention to etymology, which would frequently mislead us, but from custom, the only infallible guide in this matter, that the meanings of words in present use must be learnt. And indeed, if the want in question were material, it would equally affect all those words, no inconsiderable part of our language, whose descent is doubtful or unknown. Besides, in no case can the line of derivation be traced backwards to infinity. We must always terminate in some words of whose genealogy no account can be given †.

It

---

† Dr. Johnson, who, notwithstanding his acknowledged learning, penetration, and ingenuity, appears sometimes, if I may adopt his own expression, "lost in lexicography,' hath declared the name *punch*, which signifies a certain mixt liquor very well known, a cant word, because, being to appearance without etymology, it hath probably arisen from some silly conceit among the people. The name *sherbet*, which signifies another known mixture, he allows to be good, because it is Arabic; though, for aught we know, its origin among the Arabs, hath been equally ignoble or uncertain. By this way of reckoning, if the word *punch*, in the sense wherein we use it, should by any accident be imported into Arabia, and come into use there,

It ought, at the same time, to be observed, that what hath been said on this topic, relates only to such words as bear no distinguishable traces of the baseness of their source, the case is quite different in regard to those terms, which may be said to proclaim their vile and despicable origin, and that either by associating disagreeable and unsuitable ideas, as *bellytimber, thoroustitch, dumbfound*, or by betraying some frivolous humour in the formation of them, as *transmogrify, bamboozle, topsyturvy, pellmell, helterskelter, hurlyburly*. These may all find a place in burlesque, but ought never to show themselves in any serious performance. A person of no birth, as the phrase is, may be raised to the rank of nobility, and, which is more, may become it, but nothing can add dignity to that man, or fit him for the company of gentlemen, who bears indelible marks of the clown in his look, gait, and whole behaviour.

there, it would make good Arabic, though it be but cant English, as their *sherbet*, though in all likelihood but cant Arabic, makes good English. This, I own, appears to me very capricious.

CHAP.

CHAP. III.

Of grammatical purity.

IT was remarked formerly*, that though the grammatical art bears much the same relation to the rhetorical, which the art of the mason bears to that of the architect, there is one very memorable difference between the two cases. In architecture it is not necessary that he who designs should execute his own plans, he may therefore be an excellent artist in this way, who has neither skill nor practice in masonry: on the contrary, it is equally incumbent on the orator to design and to execute. He ought therefore to be master of the language which he speaks or writes, and to be capable of adding to grammatic purity, those higher qualities of elocution, which will give grace and energy to his discourse. I propose, then, in the first place, by way of laying the foundation †, to consider that purity which he hath in common with the grammarian,

---

* Chap. II.   † Solum quidem et quasi fundamentum oratoris, vides locutionem emendatam et Latinam. Cic. De clar. Orat. The fame holds equally of any language which the orator is obliged to use.

and then proceed to confider thofe qualities of fpeech which are peculiarly oratorical.

It was alfo obferved before*, that the art of the logician is univerfal, the art of the grammarian particular. By confequence, my prefent fubject being language, it is neceffary to make choice of fome particular tongue, to which the obfervations to be made will be adapted, and from which the illuftrations to be produced, will be taken. Let Englifh be that tongue. This is a preference to which it is furely entitled from thofe who write in it. Pure Englifh then, implies three things; *firft*, that the words be Englifh, *fecondly*, that their conftruction, under which, in our tongue, arrangement alfo is comprehended, be in the Englifh idiom, *thirdly*, that the words and phrafes be employed to exprefs the precife meaning which cuftom hath affixed to them.

From the definition now given, it will be evident on reflection, that this is one of thofe qualities, of which, though the want expofes a writer to much cenfure, the poffeffion hardly entitles him to any praife. The truth is, it is

* Book I. Chap. iv.

a kind of negative quality, as the name imports, confisting more in an exemption from certain blemishes, than in the acquisition of any excellence. It holds the same place among the virtues of elocution, that justice holds among the moral virtues. The more necessary each is, and the more blamable the transgression is, the less merit has the observance. Grace and energy, on the contrary, are like generosity and public spirit To be deficient in these virtues, is not treated as criminal, but to be eminent for the practice of them, is accounted meritorious. As, therefore, in what regards the laws of purity, the violation is much more conspicuous than the observance, I am under the disagreeable necessity of taking my illustrations on this article, solely from the former.

PURITY, it was said, implies three things. Accordingly, in three different ways it may be injured. First, the words used may not be English. This fault hath received from grammarians the denomination of *barbarism*. Secondly, the construction of the sentence may not be in the English idiom. This hath gotten the name of *solecism*. Thirdly, the words and phrases may not be employed to express the precise meaning

which

which custom hath affixed to them. This is termed *impropriety* *.

Section I.
The Barbarism.

THE reproach of barbarism may be incurred by three different ways, by the use of words entirely obsolete, by the use of words entirely new, or by new formations and compositions, from simple and primitive words in present use.

PART I. *By the use of obsolete words.*

OBSOLETE words, though they once were English, are not so now, though they were both proper and expressive in the days of our forefathers, are become as strange to our ears, as many parts of their garb would be to our eyes. And if so, such words have no more title than foreign words, to be introduced at present, for though they are not so totally unknown as to occasion obscurity, a fault which I shall consider afterwards, their appearance is so unusual, and their form is so antiquated, that, if not perfectly ridiculous, they at least suggest the notion of

---

* Quintilian hath suggested this distribution. Institut. lib. 1. cap. 5. *Deprehendat quæ barbara, quæ impropria, quæ contra legem loquendi composita.*

stiffness

stiffness and affectation. We ought, therefore, not only to avoid words, that are no longer understood by any but critics and antiquarians, such as *hight, cleped, uneath, erst, whilom*, we must also, when writing in prose, and on serious subjects, renounce the aid of those terms, which, though not unintelligible, all writers of any name have now ceased to use. Such are *behest, fantasy, tribulation, erewhile, whenas, peradventure, selfsame, anon*. All these offend more or less against the third criterion of good use formerly given*, that it be such as obtains at present.

Some indulgence, however, on this, as well as on several other articles, as was hinted already, must be given to poets, on many accounts, and particularly on account of the peculiar inconveniences to which the laws of versification subject them. Besides, in treating some topics, passages of ancient story, for example, there may be found sometimes a suitableness in the introduction of old words. In certain kinds of style, when used sparingly and with judgment, they serve to add the venerable air of antiquity to the narrative. In burlesque also, they often produce a good effect. But it is admitted on all sides, that this

* Book I Chap. xi.

species of writing is not strictly subjected to the laws of purity.

PART II. *By the use of new words.*

ANOTHER tribe of barbarisms much more numerous, is constituted by new words. Here indeed the hazard is more imminent, as the tendency to this extreme is more prevalent. Nay, our language is in greater danger of being overwhelmed by an inundation of foreign words, than of any other species of destruction. There is, doubtless, some excuse for borrowing the assistance of neighbours, when their assistance is really wanted; that is, when we cannot do our business without it; but there is certainly a meanness in choosing to be indebted to others, for what we can easily be supplied with out of our own stock. When words are introduced by any writer, from a sort of necessity, in order to avoid tedious and languid circumlocutions, there is reason to believe they will soon be adopted by others convinced of the necessity, and will at length be naturalised by the public. But it were to be wished, that the public would ever reject those which are obtruded on it merely through a licentious affectation of novelty. And of this kind certainly are most of the words and phrases which have,

have, in this century, been imported from France. Are not *pleasure, opinionative,* and *sally,* as expressive as *volupty, opiniatre,* and *sortie?* Wherein is the expression *last resort,* inferior to *dernier resort; liberal arts,* to *beaux arts;* and *polite literature,* to *belles lettres?* Yet some writers have arrived at such a pitch of futility, as to imagine, that if they can but make a few trifling changes, like *aimable* for *amiable, politesse* for *politeness, delicatesse* for *delicacy,* and *hauteur* for *haughtiness,* they have found so many gems, which are capable of adding a wonderful lustre to their works. With such, indeed, it is in vain to argue; but to others, who are not quite so unreasonable, I beg leave to suggest the following remarks.

First, it ought to be remembered, that the rules of pronunciation and orthography in French, are so different from those which obtain in English, that the far greater part of the French words lately introduced, constitute so many anomalies with us, which, by loading the grammatical rules with exceptions, greatly corrupt the simplicity and regularity of our tongue.

Nor is this the only way in which they corrupt its simplicity; let it be observed further, that one of the principal beauties of any language, and the most essential to simplicity, results from this, That a few plain and primitive words called roots, have, by an analogy, which hath insensibly established itself, given rise to an infinite number of derivative and compound words, between which and the primitive, and between the former and their conjugates, there is a resemblance in sense, corresponding to that which there is in sound. Hence it will happen, that a word may be very emphatical in the language to which it owes its birth, arising from the light that is reflected on it by the other words of the same etymology, which, when it is transplanted into another language, loses its emphasis entirely. The French word *eclaircissement*, for instance, is regularly deduced thus: *Eclaircissement, eclaircisse, eclaircir, eclair, clair*, which is the etymon, whence also are descended, *clairement, clarté, clarifies, clarification, eclairer*. The like may be observed in regard to *connoisseur, reconnoitre, agrémens*, and a thousand others. Whereas, such words with us, look rather like strays than like any part of our own property. They

They are very much in the condition of exiles, who, having been driven from their families, relations, and friends, are compelled to take refuge in a country where there is not a single person with whom they can claim a connexion, either by blood or by alliance.

But the patrons of this practice will probably plead, that as the French is the finer language, ours must certainly be improved by the mixture. Into the truth of the hypothesis from which they argue, I shall not now inquire. It sufficeth for my present purpose, to observe, that the consequence is not logical, though the plea were just. A liquor produced by the mixture of two liquors of different qualities, will often prove worse than either. The Greek is, doubtless, a language much superior, in riches, harmony, and variety, to the Latin, yet, by an affectation in the Romans of Greek words and idioms, (like the passion of the English for whatever is imported from France) as much, perhaps, as by any thing, the Latin was not only viciated, but lost almost entirely, in a few centuries, that beauty and majesty which we discover in the writings of the Augustan age. On the contrary, nothing contributed more to the preservation of
the

the Greek tongue in its native purity for such an amazing number of centuries, unexampled in the history of any other language, than the contempt they had of this practice. It was in consequence of this contempt, that they were the first who branded a foreign term in any of their writers with the odious name of *barbarism*.

But there are two considerations which ought especially to weigh with authors, and hinder them from wantonly admitting such extraneous productions into their performances. One is, if these foreigners be allowed to settle amongst us, they will infallibly supplant the old inhabitants. Whatever ground is given to the one, is so much taken from the other. Is it then prudent in a writer, to foment a humour of innovation which tends to make the language of his country still more changeable, and consequently to render the style of his own writings the sooner obsolete? Nor let it be imagined, that this is not a necessary consequence. Nothing can be juster than Johnson's manner of arguing on this subject, in regard to what Swift a little chimerically proposeth, that though new words be introduced, none should be permitted to become obsolete [*].

[*] Preface to the Dictionary.

For what makes a word obfolete, but a general, though tacit agreement to forbear it? And what fo readily produces this agreement, as another term which hath gotten a vogue and currency, and is always at hand to fupply its place? And if thus, for fome time, a word is overlooked or neglected, how fhall it be recalled, when it hath once, by difufe, become unfamiliar, and, by unfamiliarity, unpleafing?

THE other confideration is, that if he fhould not be followed in the ufe of thofe foreign words, which he hath endeavoured to ufher into the language, if they meet not with a favourable reception from the Public, they will ever appear as fpots in his work. Such is the appearance which the terms *opine, ignore, fraicheur, adroitnefs, opiniatry,* and *opiniatrety,* have at prefent in the writings of fome ingenious men. Whether, therefore, he be, or be not, imitated, he will himfelf prove a lofer at laft. I might add to thefe, that as borrowing naturally expofeth to the fufpicion of poverty, this poverty will much more readily, and more juftly too, be imputed to the writer than to the language.

INVENTORS in the arts, and difcoverers in fcience, have an indifputable title to give names to their own inventions and discoveries. When foreign inventions and discoveries are imported into this island, it is both natural and reasonable that the name should accompany the thing. Nay, in regard even to evils of foreign growth, I should not object to the observance of the same rule. Were any one to insist, that we have not in our language words precisely corresponding to the French *galimatias, phebus, verbiage,* I should not contend with him about it; nor should I perhaps dislike, that the very name served to show, that these plants are the natives of a ranker soil, and did not originally belong to us. But if the introduction of exotic words were never admitted, except in such cases, or in order to supply an evident want amongst ourselves, we should not at present have one such term where we have fifty. The advice of the poet with regard to both the beforementioned sorts of barbarism, is extremely good.

> In words, as fashions, the same rule will hold,
> Alike fantastic, if too new or old·
> Be not the first by whom the new are try'd,
> Nor yet the last to lay the old aside*.

* Pope's Essay on Criticism.

PART III. *By the use of good words new-modelled.*

THE third species of barbarism, is that produced by new formations and compositions, from primitives in present use. I acknowledge, that when the English analogy is observed in the derivation or composition, and when the new-coined word is wanted in the language, greater liberty ought to be given on this article than on the former. The reason of the difference will appear from what hath been said already. But still this is a liberty which needs an excuse from necessity, and is in no case pardonable, unless the words be at least not disagreeable to the ear, and be so analogically formed, that a reader, without the help of the context, may easily discover the meaning.

Now, if the plea of necessity be requisite, what quarter is due to such frivolous innovations as these, *incumberment* *, *portic* *, *martyrised* *, *eucharisty* *, *analyse* *, *connexity* *, *stoician* *, *platonician* *, *peripatetician* *, *pythagorician* *, *fictious* †, *majestatic* ‡, *acception* §, which were intended solely to express what had always been at

* Bolingbroke.   † Prior.
‡ Spectator, N°. 580   § Hammond.

least as well expressed by *encumbrance, portico, martyr'd, eucharist, analysis, connexion, stoic, platonist, peripatetic, pythagorean, fictitious, majestic, acceptation.* And if any regard is due to the ear, what shall we say of——I cannot call it the composition, but——the collision of words which are naturally the most unfit for coalescing, like *saintauthors, saintprotectrices, architectcapacity, commentatorcapacity, authorcharacter,* and many others forged in the same taste, to be found in the pages of a late right honourable author[*]? And lastly, if the analogy of the language must be preserved in composition, to what kind of reception are the following entitled, which have issued from the same source, *selfend, selfpassion, selfaffections, selfpractice, homedialect, bellysense,* and *mirrourwriting?*

It may, indeed, be urged, that the pronoun *self* is used in composition with such latitude, that one can scarcely err in forming new words with its assistance. But this is a mistake. New words may be formed by it; but they must be formed analogically. And the analogy of these formations may be understood from observing, that when analysed thus, they ought regularly

[*] Shaftesbury.

to exhibit the same meaning. Make *one's self, himself, herself, itself,* or *themselves,* as the sense requires, follow the last word in the compound, with the preposition intervening, with which the word, whether noun or participle, is usually construed. If the word be a substantive, the preposition is commonly *of,* if the passive participle, *by,* and if the active participle, no preposition is requisite. Thus *selflove* is *the love of one's self.* In the same way are resolved, *selfhate, selfmurder, selfpreservation.* When we say of a man that he is *selfcondemned,* we mean, that he is *condemned by himself.* A *selfconsuming* fire, is a fire *consuming itself.*

Now to apply this observation, what is the meaning of *the end of one's self, the passion of one's self, the affections of one's self,* and *the practice of one's self?* And if some meaning may be affixed to any of these expressions, it is easy to perceive, that it is not the meaning of the author. Yet I can remember but two compounds that have obtained in English, which are not formed according to the analogy above explained. One is *selfwilled,* signifying *perverse,* and now little used; the other is *selfexistence,* a favourite word of some metaphysicians, which, if it signify any thing more than what is properly and clearly expressed by independency and eternity, signifies I know not what. In new formations, however, the rule ought to be followed, and not the exceptions. But what shall be said of such monsters, as *self-practice*, *bellysense*, and *mirrourwriting*? These, indeed, might have been regarded as flowers of rhetoric in the days of Cromwell, when a jargon of this sort was much in vogue, but are extremely unsuitable to the chaster language of the present age.

AGAIN, under this class may be ranked another modern refinement, I mean the alterations that have been made by some late writers on proper names and some other words of foreign extraction, and on their derivations, on pretence of bringing them nearer, both in pronunciation and in spelling, to the original names, as they appear in the language from which those words were taken. In order to answer this important purpose, several terms which have maintained their place in our tongue for many centuries, and which are known to every body, must be expelled, that room may be made for a set of uncouth and barbarous sounds, with which our ears are unacquainted, and to some of which it is impossible

for

for us so to adapt our organs, accustomed only to English, as rightly to articulate them.

It hath been the invariable custom of all nations, as far as I know; it was particularly the custom of the Grecians and the Romans, when they introduced a foreign name into their language, to make such alterations on it, as would facilitate the pronunciation to their own people, and render it more analogous to the other words of their tongue. There is an evident convenience in this practice; but where the harm of it is, I am not able to discover. No more can I divine what good reason can be alleged for proscribing the name *Zoroaster*, till of late universally adopted by English authors who had occasion to mention that eastern sage, and the same, except in termination, that is used in Greek and Latin classics. Is *Zerdusht*, which those people would substitute in its place, a more musical word? Or is it of any consequence to us, that it is nearer the Persian original? Will this sound give us a deeper insight than the other into the character, the philosophy, and the history of the man? On the same principles we are commanded by these refiners to banish *Confucius* for the sake of *Con-fut-cee*, and never again, on pain of the charge of grofs ignorance, to mention *Mahomet, Mahometan, Mahometifm,* fince *Mohammed, Mohammedan, Mohammedifm,* are ready to fupply their room. *Muffulman* muft give place to *moflem, hegira* to *hejra,* and *alcoran* to *koran.* The *dervis* too is turned a *dirvefh,* and the *bafhaw* is transformed into a *pacha.*

But why do our modern reformers ftop here? Ought not this reformation, if good for any thing, to be rendered more extenfively ufeful? How much more edifying would holy writ prove to readers of every capacity, if, inftead of thofe vulgar corruptions, Jacob and Judah, and Mofes and Elijah, we had the fatisfaction to find in our Bibles, as fome affure us that the words ought to be pronounced, Yagnhakob, and Yehudah, and Mofcheh, and Eliyahu? Nay, fince it feems to be agreed amongft our oriental fcholars, that the Hebrew *jod* founds like the Englifh *y* before a vowel, and that their *vau,* is the fame with the German *w,* the word *Jehovah* ought alfo to be exploded, that we may henceforth fpeak of the Deity more reverently and intelligibly by the only authentic name *Yehowah.* A reform of this kind was indeed, for the benefit of the learned, attempted abroad more than two centuries ago, by by a kindred genius of those modern English critics, one Pagninus a Dominican friar. In a translation which this man made of the scriptures, into a sort of Monkish gibberish that he called Latin, he hath, in order to satisfy the world of the vast importance and utility of his work, instead of *Eve*, written *Chauva*, and for *Isaiah, Jeremiah, Ezekiel*——given us *Jesahiahu, Irmeiahu, Jechezechel.*——But I know not how it hath happened, that in this he hath had no imitators among men of letters. Probably upon the trial, people have discovered that they were just as much edified by the old names as by the new.

AGAIN, why this reformation should be confined almost entirely to proper names, for my part, I can discover no good reason. Appellatives are doubtless entitled to a share. Critics of this stamp ought, for example, boldly to resolve, in spite of inveterate abuses and plebeian prejudices, never, whilst they breathe, either to write or to pronounce the words *pope, popery,* and *popedom,* but instead of them, *pape, papery,* and *papedom;* since, whether we derive these words immediately from the French *, the Latin †, or the Greek ‡, still it appears that the *o* is but a

* Pape.   † Papa.   ‡ παππας.

base

base usurper of a place which rightfully belongs to the *a*. The reason assigned for saying *koran*, and not *alcoran*, is truly curious. *Al*, say they, is the Arabic article, and signifies *the*, consequently, if we should say *the alcoran*, we should fall into a gross patissology. It is just as if we said *the the book*. A plain illiterate man would think it sufficient to reply, What though *al* signifies *the* in Arabic, it hath no signification in English, and is only here the first syllable of a name which use hath appropriated, no matter how, to a particular book. But if ye who are such deep scholars, and wonderful improvers of your mother-tongue, are determined to exclude this harmless syllable from *alcoran*, act at least consistently, and dismiss it also from *alchymy*, *alcove*, *alembic*, *algebra*, *almanac*, and all the other words in the language that are derived in the same way, and from the same source. Indeed, it is not easy to say where ye will stop; for if ye attend to it, ye will find many words of Latin or French origin, which stand equally in need of reformation*.

It

---

* Suppose one of these Aristarchs advancing in such ingenious refinements, and thus criticising on the word *aversion*
' This substantive is by divers authors diversely construed.
' Some say *aversion to a change*, others *aversion from a change*
' both,

It is necessary to add, that if the Public give way to a humour of this kind, there will be no end of innovating. When some critics first thought of reforming the word *bashaw*, one would have it *bassa*, another *pacha*, and a third *pasha*, and how many more shapes it may yet be transformed into, it is impossible to say. A late historiographer hath adopted just the half of Sale's reformation of the name Mahomet. He restores the vowels to the places which they for-

'both, I affirm, from a blind attachment to vernacular idioms,
'have alike deviated into the most ugly and deformed faults.
'This judgment, how severe soever, I am able to support by
'an irrefragable argument. *Aversion*, according to its etymo-
'logy, denotes *turning from* The first syllable *a* is, in the
'original language, a preposition signifying *from* It would
'therefore be absurd to conjoin in the same phrase with it,
'the preposition *to*, which hath a contrary signification. and to
'use *from* after aversion, would render the expression hide-
'ously pleonastic. In defiance therefore of a habitude, which,
'however ancient and universal, is the offspring of ignorance,
'we must, if we would speak correctly, either say *aversion a*
'*change*, the first syllable *a* having the force of the preposition,
'or, cutting off this prepositive, we must say *version from a*
'*change*.' If any should think this representation exaggerated, let him compare the reasoning with that which hath been seriously used for mutilating the word *alcoran*, and he will find it in all respects the same. It is, I acknowledge, of no consequence, whether we say *alcoran*, or *koran*, but it is of consequence that such a silly argument shall not be held a sufficient ground for innovation.

merly

merly held, but admits his alteration of the confonants, never writing either Mahomet or Mohammed, but Mahommed. In regard to such foreign names of persons, offices, eras, and rites, it would be obliging in writers of this stamp, to annex to their works a glossary, for the sake of the unlearned, who cannot divine whether their newfangled terms belong to things formerly unknown, or are no more than the old names of things familiar to them, newly vamped and dressed. Surely, if any thing deserves to be branded with the name of pedantry, it is an ostentation of erudition, to the reproach of learning, by affecting singularity in trifles.

I shall just mention another set of barbarisms, which also comes under this class, and arises from the abbreviation of polysyllables, by lopping off all the syllables except the first, or the first and second. Instances of this are, *hyp* for *hypochondriac*, *rep* for *reputation*, *ult* for *ultimate*, *penult* for *penultimate*, *incog* for *incognito*, *hyper* for *hypercritic*, *extra* for *extraordinary*. Happily all these affected terms have been denied the public suffrage. I scarcely know any such that have established themselves, except *mob* for *mobile*,

mobile*. And this it hath effected at last, notwithstanding the unrelenting zeal with which it was persecuted by Dr. Swift, wherever he met with it. But as the word in question hath gotten use, the supreme arbitress of language, on its side, there would be as much obstinacy in rejecting it at present, as there was perhaps folly at first in ushering it upon the public stage.

As to the humour of abbreviating, we need say very little, as it seems hardly now to subsist amongst us. It only arose in this island about the end of the last century, and when, in the beginning of the present, it assumed to figure in conversation, and even sometimes to appear in print, it was so warmly attacked by Addison and Swift, and other writers of eminence, that since then it hath been in general disgrace, hardly daring

---

* As I am disposed to think that, in matters of this kind, the Public is rarely in the wrong, it would not be difficult to assign a plausible reason for this preference. First, the word *mobile*, from which it is contracted, can scarcely be called English, and, I suspect, never had the sanction of the public voice. Secondly, there is not another word in the language that expresseth precisely the same idea, *a tumultuous and seditious rout*: the word *mobility*, adopted by some writers, is a gross misapplication of a philosophical term, which means only *susceptibility of motion*, lastly, the word *mob* is fitter than either of those for giving rise, according to the analogy of our tongue, to such convenient derivatives as *to mob, mobbed, mobbish, mobber*.

to appear in good company, and never showing itself in books of any name.

The two classes of barbarisms last mentioned, comprehending new words, and new formations from words still current, offend against use, considered both as reputable and as national. There are many other sorts of transgression which might be enumerated here, such as vulgarisms, provincial idioms, and the cant of particular professions. But these are more commonly ranked among the offences against elegance, than among the violations of grammatical purity, and will therefore be considered afterwards.

Section II.

The Solecism.

I now enter on the consideration of the second way by which the purity of the style is injured, the *solecism*. This is accounted by grammarians a much greater fault than the former, as it displays a greater ignorance of the fundamental rules of the language. The sole aim of grammar is to convey the knowledge of the language; consequently, the degree of grammatical demerit in every blunder, can only be ascertained ed by the degree of deficiency in this knowledge which it betrays. But the aim of eloquence is quite another thing. The speaker or the writer doth not purpose to display his knowledge in the language, but only to employ the language which he speaks or writes, in order to the attainment of some further end. This knowledge he useth solely as the instrument or means by which he intends to instruct, to please, to move, or to persuade. The degree of demerit therefore, which, by the orator's account, is to be found in every blunder, must be ascertained by a very different measure. Such offence is more or less heinous, precisely in proportion as it proves a greater or smaller obstruction to the speaker's or writer's aim. Hence it happens, that when solecisms are not very glaring, when they do not darken the sense, or suggest some ridiculous idea, the rhetorician regards them as much more excusable than barbarisms. The reason is, the former is accounted solely the effect of negligence, the latter of affectation. Negligence in expression, often the consequence of a noble ardour in regard to the sentiments, is at the worst a venial trespass, sometimes it is even not without energy; affectation is always a deadly sin against the laws of rhetoric.

It ought also to be observed, that in the article of solecisms, much greater indulgence is given to the speaker than to the writer; and to the writer who proposeth to persuade or move, greater allowances are made, than to him who proposeth barely to instruct or please. The more vehemence is required by the nature of the subject, the less correctness is exacted in the manner of treating it. Nay, a remarkable deficiency in this respect is not near so prejudicial to the scope of the orator, as a scrupulous accuracy, which bears in it the symptoms of study and art. Eschines is said to have remarked, that the orations of his rival and antagonist Demosthenes, smelled of the lamp; thereby intimating that their style and composition were too elaborate. If the remark is just, it contains the greatest censure that ever was passed on that eminent orator. But, as the intermediate degrees between the two extremes are innumerable, both doubtless ought to be avoided.

Grammatical inaccuracies ought to be avoided by a writer, for two reasons. One is, that a reader will much sooner discover them than a hearer, however attentive he be. The other is, as writing implies more leisure and greater

greater coolness than is implied in speaking, defects of this kind, when discovered in the former, will be less excused, than they would be in the latter.

To enumerate all the kinds of solecism into which it is possible to fall, would be both a useless and an endless task. The transgression of any of the syntactic rules is a solecism; and almost every rule may be transgressed in various ways. But as novices only are capable of falling into the most flagrant solecisms, such, I mean, as betray ignorance in the rudiments of the tongue, I shall leave it to grammarians to exemplify, and class the various blunders of this sort which may be committed by the learner. All I propose to do at present, is to take notice of a few less observable, which writers of great name, and even of critical skill in the language, have slidden into through inattention; and which, though of the nature of solecism, ought perhaps to be distinguished by the softer name *inaccuracy*[*].

[*] I am sensible, that in what concerns the subject of this section, I have been in a great measure prevented by the remarks of Lowth and Priestley, and some other critics and grammarians, who have lately favoured the world with their observations. Since reading their publications, I have curtailed considerably what I had prepared on this article; for though I had rarely hit

The first of this kind I shall observe is a mistake of the plural number for the singular, "The zeal of the *seraphim* breaks forth in a becoming warmth of sentiments and expressions, as the character which is given us of *him* denotes that generous scorn and intrepidity which attends heroic virtue †." *Cherub* and *seraph* are two nouns in the singular number transplanted into our language, directly from the Hebrew. In the plural we are authorised, both by use and by analogy, to say either *cherubs* and *seraphs*, according to the English idiom, or *cherubim* and *seraphim*, according to the oriental. The former suits better the familiar, the latter the solemn style. It is surprising that an author of Mr. Addison's discernment, did not, in criticising Milton, take notice of a distinction which is every where so carefully observed by the poet. I shall add to this remark, that as the words *cherubim* and *seraphim* are plural, the

upon the same examples, there was often a coincidence in the matter, inasmuch as the species of fault animadverted on, was frequently the same. I have now almost entirely confined myself to such slips as have been overlooked by others, I say *almost entirely*; for when any error begins to prevail, even a single additional remonstrance may be of consequence, and in points on which critics are divided, I thought it not unreasonable to offer my opinion.

† Spectator, N°. 327.

terms *cherubims* and *seraphims*, as expressing the plural, are quite improper. Yet these barbarisms occur sometimes in our translation of the Bible; which, nevertheless, doth not once adopt the plural form *cherubim* and *seraphim*, to express the singular; though one would naturally imagine, that this error must originally have given rise to the other.

INACCURACIES are often found in the way wherein the degrees of comparison are applied and construed. Some of these, I suspect, have as yet escaped the animadversion of all our critics. Before I produce examples, it will be proper to observe, that the comparative degree implies commonly a comparison of one thing with one other thing; the superlative, on the contrary, always implies a comparison of one thing with many others. The former, consequently, requires to be followed by the singular number, the latter by the plural. In our language, the conjunction *than* must be interposed between the things compared in the former case, the preposition *of* is always used in the latter.

THE following is an example of wrong construction in the comparative: " This noble na-

"tion hath *of all others* admitted *fewer* corrup-
"tions*." The word *fewer* is here construed precisely as if it were the superlative. Grammatically thus. 'This noble nation hath admitted 'fewer corruptions *than any other*.' Sometimes indeed the comparative is rightly followed by a plural, as in these words, ' He is wiser than we.' But it cannot be construed with the preposition *of*, before that to which the subject is compared. There is one case, and but one, wherein the aforesaid preposition is proper after the comparative, and that is, when the words following the preposition comprehend both sides of the comparison; as, ' He is the taller man of the ' two.' In these words *the two* are included he and the person to whom he is compared. It deserves our notice also, that in such cases, and only in such, the comparative has the definite article *the* prefixed to it, and is construed precisely as the superlative, nay, both degrees are in such cases used indiscriminately. We say rightly, either ' This is the weaker of the two,' or— ' the weakest of the two.' If, however, we may form a judgment from the most general principles of analogy, the former is preferable, because there are only two things compared.

* Swift's Mechanical Operations.

I shall subjoin to this an inaccuracy in a comparison of equality, where, though the positive degree only is used, the construction must be similar to that of the comparative, both being followed by conjunctions which govern no case. "Such notions would be avowed at this time "by none but rosicrucians, and fanatics as mad "as them †." Grammatically *they*, the verb *are* being understood.

That the particles, *as* after the positive, and *than* after the comparative, are conjunctions and not prepositions, seems never to have been questioned by any grammarian or critic before Dr. Priestley. I readily acknowledge, that it is use which must decide the point, nor should I hesitate a moment in agreeing to the notion he suggests, if it were supported by what could be justly denominated general and reputable use. But to me it is manifest, that both the most numerous and the most considerable authorities are on the opposite side, and therefore, that those instances which he produceth in favour of that hypothesis, ought to be regarded merely as negligences of style, into which (as I shall have occasion to observe more fully in the sequel)

† Bolingbroke's Ph. Fr. 24.

even the best writers will sometimes fall. That in the colloquial dialect, as Johnson calls it, such idioms frequently occur, is undeniable. In conversation you will perhaps ten times oftener hear people say, 'There's the books you wanted,' than 'There are the books——;' and 'You was 'present,' when a single person is addressed, than 'you were present.' Yet good use is always considered as declaring solely for the last mode of expression in both cases. The argument drawn from the French usage, (which, by the way, hath no authority in our tongue) is not at all apposite †.

BUT

---

† The oblique cases of their personal pronouns, answering to our *me*, *thee*, and *him*, are *me*, *te*, and *le*, not *moi*, *toi*, and *lui*. In these last we have the indefinite form which serves indifferently as occasion requires, for either nominative or accusative, and to which there is nothing in our language that exactly corresponds. Thus, to express in French, 'He and I 'are relations,' we must say, 'Lui et moi, nous sommes parens.' But in English, 'Him and me, we are relations,' would be insufferable. The nominatives *je*, *tu*, *il*, are never used by them, but when immediately adjoined to the verb, prefixed in affirming, or affixed in interrogating. In every other situation the indefinite form must supply their place. *Le Clerc* thus renders a passage of Scripture, (Rev. i. 18) "Moi qui vis présentement, j'ai été mort." But who that understands English would say, "Me who live at present, I have been dead." Let this serve also as an answer to the plea for these vulgar, but unauthorised idioms, *It is me*, *it is him*, from the *C'est moi*, *c'est lui*, of the French. I shall observe in passing, that one of

Priestley's

But supposing good use were divided on the present question, I acknowledge that the first and second canons proposed on this subject *, would determine me to prefer the opinion of those who consider the aforesaid particles as conjunctions. The first directs us in doubtful cases to incline to that side in which there is the least danger of ambiguity. In order to illustrate this point, it will be necessary to observe, that the doubt is not properly stated by saying with Dr. Priestley, that the question is, whether the nominative or accusative ought to follow the particles *than* and *as*; but, whether these particles are, in such particular cases, to be regarded as conjunctions or prepositions. For, on either supposition, it must be admitted, that in certain circumstances the accusative ought to follow, and not the nominative. But I insist, that as in such cases there is a difference in the sense, uniformly to consider those particles as conjunctions, is the only way of removing the ambiguity. Thus I say properly, 'I esteem you more than they.'

Priestley's quotations in support of these phrases, is defensible on a different principle, and therefore not to his purpose. "It is not *me* you are in love with." The *me* is here governed by the preposition *with*." "It is not *with me* you are in love." Such transpositions are frequent in our language.

* Chap X. Part i.

I say properly also, 'I esteem you more than
'them,' but in a sense quite different. If *than* is
understood as a conjunction, there can be nothing
ambiguous in either sentence. The case of the
pronoun determines at once the words to be supplied. The first is, 'I esteem you more than they
'esteem you.' The second is, 'I esteem you more
'than I esteem them.' But this distinction is confounded, if you make *than* a preposition, which, as
in every instance it will require the oblique case,
will by consequence render the expression perfectly equivocal. For this reason, I consider that
quotation from Smollet, (who is, by the bye, the
only authority alleged on this question)—" Tell
" the cardinal, that I understand poetry better
" than him," as chargeable not so much with
inaccuracy, as with impropriety. The sense it
expresseth, is clearly, " I understand poetry bet-
" ter than I understand him." But this is not
the sense of the author. The second canon leads
directly to the same decision, as it teacheth us to
prefer what is most agreeable to analogy. Now
that is always most repugnant to analogy, which
tends most to multiply exceptions. Consequently,
to consider the particles employed in this manner, of stating a comparison as conjunctions,
(which they are universally admitted to be in

every

every other case) is more analogical, than to consider them as changing their usual denomination and character, in such instances.

But to proceed; incorrectness in using the superlative degree, appears in the subsequent quotation: " The vice of covetousness is what " enters *deepest* into the soul *of any other* *." An instance of the same fault I shall give from a writer of no small merit for harmony and elegance. " We have a profession set apart for the " purposes of persuasion, wherein a talent of this " kind would prove *the likeliest* perhaps *of any* " *other* †." I do not here criticise on the word *other* in those examples, which, in my opinion, is likewise faulty, after the superlative; but this fault comes under another category. The error I mean at present to point out, is the superlative followed by the singular number, " the deepest " of any other," " the likeliest of any other." We should not say, " the best of any man," or " the best of any other man," for " the best of " men." We may indeed say, " He is the oldest " of the family." But the word family is a collective noun, and equivalent to *all in the house*. In like manner it may be said, " The eyes are " the worst of his face." But this expression is

* Guardian, N°. 19. † Fitz-Osborn's Letters, B. 1 L. 24.

evidently

evidently deficient. The face is not the thing with which the eyes are compared, but contains the things with which they are compared. The sentence, when the ellipsis is supplied, stands thus, " Of all the features of his face, the eyes " are the worst."

Both the expressions above censured, may be corrected by substituting the comparative in room of the superlative. " The vice of covet-" ousness is what enters *deeper* into the soul *than* " *any other*," and " We have a profession set " apart for the purposes of persuasion, wherein " a talent of this kind would prove *likelier* per-" haps *than any other*." It is also possible to retain the superlative, and render the expression grammatical. " Covetousness is what *of all vices* " enters *the deepest* into the soul ;"——and, " wherein a talent of this kind would perhaps *of* " *all talents* prove the *likeliest*."

In the following example we have a numeral adjective, which doth not belong to any entire word in the sentence as its substantive, but to a part of a word. " The first project was to " shorten discourse by cutting polysyllables into " one *." The term *one* relates to *syllable*, a

* Voyage to Laputa.

part of the word polysyllables. This is quite ungrammatical. The expression is likewise exceptionable on the score of propriety, but of this afterwards.

There is an error of the same kind in the following passage from Addison, " My christian " and sirname begin and end with the same let-" ters *." The word christian is here an adjective, which hath for its substantive the last syllable of the word sirname. The expression is also exceptionable on the score of perspicuity, of which afterwards.

Sometimes the possessive pronoun does not suit the antecedent. "*Each* of the sexes," says Addison, " should keep within *its* particular " bounds, and content *themselves* to exult with-" in *their* respective districts †." *Themselves* and *their* cannot grammatically refer to *each*, a singular. Besides the trespass here is the more glaring, that these pronouns are coupled with *its*, referring to the same noun.

In no part of speech do good writers more frequently fall into mistakes than in the verbs.

* Spectator, N°. 505. O.   † Freeholder, N°. 38

Of these I shall give some specimens out of a much greater number which might be collected. The first shall be of a wrong tense, "Ye *will* not "come unto me that ye *might* have life*." In two clauses thus connected, when the first verb is in the present or the future, the second which is dependent on it, cannot be in the past. The words, therefore, ought to have been translated, "that ye *may* have life." On the contrary, had the first verb been in the preterit, the second ought to have been so too. Thus, "Ye *would* "not come to me," or, "Ye *did* not come to "me, that ye *might* have life," is entirely grammatical. In either of these instances, to use the present tense would be erroneous. When the first verb is in the preterperfect, or the present perfect, as some call it, because it hath a reference both to the past and to the present, the second, I imagine, may be in either tense. Thus, "Ye *have* not *come* to me that ye *might*,"—or, "that ye *may*—have life," seem equally unexceptionable.

LET it be observed, that, in expressing abstract or universal truths, the present tense of the verb ought, according to the idiom of our language,

* John v. 40.

and perhaps of every language, always to be employed. In such cases, the verb in that form has no relation to time, but serves merely as a copula to the two terms of the proposition. The case is different with the past and the future, in which the notion of time is always comprehended. Yet this peculiarity in the present hath sometimes been overlooked, even by good authors, who, when speaking of a past event which occasions the mention of some general truth, are led to use the same tense in enunciating the general truth, with that which had been employed in the preceding part of the sentence. Of this we have the following example from Swift, which shall serve for the second instance of inaccuracy in the verbs. " It is confidently report-
" ed, that two young gentlemen of real hopes,
" bright wit, and profound judgment, who,
" upon a thorough examination of causes and
" effects, and by the mere force of natural abi-
" lities, without the least tincture of learning,
" have made a discovery, that there *was* no
" God, and generously communicating their
" thoughts for the good of the Public, were
" some time ago, by an unparalleled severity,
" and upon I know not what obsolete law, broke
" for

"for blasphemy*." Properly—"have made
"a discovery that there is no God."

The third example shall be of a wrong mood,
"*If* thou *bring* thy gift to the altar, and there
"*rememberest* that thy brother hath ought against
"thee †."——The construction of the two verbs
bring and *rememberest* ought to be the same,
as they are both under the regimen of the
same conjunction *if*. Yet the one is in the
subjunctive mood, the other in the indicative.

The fourth instance shall be the omission of
an essential part of one of the complex tenses, the
writer apparently referring to a part of the verb
occurring in a former clause of the sentence,
although the part referred to will not supply the
defect, but some other part not produced. Of
this the following is an example: "I shall do all
'I can to persuade others to *take* the same mea-
"sures for their cure which I *have* ‡." Here
we have a reference in the end to the preceding
verb *take*. Yet it is not the word *take* which will
supply the sense, but *taken*. This participle,
therefore, ought to have been added.

* An Argument against abolishing Christianity.
† Matt. v. 23.   ‡ Guardian, N°. 1.

THE fifth specimen in the verbs shall be of a faulty reference to a part to be mentioned. "This dedication may serve for almost any book, that *has*, is, or shall be, published." *Has* in this place being merely a part of a complex tense, means nothing without the rest of the tense. Yet the rest of the tense is not to be found in the sentence. We cannot say, "any book that *has published*," no more can we say, "that *has be published*." Corrected it would run thus, "that *has been*, or *shall be* published." The word *is* ought to be expunged, as adding nothing to the sense.

I SHALL next produce a few instances of inaccuracy, which result from coupling words together, and assigning to them a common regimen, when use will not admit that they be construed in the same manner. The following is an example in the construction of adjectives: "Will it be urged, that the four gospels are *as old*, or even *older than* tradition*?" The words *as old* and *older* cannot have a common regimen, the one requires to be followed by the conjunction *as*, the other by *than*. If he had said, "*as old as* tradition, and even *older*," there

* Bolingb. Phil. Ef. iv. S. 19.

would

would have been no error. The comparative, in this cafe, is not conftrued with the preceding words, but with words which, being afcertained by the preceding, are properly enough underftood.

I shall exemplify the fame inaccuracy in the conftruction of verbs. " It requireth few talents " *to which* moft men are not *born*, or at leaft " may not *acquire**." Admitting that the words *to which* are rightly conftrued with the paffive participle *born*, they cannot be conftrued with the active verb *acquire*. For it ought to be noted, that the connexion between the prepofition and the noun or pronoun governed by it, is fo intimate, that there cannot be a reference to the one without the other. The laft claufe, therefore, ought to run thus, " or *which* at leaft *they* may " not acquire." The repetition of the relative makes the infertion of the perfonal pronoun neceffary.

There is an error of the fame kind in the fentence following: " The court of Chancery " frequently *mitigates*, and breaks the teeth of " the common law †." What is the regimen of

* Swift on Converfation.   † Spectator, N° 564.

the active verb *mitigates?* Regularly it ought to be, *the teeth of the common law,* as these words make the regimen of the other active verb *breaks,* with which the former is coupled. But as this manner of construing the sentence would render the expression highly improper, if not nonsensical, it is evidently the author's view, that the verb *mitigates* should be construed with these words *the common law,* which, being in construction with the preposition *of,* (or, as some would call it, in the genitive) cannot serve grammatically as the regimen of an active verb.

"GIVE the Whigs," says the candid Dean of Saint Patrick's, "but power enough to insult "their sovereign, engross his favours to them-"selves, and to oppress and plunder their fellow-"subjects, they presently *grow into* good hu-"mour, and *good language* towards the crown*." I do not like much *grow into good humour,* for growing good-humoured, but *grow into good language* is insufferable.

I SHALL add to these an instance in the syntax of nouns. "There is never wanting a set of "evil instruments, who, either *out of* mad zeal,

* Examiner, N°. 35.

"private

" private hatred, or *filthy lucre*, are always
" ready †."——We say properly, " a man acts
" *out of mad zeal*, or *out of private hatred*," but
we cannot say, if we would speak English, " he
" acts *out of filthy lucre*." He ought, therefore, to
have substituted in the place of the two last words
the term *avarice*; or *love of filthy lucre*, either of
which expressions would have been rightly construed with the preposition.

Of the same kind nearly is the following specimen in the government of a substantive:
" There is one that will think herself obliged to
" double her *kindness* and *caresses* of me ‡." The
word *kindness* requires to be followed by either *to*
or *for*, and cannot be construed with the preposition *of*.

We often find something irregular in the management of the prepositions: for instance, in
the omission of one altogether: " He lamented
" the fatal mistake the world had been so long
" *in* using silk-worms ‖." Another *in* is necessary to complete the construction, whether we
suppose the *in* mentioned to belong to the pre-

---

† Swift's Sermon on False Witness
‡ Spect. N°. 490. T.   ‖ Voyage to Laputa.

ceding words, or to the succeeding. But as it would have sounded harshly to subjoin another *in* immediately after the former, it would have been better to give the sentence another turn; as, " He lamented the fatal mistake *in* " which the world had been so long, *in* using " silk-worms *."

We have a similar omission, though not of a preposition, in the expression following: " That " the discoursing on politics shall be looked upon " *as* dull *as* talking on the weather †." Syntax absolutely requires, that the sentence in this form should have another *as* immediately before the first. At the same time it must be owned, that this would render the expression very inelegant. This dilemma might have been avoided by giving another turn to the concluding part, as thus, " ―――shall be looked upon as equally dull with " talking on the weather."

Of an error in the wrong choice of a preposition, these words of the same author will furnish an example. " The greatest masters of cri- " tical learning differ *among one another* ‡." Had

* Voyage to Laputa.　　† Freeholder, N°. 38.
‡ Spectator, N°. 321.

he said, "differ *among themselves*," the expression would have been faultless. But the terms *themselves* and *one another*, though frequently synonymous, rarely admit the same construction. We cannot say "one differs *among another*." But we may say, "one differs *from another*," or "*with another*;" the former to express a difference in opinion, the latter a quarrel or breach. It ought, therefore, to have been in the above-cited passage, "differ *from one another*."

I shall only add an instance or two of inaccuracy in the conjunctions and the adverbs; first, in the conjunctions: "A petty constable will "*neither* act cheerfully *or* wisely*."—Properly —"act *neither* cheerfully *nor* wisely." *Neither* cannot grammatically be followed by *or*.

An example of incorrectness in the adverbs, you have in the passage following: "Lest I "should be charged for being worse than my "word, I shall endeavour to satisfy my reader, "by pursuing my method proposed; *if perad-* "*venture* he can call to mind what that method "was †." The adverb *peradventure*, expressing

* Swift's Free Thoughts, &c.
† Shaftesbury, Vol. III. Misc. n. Ch 3.

a degree

a degree of evidence or credibility, cannot regularly be construed with the hypothetical conjunction *if*. It is only to affirmations and negations, not to bare suppositions, that all the adverbs denoting certainty, probability, or possibility, properly belong.

The following passage in the common version of the Bible is liable to the same censure: " Mi-
" caiah said, *If* thou *certainly* return in peace,
" then hath not the Lord spoken by me †." The translators in this, as in some other places, have been misled by a well-meant attempt to express the force of a hebraism, which in many cases cannot be expressed in our language.

I shall conclude this article with a quotation from an excellent author, of which, indeed, it would not be easy to say in what part the solecism may be discovered, the whole passage being so perfectly solecistical. " As he that would
" keep his house in repair, must attend every
" little breach or flaw, and supply it immedi-
" ately, else time alone will bring all to ruin;

---

† 2 Chron xviii. 27. Saci, in his French translation, hath expressed the sense of the original with more simplicity and propriety. " Michée repartit, Si vous revenez en paix, le
" seigneur n'a point parlé par ma bouche."

"how much more the common accidents of
"storms and rain? He must live in perpetual
"danger of his house falling about his ears; and
"will find it cheaper to throw it quite down,
"and build it again from the ground, perhaps
"upon a new foundation, or at least in a new
"form, which may neither be so safe nor so
"convenient as the old †." It is impossible to
analyse this sentence grammatically, or to say
whether it be one sentence or more. It seems,
by the conjunction *as*, to begin with a comparison, but we have not a single hint of the subject illustrated. Besides, the introducing of the interrogation, How much more——? after *else*, which could be regularly followed only by an affirmation or negation; and the incoherency of the next clause, *He must live*——render it indeed —all of a piece.

So much for the solecism, of which examples might be multiplied almost without end. Let those produced suffice for a specimen. It is acknowledged, that such negligences are not to be considered as blemishes of any moment in a work of genius, since those, and even worse, may be discovered, on a careful examination, in the most

† Project for the Advancement of Religion. Last sentence.

celebrated

celebrated writings. It is for this reason acknowledged also, that it is neither candid nor judicious, to form an opinion of a book from a few such specks, selected perhaps from the distant parts of a large performance, and brought into our view at once. Yet, on the other hand, it is certain, that an attention to these little things ought not to be altogether disregarded by any writer. Purity of expression hath but a small share of merit; it hath, however, some share. But it ought especially to be remembered, that, on the account of purity, a considerable part of the merit discovered in the other virtues of elocution, to which it contributes, ought undoubtedly to be charged. The words of the language constitute the materials with which the orator must work; the rules of the language teach him, by what management those materials are rendered useful. And what is purity but the right using of the words of the language by a careful observance of the rules. It is therefore justly considered as essential to all the other graces of expression. Hence, not only perspicuity and vivacity, but even elegance and animation derive a lustre.

Section III.

The Impropriety.

I come now to consider the third and last class of faults against purity, to which I gave the name of *impropriety*. The barbarism is an offence against etymology, the solecism against syntax, the impropriety against lexicography. The business of the lexicographer is to assign to every word of the language, the precise meaning or meanings which use hath assigned to it. To do this is as really a part of the grammarian's province, though commonly executed by a different hand, as etymology and syntax. The end of every grammar is to convey the knowledge of that language of which it is the grammar. But the knowledge of all the rules, both of derivation, under which inflection is included, and of construction, nay, and of all the words in the language, is not the knowledge of the language. The words must be known, not barely as sounds, but as signs. We must know to what things respectively they are appropriated. Thus, in our own tongue, we may err egregiously against propriety, and consequently against purity, though all the words we employ be English, and though they be construed in the English idiom. The reason is evident, they may be misapplied; they may be employed as signs of things to which use hath not affixed them. This fault may be committed either in single words or in phrases.

PART I. *Impropriety in single words.*

I BEGIN with single words. As none but such as are grosly ignorant of our tongue, can misapply the words that have no affinity to those whose place they are made to occupy, I shall take notice only of such improprieties, as by some resemblance or proximity in sound, or sense, or both, a writer is apt unwarily to be seduced into.

It is by proximity in sound that several are misled to use the word *observation* for *observance*, as when they speak of the religious observation of a festival, for the religious observance of it. Both words spring from the root *observe*, but they spring from the same word in different significations. When to observe signifies to *remark*, the verbal noun is *observation*; when it signifies to *obey* or to keep, the verbal is *observance*.

By

By a similar mistake *endurance* hath been used for *duration*, and confounded with it; whereas its proper sense is *patience*. It is derived from the active verb to endure, which signifies to *suffer*, and not from the neuter which signifies to *last*. As far back as the days of queen Elizabeth, the word endurance was synonymous with duration, whereas now it is in this acceptation obsolete. Nay, even in a later period, about the middle of the last century, several words were used synonymously, which we now invariably discriminate. Such are the terms *state* and *estate*, *property* and *propriety*.

HUMAN and *humane* are sometimes confounded, though the only authorised sense of the former is, *belonging to man*; of the latter, *kind and compassionate*. *Humanly* is improperly put for *humanely* in these lines of Pope.

> Tho' learn'd, well-bred, and tho' well-bred, sincere;
> Modestly bold, and *humanly* severe*.

The abstract *humanity* is equally adapted to both senses.

By an error of the same kind with the former, the adjectives *ceremonious* and *ceremonial* are some-

---

* Essay on Criticism.

times used promiscuously, though by the best and most general use they are distinguished. They come from the same noun *ceremony*, which signifies both a *form of civility*, and a *religious rite*. The epithet expressive of the first signification is *ceremonious*, of the second *ceremonial*.

THE word *construction* serves as the verbal noun of two different verbs, to *construe* and to *construct*. The first is a grammatical term, relating solely to the disposition of words in a sentence; the second signifies to *fabricate* or *build*. The common relation in which the two verbs stand to the same appellative, hath misled some writers to confound them, so far at least as to use improperly the word *construct*, and speak of *constructing*, instead of construing a sentence; for I have not observed the like misapplication of the other verb. We never hear of *construing* a fabric or machine.

ACADEMICIAN is frequently to be found in Bolingbroke's works for *academic*. The former denotes solely with us a member of a French academy, or of one established on a similar footing; the latter a Platonic philosopher, one of that sect which took its denomination from the Grecian academy; or more properly, from the

grove

grove of Academus, where the principles of that philosophy were first inculcated.

By a like error, the words *sophist* and *sophister* are sometimes confounded; the proper sense of the former being a teacher of philosophy in ancient Greece; of the latter, a specious, but false reasoner.

E'ER, a contraction of the adverb *ever*, hath, from a resemblance, or rather an identity in sound, been mistaken for the conjunction *ere*, before; and in like manner *it's*, the genitive of the pronoun *it*, for *'tis*, a contraction of *it is*.

IN the same way *bad* is sometimes very improperly used for *bade*, the preterit of the verb *bid*, and *sate* for *sat*, the preterit of *sit*. The only proper use of the word *bad* is as a synonyma for *ill*; and to *sate* is the same in signification as to *glut*.

THE word *genii* hath by some writers been erroneously adopted for *geniuses*. Each is a plural of the same word *genius*, but in different senses. When genius in the singular means a separate spirit or demon good or bad, the plural

ral is *genii*; when it denotes mental abilities, or a person eminently possessed of these, the plural is *geniuses*. There are some similar instances in our tongue of different plurals belonging to the same singular in different significations. The word *brother* is one. The plural in modern language, when used literally for male children of the same parent or parents, is *brothers*; when used figuratively for people of the same profession, nation, religion, or people, considered as related by sharing jointly in the same human nature, is *brethren*. Anciently this last term was the only plural.

I shall next specify improprieties arising from a similitude in sense, into which writers of considerable reputation have sometimes fallen. *Veracity* you will find, even among such, applied to things, and used for *reality*; whereas in strict propriety, the word is only applicable to persons, and signifies not physical, but moral truth.

Epithet hath been used corruptly to denote *title* or *appellation*; whereas it only signifies some attribute expressed by an adjective.

In the same way, *verdict* hath been made to usurp the place of *testimony*; and the word *risible*

sible hath of late been perverted from its original sense, which is *capable of laughing*, to denote *ridiculous, laughable*, or *fit to be laughed at*. Hence these newfangled phrases *risible jests*, and *risible absurdities*. The proper discrimination between *risible* and *ridiculous*, is that the former hath an active, the latter a passive signification. Thus we say, 'Man is a *risible* animal.' 'A fop is a 'ridiculous character.' To substitute the former instead of the latter, and say 'A fop is a *risible* 'character,' is, I suspect, no better English, than to substitute the latter instead of the former, and say ' Man is a *ridiculous* animal.' In confirmation of this distinction, it may be further remarked, that the abstract *risibility*, which analogically ought to determine the import of the concrete, is still limited to its original and active sense, the *faculty of laughter*. Where our language hath provided us with distinct names for the active verbal and the passive, as no distinction is more useful for preventing ambiguity, so no distinction ought to be more sacredly observed.

But to proceed; the word *together* often supplies the place of *successively*, sometimes awkwardly enough, as in the following sentence, " I do not remember that I ever spoke three sen-
" tences

" tences *together* in my whole life*." The resemblance which continuity in time bears to continuity in place, is the source of this impropriety, which, by the way, is become so frequent, that I am doubtful whether it ought to be included in the number. Yet, should this application generally obtain, it would, by confounding things different, often occasion ambiguity. If, for example, one should say ' Charles, ' William, and David, lived *together* in the same ' house,' in order to denote that William immediately succeeded Charles, and David succeeded William, every one would be sensible of the impropriety. But if such a use of the word be improper in one case, it is so in every case.

By an error not unlike, the word *everlasting* hath been employed to denote time without beginning, though the only proper sense of it be time without end; as in these words, "From " *everlasting* to everlasting thou art God †." It may further be remarked of this term, that the true meaning is so strongly marked in its composition, that very frequent use will not be sufficient to prevent the misapplication from appearing awkward. I think, besides, that there is a

* Spect. N°. 1.   † Ps. xc. 2.

want of correctness in using the word substantively. The proper expression is "From *eternity* to eternity thou art God."

ABUNDANCE, in the following quotation, is, I imagine, improperly used for *a great deal*. "I will only mention that passage of the buskins, which, after *abundance* of persuasion, you would hardly suffer to be cut from your legs ‡."

THE word *due*, in the citation subjoined, is not only improperly, but preposterously employed. "What right the first observers of nature, and instructors of mankind, had to the title of sages, we cannot say. It was *due* perhaps more to the ignorance of the scholars, than to the knowledge of the masters *." The author hath doubtless adopted the word *due* in this place, as preferable at least to the word *owing*, which, though an active participle, is frequently, and as some think inaccurately, employed in a passive sense. Thus, in order to avoid a latent error, if it be an error, he hath run into a palpable absurdity; for what can be more absurd than to say, that the title of sages is due more to ignorance than to knowledge? It

‡ Swift's Examiner, N°. 27.   * Bolingb. Phil. Ef. ii. Sect. 1.

had

had been better to give the sentence another turn, and to say, "It took its rise perhaps "more from the ignorance of the scholars, than "from the knowledge of the masters."

I shall add the improper use of the word *surfeit* in the following quotation from Anson's Voyage round the World: "We thought it "prudent totally to abstain from fish, the few "we caught at our first arrival, having *surfeited* "those who eat of them*." I should not have mentioned, indeed I should not have discovered this impropriety in that excellent performance, which would have passed with me for an expression somewhat indefinite, had it not been for the following passage in a late publication. "Se- "veral of our people were so much disordered "by eating of a very fine-looking fish, which "we caught here, that their recovery was for a "long time doubtful. The author of the ac- "count of Lord Anson's Voyage says, that the "people on board the Centurion, thought it "prudent to abstain from fish, as the few which "they caught at their first arrival, surfeited "those who eat of them. But not attending "sufficiently to this caution, and too hastily

* Anson's Voyage, B. iii. c. 2.

"taking the word *surfeit* in its literal and com-
"mon acceptation, we imagined that those who
"tasted the fish, when Lord Anson first came
"hither, were made sick merely by eating too
"much; whereas, if that had been the case,
"there would have been no reason for totally
"abstaining, but only eating temperately. We,
"however, bought our knowledge by expe-
"rience, which we might have had cheaper;
"for though all our people who tasted this fish,
"eat sparingly, they were all soon afterwards
"dangerously ill*." I have given this passage
entire, chiefly because it serves to show, both
that an inaccuracy, apparently trifling, may, by
misleading the reader, be productive of very bad
consequences; and that those remarks which
tend to add precision and perspicuity to our language, are not of so little moment as some, who
have not duly considered the subject, would affect to represent them.

To this class we may reduce the *idiotism*, or
the employing of an English word in a sense
which it bears in some provincial dialect, in low
and partial use, or which perhaps the corresponding word bears in some foreign tongue, but

* Byron's Voyage, Chap. xi.

unsupported by general use in our own language. An example of this we have in the word *impracticable*, when it is used for *impassable*, and applied to roads, an application which suits the French idiom, but not the English. Of the same kind, are the following gallicisms of Bolingbroke: " All this was done, at the time, on the occasion, " and by the persons, I *intend**," properly *mean*. " When we learn the names of complex ideas " and notions, we should accustom the mind to " *decompound* them, that we may verify them, " and so make them our own, as well as to " learn to compound others †." *Decompound* he hath used here for *analyse*, misled by the meaning of the French word *decomposer*, which is not only different from the sense of the English word, but contrary to it. *To decompound*, is to compound of materials already compounded.

The use made of the verb *arrive* in the subsequent passage, is also exceptionable in the same way: " I am a man, and cannot help feeling any " sorrow that can *arrive at* man ‡." In English, it should be, " *happen* to man."

* Of the State of Parties. † Phil. Ef. i. Sect. 4.
‡ Spectator, N°. 502. T.

To hold, signifying *to use*, and applied to language, *to give into*, signifying *to adopt*, in the figurative sense of that word, are other expressions frequently employed by this author, and of late by several others, which fall under the same censure. Even our celebrated translator of the Iliad hath not been clear of this charge. Witness the title he hath given to a small dissertation prefixed to that work. "A view," he calls it, "of *the* epic *poem*," in which short title there are no less than two improprieties. First, the word *poem*, which always denotes with us, a particular performance, is here used, agreeably to the French idiom, for *poetry* in general, or the art which characterises the performance, secondly, the definite article *the* is employed, which, though it be always given to abstracts in French, is never so applied in English, unless with a view to appropriate them to some subject. And this, by the way, renders the article with us more determinative than it is in French, or perhaps in any other tongue*. Accordingly, on the first hearing of the title above mentioned, there is no English reader who would not suppose, that it

---

* Accordingly Bossu hath styled his performance on the same subject, *Traité du poëme epique*. It is this title, I suppose, which hath misled the English poet.

were a critical tract on some particular epic poem, and not on that species of poesy.

ANOTHER error of the same kind is the *latinism*. Of this, indeed, the examples are not so frequent. Foppery is a sort of folly much more contagious than pedantry, but as they result alike from affectation, they deserve alike to be proscribed. An instance of the latter is the word *affection*, when applied to things inanimate, and signifying the state of being affected by any cause. Another instance is the word *integrity*, when used for entireness. But here, I think, a distinction ought to be made between the familiar style and that of philosophical disquisition. In the latter, it will be reasonable to allow a greater latitude, especially in cases wherein there may be a penury of proper terms, and wherein, without such indulgence, there would be a necessity of recurring too often to periphrasis. But the less, even here, this liberty is used, it is the better.

To these properly succeeds, that sort of the *vulgarism* †, in which only a low and partial use can

---

† I say that sort of the vulgarism, because, when the word is in no acceptation in good use, it is a sort that partakes of the barbarism, but when a particular application of a good word is current only among the lower classes, it belongs to the impropriety.

be pleaded in support of the application that is made of a particular word. Of this you have an example in the following quotation: " 'Tis "my humble request you will be particular in "speaking *to* the following points ‡." The preposition ought to have been *on*. Precisely of the same stamp is the *on't* for *of it*, so much used by one class of writers. The pronoun *it* is by a like idiom made sometimes to follow neuter verbs, as in the following passage: " He is an " assertor of liberty and property; he rattles *it* " out against popery and arbitrary power, and " priestcraft and high church ||."

THE auxiliaries *should*, *should have*, and *should be*, are sometimes used in the same improper manner. I am not sensible of the elegance which Dr. Priestley seems to have discovered in the expression—" The general report is that *he should* " *have said*"—for " that *he said*." It appears to me not only as an idiomatical expression, but as chargeable both with pleonasm, and with ambiguity. For what a man said, is often very different from what he should have said.

I SHALL finish all that I propose to offer on the idiotism, when I have observed, that these

‡ Guardian, N°. 57.
|| Swift's Project for the Advancement of Religion.

remarks are not to be extended to the precincts of satire and burlesque. There indeed a vulgar, or even what is called a cant expression, will sometimes be more emphatical than any proper term whatsoever. The satirist may plead his privilege. For this reason the following lines are not to be considered as falling under this criticism,

> Whether the charmer sinner it, or saint it,
> If folly grows romantic, I must paint it*.

It remains to give some instances wherein sound and sense both concur in misleading us. Of this the word *enough* is an example, which is frequently confounded with *enow*, and used for it. Both denote sufficiency, the former in quantity or in degrees of quality, the latter in number. Thus we say properly, " We have courage " *enough*, and ammunition *enough*; but we have " not men *enow*."

The derivatives *falseness*, *falsity*, *falsehood*, from the root *false*, are often by mistake employed for one another, though in the best use they are evidently distinguished. The first *falseness* is properly used in a moral sense for want of veracity, and applied only to persons, the other two are

* Pope.

applied only to things. *Falsity* denotes that quality in the abstract, which may be defined contrariety to truth. *Falsehood* is an untrue assertion. The word *negligence* is improperly used in the following passage. "The *negligence* of this "leaves us exposed to an uncommon levity in our "usual conversation †." He ought to have said *neglect*. The former implies the habit, the latter denotes the act; perhaps in this case I should say the instance; for an act of a habit of not doing, hath itself the appearance of impropriety.

PRECISELY of the same kind is the misapplication of the word *conscience* in this quotation. "The *conscience* of approving one's self a bene- "factor to mankind, is the noblest recompence "for being so ‡." Properly the consciousness; the former denotes the faculty, the latter a particular exertion.

THIS impropriety is reversed in the citation following: "I apprehend that all the *sophism*, "which has been, or can be employed, will not "be sufficient to acquit this system at the tri- "bunal of reason §." For *sophism* he should have said *sophistry*, this denotes fallacious rea-

† Spect. N°. 76. ‡ Spect. N°. 588. § Bol. Ph. F. 20.

soning,

soning, that only a fallacious argument. This error is of the same kind with *poem* for *poetry*, which was remarked above.

Sometimes the neuter verb is mistaken for the active. " What Tully says of war, may be " applied to disputing, it should be always so " managed, as to *remember*, that the only end of " it is peace *." Properly *remind us*.

Sometimes again, the active verb is mistaken for the neuter. " I may say without vanity, that " there is not a gentleman in England better " read in tomb-stones than myself, my studies " having *laid* very much in church-yards †." Properly *lien* or *lain*. The active verb *lay* for the neuter *lie*, is so frequently to be met with in some very modern compositions, as to give room for suspecting that it is an idiom of the cockney language, or of some provincial dialect. In that case it might have been classed under the idiotism.

Perhaps under the same predicament ought also to be ranked the word *plenty*, used adjectively for *plentiful*, which indeed appears to me so gross a vulgarism, that I should not have thought it worthy a place here, if I had not

* Pope's Thoughts on various Subjects. † Spect. N° 518.

sometimes found it in works of considerable merit. The relative *whom*, in the following quotation, is improperly used for *which*, the former always regarding persons, the latter always things. "The exercise of reason appears as little in them, "as in the beasts they sometimes hunt, and by "*whom* they are sometimes hunted *."

I shall add but two instances more of impropriety in single words, instances which I have reserved for this place, as being somewhat peculiar, and therefore not strictly reducible to any of the classes above mentioned, instances too, from authors of such eminence in respect of style, as may fully convince us, if we are not already convinced, that infallibility is not more attainable here than in other articles. "As I firmly "believe the divine *precept*, delivered by the "Author of Christianity, *there is not a sparrow* "*falls to the ground without my Father*, and can- "not admit the agency of chance in the govern- "ment of the world, I must necessarily refer "every event to one cause, as well the danger as "the escape, as well the sufferings as the enjoy- "ments of life †." There is very little affinity,

---

* Bolingb Ph Es. ii Sect. 2. † General Introduction to the Account of the Voyages of Commodore Byron, &c. by Hawkesworth.

either

either in sense or in sound, between *precept* and *doctrine*; and nothing but an oscitancy, from which no writer whatever is uniformly exempted, can account for so odd a misapplication of a familiar term. The words in connexion might have shown the error. It is the *doctrines* of our religion that we are required to believe, and the *precepts* that we are required to obey. The other example is, " Their success may be com-
" pared to that of a certain prince, who placed,
" it is said, cats, and other animals, adored by
" the Egyptians, in the front of his army, when
" he invaded that people. A reverence for these
" *phantoms* made the Egyptians lay down their
" arms, and become an easy conquest *." What the author here intended to say, it is hard to conjecture, but it is unquestionable, that in no sense whatever can cats and other animals be called *phantoms*.

I shall now, before I proceed to consider impropriety, as it appears in phrases, make a few reflections on those principles which most frequently betray authors into such misapplications in the use of single words. As to that which hath been denominated the *vulgarism*, its genuine

* Bolngb. Ph. Ef. iv. Sect. 1.

source seems to be the affectation of an easy, familiar, and careless manner. The writers who abound in this idiom generally imagine, that their style must appear the more natural, the less pains they bestow upon it. Addison hath exactly hit their notion of easy writing. "It is," says he, "what any man may easily write." But these people, it would seem, need to be informed, that ease is one thing, and carelessness is another; nay, that these two are so widely different, that the former is most commonly the result of the greatest care. It is like ease in motion, which, though originally the effect of discipline, when once it hath become habitual, has a more simple and more natural appearance, than is to be observed in any manner which untutored Nature can produce. This sentiment is well expressed by the poet:

But ease in writing flows from art, not chance;
As those move easiest who have learn'd to dance †

True ease in composition, accompanied with purity, differs as much from that homely manner which affects the familiarity of low phrases and vulgar idioms, as the appearance of a woman that is plainly but neatly dressed, differs from

---

† Pope's Imitations.

that

that of a flattern. But this affectation is to be considered as the spring of one species of impropriety only.

ALL the rest, unless when chargeable on inadvertency, as they sometimes doubtless are, seem naturally to flow from one or other of these two sources, which are almost diametrically opposite to the former. One is, the love of novelty; the other, a fondness for variety. The former, when excessive, tends directly to misguide us, by making us disdain the beaten track, for no other reason but because it is the beaten track. The idea of vulgarity in the imaginations of those who are affected by this principle, is connected with every thing that is conceived as customary. The genuine issue of this extreme, much worse, I acknowledge, than the former, is not only improprieties, but even absurdities, and fustian, and bombast. The latter, to wit, a fondness for variety, produceth often the same effect, though more indirectly. It begets an immoderate dread of becoming tedious, by repeating too frequently the same sound. In order to avoid this, a writer resolves at any rate to diversify his style, let it cost what it will. And, indeed, this fancied excellence usually costs more than it is worth.

Very

Very often propriety and perspicuity both are sacrificed to it.

It is justly observed by Abbé Girard[*], that when a performance grows dull through an excess of uniformity, it is not so much because the ear is tired by the frequent repetition of the same sound, as because the mind is fatigued by the frequent recurrence of the same idea. If, therefore, there be a remarkable paucity of ideas, a diversity of words will not answer the purpose, or give to the work the agreeable appearance of variety. On the contrary, when an author is at great pains to vary his expressions, and for this purpose even deserts the common road, he will, to an intelligent reader, but the more expose his poverty, the more he is solicitous to conceal it. And, indeed, what can more effectually betray a penury of words, than to be always recurring to such as custom hath appropriated to purposes different from those for which we use them? Would the glitter of jewels which we know to be stolen, produce an opinion of the wearer's affluence? And must not such alienations of words, if I may be allowed the metaphor, awaken a suspicion of some original defect which

[*] Synonymes François. Preface.

have given occasion to them? We should hardly say that a house were richly furnished, I am sure we could not say that it were well furnished, where we found a superfluity of utensils for answering some purposes, and a total want of those adapted to other purposes not less necessary and important. We should think, on the contrary, that there were much greater appearance both of opulence and of taste, where, though there were little or nothing superfluous, no vessel or piece of furniture useful in a family were wanting. When one is obliged to make some utensils supply purposes to which they were not originally destined; when, for instance, " the copper pot " boils milk, heats porridge, holds small beer, " and, in case of necessity, serves for a jorden [*]," there are always, it must be confessed, the strongest indications of indigence. On the contrary, when every real use hath some instrument or utensil adapted to it, there is the appearance, if not of profusion, of what is much more valuable, plenty.

In a language there may be great redundancies, and at the same time great defects. It is infinitely less important to have a number of sy-

[*] Swift.

nonymous words, which are even sometimes cumberfome, than to have very few that can be called homonymous, and confequently to have all the differences which there are in things, as much as poffible, marked by correfponding differences in their figns. That this fhould be perfectly attained, I own is impoffible. The varieties in things are infinite, whereas the richeft language hath its limits. Indeed, the more a people improve in tafte and knowledge, they come the more, though by imperceptible degrees, to make diftinctions in the application of words which were ufed promifcuoufly before. And it is by thus marking the delicate differences of things, which in a ruder ftate they overlooked, more than by any other means, that their language is refined and polifhed. Hence it acquires precifion, perfpicuity, vivacity, energy. It would be no difficult tafk to evince, as partly it may be collected from what hath been obferved already, that our own language hath from this fource received greater improvements in the courfe of the laft century and of the prefent, than from the acceffion of new words, or perhaps from any other caufe. Nothing then, furely, can ferve more to corrupt it, than to overturn the barriers ufe hath erected, by confounding

words

words as synonymous to which distinct significations have been assigned. This conduct is as bad policy with regard to style, as it would be with regard to land, to convert a great part of the property into a common. On the contrary, as it conduceth to the advancement of agriculture, and to the increase of the annual produce of a country, to divide the commons and turn them into property, a similar conduct in the appropriation of words, renders a language more useful and expressive.

PART II. *Impropriety in phrases.*

I come now to consider the improprieties which occur in phrases. The first of this kind of which I shall take notice, is, when the expression, on being grammatically analysed, is discovered to contain some inconsistency. Such is the phrase *of all others* after the superlative, common with many English writers. Interpreted by the rules of syntax, it implies that a thing is different from itself. Take these words for an example, " It celebrates the church of " England, as the *most perfect of all others**." Properly, either—" as more perfect than any " other," or—" as the most perfect of all

* Swift's Apology for the Tale of a Tub.

" churches."

"churches." This is precisely the same sort of impropriety into which Milton hath fallen, in these words,

>———————————Adam,
>The comeliest man of men *since born*
>His sons. The fairest of *her daughters* Eve †.

And in these

>———————————The loveliest pair
>That ever *since* in love's embraces met *.

Use indeed may be pleaded for such expressions, which, it must be acknowledged, use hath rendered intelligible. But still the general laws of the language, which constitute the most extensive and important use, may be pleaded against them. Now it is one principal method of purifying a language, to lay aside such idioms as are inconsistent with its radical principles and constituent rules, or as, when interpreted by such principles and rules, exhibit manifest nonsense. Nor does the least inconvenience result from this conduct, as we can be at no loss to find expressions of our meaning, altogether as natural, and entirely unexceptionable.

Sometimes, indeed, through mere inattention, slips of this kind are committed, as in the

† Paradise Lost.   * Ib. B. iv

following

following instance; "I do not reckon that we want a genius more than *the rest of* our neighbours ‡." The impropriety here is corrected by omitting the words in Italics.

Another oversight of much the same kind, and by the same author, we have in the following passage "I had like to have gotten one or two broken heads for my impertinence *." This unavoidably suggests the question, How many heads was he possessed of? Properly, "I was once or twice like to have gotten my head broken."

Another from the same work, being a passage formerly quoted for another purpose, is this, "The first project was to shorten discourse by cutting polysyllables into one †." One thing may be cut into two or more, but it is inconceivable that, by cutting, two or more things should be made one.

Another, still from the same hand, "I solemnly declare, that I have not *wilfully* committed the least *mistake* ‖." The words used

‡ Swift's Proposal for ascertaining the English Tongue.
* Voyage to Brobdignag. † Voyage to Laputa.
‖ Remarks on the Barrier Treaty.

here are incompatible. A wrong wilfully committed is no miſtake.

Addison hath fallen into an inaccuracy of the ſame kind, in the following lines:

> So the *pure limpid* ſtream, when *foul with ſtains*
> Of ruſhing torrents and deſcending rains*.

A ſtream may doubtleſs be at one time limpid, and at another foul, which is all that the author meant; but we cannot properly call it a *pure limpid* ſtream, when it is *foul with ſtains*. So much for thoſe improprieties which involve in them ſome abſurdity.

I shall next illuſtrate thoſe by which an author is made to ſay one thing when he means another. Of this kind I ſhall produce only one example at preſent, as I ſhall have occaſion afterwards of conſidering the ſame fault under the article of perſpicuity. "I will inſtance in
" one opinion, which I look upon every man
" obliged in conſcience to quit, or in prudence
" to conceal, I mean, that whoever argues in
" defence of abſolute power in a ſingle perſon,
" though he offers the old plauſible plea, that it

* Cato.

"is his opinion, which he cannot help, unless he
"be convinced, ought in all free states to be
"treated as the common enemy of mankind †."
From the scope of the discourse it is evident,
he means, that whoever hath it for his opinion, that a single person is entitled to absolute authority, ought to quit or conceal that opinion; because, otherwise, he will in a free state deserve to be treated as a common enemy. Whereas, if he says any thing, he says, that whoever thinks that the advocates for absolute power ought to be treated as common enemies, is obliged to quit or conceal that opinion; a sentiment very different from the former.

THE only species of impropriety that remains to be exemplified, is that wherein there appears some slight incongruity in the combination of the words, as in the quotations following: "When you fall *into a man's conversation*, the "first thing you should consider, is——*" Properly "fall *into conversation with a man*." "I "wish, Sir, you would animadvert frequently "on the false taste *the town is in*, with relation "to plays as well as operas ‡." Properly, "the "false taste *of the town*."

† Sentiments of a Church of England man.
* Spect. N°. 49.   ‡ Ib. N°. 22.

"THE presence of the deity, and the *care* "such an august *cause* is to be supposed to *take* "about any action *." The impropriety here is best corrected by substituting the word *being* in the place of *cause*, for though there be nothing improper, in calling the deity an august Cause, the author hath very improperly connected with this appellative some words totally unsuitable, for who ever heard of a *cause taking care about an action*.

I shall produce but one other instance— "Neither implies that there are virtuous habits "and accomplishments already *attained* by the "*possessor*, but they certainly show an *unpreju-* "*diced* capacity *towards* them †." In the first clause of this sentence, there is a gross inconsistency; we are informed of habits and accomplishments that are *possessed*, but not *attained*, in the second clause there is a double impropriety, the participle adjective is not suited to the substantive with which it is construed, nor is the subsequent preposition expressive of the sense. Supposing, then, that the word *possessor* hath been used inadvertently for *person*, or some other general term, the sense may be exhibited thus:

---

* Pope's View of the Epic Poem.   † Guardian, N° 34.

'Neither

'Neither implies that there are virtuous habits
'and accomplishments already attained by this
'person, but they certainly show that his mind
'is not prejudiced against them, and that it hath
'a capacity of attaining them.'

UNDER this head I might consider that impropriety which results from the use of metaphors, or other tropes, wherein the similitude to the subject, or connection with it, is too remote, also, that which results from the construction of words with any trope, which are not applicable in the literal sense. The former errs chiefly against vivacity, the latter against elegance. Of the one, therefore, I shall have occasion to speak, when I consider the *catachresis*, of the other when I treat of *mixed metaphor*.

I HAVE now finished what was intended on the subject of grammatical purity; the first, and in some respect the most essential of all the virtues of elocution. I have illustrated the three different ways in which it may be violated, the *barbarism*, when the words employed are not English, the *solecism*, when the construction is not English, the *impropriety*, when the meaning in which any English word or phrase is used, by a writer or speaker, is not the sense which good use hath assigned to it.

CHAP. IV

Some grammatical Doubts in regard to English Construction stated and examined.

BEFORE I dismiss this article altogether, it will not be amiss to consider a little some dubious points in construction, on which our critics appear not to be agreed.

One of the most eminent of them makes this remark upon the neuter verbs. " A neuter verb " cannot become a passive. In a neuter verb " the agent and object are the same, and can- " not be separated even in imagination, as in " the examples *to sleep, to walk*, but when the " verb is passive, one thing is acted upon by " another, really or by supposition different " from it*." To this is subjoined in the margin the following note. " That some neuter " verbs take a passive form, but without a pas- " sive signification, has been observed above " Here we speak of their becoming both in form

* Short Introduction, &c. Sentences.

" and

" and signification passive, and shall endeavour
" further to illustrate the rule by example.
" *To split*, like many other English verbs, has
" both an active and a neuter signification; ac-
" cording to the former we say, The force of
" gunpowder *split* the rock, according to the
" latter, The ship *split* upon the rock:—and
" converting the verb active into a passive, we
" may say, The rock was *split* by the force of
" gunpowder, or, The ship was *split* upon the
" rock. But we cannot say with any propriety,
" turning the verb neuter into a passive, The
" rock *was split* upon by the ship."

THIS author's reasoning, so far as concerns verbs properly neuter, is so manifestly just, that it commands a full assent from every one that understands it. I differ from him only in regard to the application. In my apprehension, what may grammatically be named the neuter verbs, are not near so numerous in our tongue as he imagines. I do not enter into the difference between verbs absolutely neuter, and intransitively active. I concur with him in thinking, that this distinction holds more of metaphysics than of grammar. But by verbs grammatically neuter, I mean such as are not followed either by an accusative, or by a prepofition and a noun; for I take this to be the only grammatical criterion with us. Of this kind is the simple and primitive verb *to laugh*; accordingly to say *he was laughed*, would be repugnant alike to grammar and to fenfe. But give this verb a regimen, and fay, *To laugh at*, and you alter its nature, by adding to its fignification. It were an abufe of words to call this a neuter, being as truly a compound active verb in Englifh, as *deridere* is in Latin, to, which it exactly correfponds in meaning. Nor doth it make any odds that the prepofition in the one language precedes the verb, and is conjoined with it, and in the other follows it, and is detached from it. The real union is the fame in both. Accordingly *he was laughed at* is as evidently good Englifh, as *derifus fuit* is good Latin.

Let us hear this author himfelf, who, fpeaking of verbs compounded with a prepofition, fays exprefsly, " In Englifh the prepofition is
" more frequently placed after the verb, and fe-
" parate from it, like an adverb, in which fitu-
" ation it is no lefs apt to affect the fenfe of it,
" and to give it a new meaning, and may ftill
" be confidered as belonging to the verb, and a
" part

" part of it. As, *to cast* is to throw ; but *to cast
" up*, or to compute, *an account*, is quite a dif-
" ferent thing : thus, *to fall on, to bear out, to
" give over*, &c." Innumerable examples might be produced, to show that such verbs have been always used as active or transitive compounds, call them which you please, and therefore as properly susceptible of the passive voice. I shall produce only one authority, which, I am persuaded, the intelligent reader will admit to be a good one. It is no other than this ingenious critic himself, and the passage of his which I have in view will be found in the very quotation above made. " When the verb is passive, one
" thing *is acted upon* by another." Here the verb *to act upon* is undoubtedly neuter, if the verb *to split upon* be neuter in the expression censured ; and conversely, the verb *to split upon* is undoubtedly active, if the verb *to act upon* be active in the passage quoted. Nor can any thing be more similar than the construction. " One
" thing *is acted upon* by another." " The rock
' *is split upon* by the ship."

After all, I am sensible that the latter expression is liable to an exception, which cannot be made against the former. I therefore agree with the author in condemning it, but not in the reason

son of pronouncing this sentence. The only reason that weighs with me is this. The active sense of the simple verb *to split*, and the sense of the compound *to split upon*, are, in such a phrase as that above mentioned, apt to be confounded. Nay, what is more, the false sense is that which is first suggested to the mind, as if the rock and not the ship had been *split*. And though the subsequent words remove the ambiguity, yet the very hesitancy which it occasions, renders the expression justly chargeable, though not with solecism, with what is perhaps worse, obscurity and inelegance.

That we may be satisfied, that this and no other is the genuine cause of censure, let us borrow an example from some verb, which in the simple form is properly univocal. *To smile* is such a verb, being a neuter, which, in its primitive and uncompounded state, never receives an active signification; but *to smile on* is with us, according to the definition given above, a compound active verb, just as *arridere* *; to which it

---

* I know that the verb *arrideo* is accounted neuter by Latin lexicographers. The reason lies not in the signification of the word, but purely in this circumstance, that it governs the dative and not the accusative. But with this distinction we have no concern. That it is active in its import is evident from this, that it is used by good authors in the passive.

corre-

corresponds alike in etymology and meaning, is in Latin. Accordingly, we cannot say, *he was smiled*, in any sense. But to say, *he was smiled on*, as in the following example, "He was *smiled on* by fortune in every stage of life," is entirely unexceptionable. Yet the only difference between this and the phrase above criticised, ariseth hence, that there is something ambiguous in the first appearance of the one, which is not to be found in the other. And, indeed, when the simple and primitive verb has both an active signification and a neuter (as is the case with the verb *split*), such an ambiguous appearance of the compound in the passive, is an invariable consequence.

I shall observe further, in order to prevent mistakes on this subject, that there are also in our language compound neuter, as well as compound active verbs. Such are, *to go up, to come down, to fall out*. These properly have no passive voice; and though some of them admit a passive form, it is without a passive signification. Thus *he is gone up*, and *he has gone up*, are nearly of the same import. Now the only distinction in English between the active compound and the neuter compound, is this; the preposition in the former,

former, or more properly the compound verb itself, hath a regimen, in the latter it hath none. Indeed these last may be further compounded, by the addition of a preposition with a noun, in which case, they also become active or transitive verbs; as in these instances, "He *went up to* her;" "She *fell out with* them." Consequently, in giving a passive voice to these there is no solecism. We may say, "She *was gone up to* by "him;" "They *were fallen out with* by her." But it must be owned, that the passive form, in this kind of decomposite verbs, ought always to be avoided as inelegant, if not obscure. By bringing three prepositions thus together, one inevitably creates a certain confusion of thought; and it is not till after some painful attention, that the reader discovers two of the prepositions to belong to the preceding verb, and the third to the succeeding noun. The principal scope of the foregoing observations on the passage quoted from Dr. Lowth, is to point out the only characteristical distinction between verbs neuter and verbs active, which obtains in our language.

To these I shall subjoin a few things, which may serve for ascertaining another distinction in regard to verbs. When a verb is used imperfonally, sonally, it ought undoubtedly to be in the singular number, whether the neuter pronoun be expressed or understood; and when no nominative in the sentence can regularly be construed with the verb, it ought to be considered as impersonal. For this reason, analogy as well as usage favour this mode of expression. "The conditions of the "agreement were *as follows*;" and not *as follow*. A few late writers have inconsiderately adopted this last form through a mistake of the construction. For the same reason we ought to say, "I "shall consider his censures so far only as *concerns* my friend's conduct;" and not ' so far ' as *concern*.' It is manifest that the word *conditions* in the first case, and *censures* in the second, cannot serve as nominatives. If we give either sentence another turn, and instead of *as*, say *such as*, the verb is no longer impersonal. The pronoun *such* is the nominative, whose number is determined by its antecedent. Thus we must say, ' They were such as follow,'——' such of his ' censures only as concern my friend.' In this I entirely concur with a late anonymous remarker on the language.

I SHALL only add on this subject, that the use of impersonal verbs was much more frequent
with

with us formerly than it is now. Thus *it pleaseth me, it grieveth me, it repenteth me*, were a sort of imperſonals, for which we ſhould now ſay, *I pleaſe, I grieve, I repent*. *Methinks* and *methought* at preſent, as *meſeemeth* and *meſeemed* anciently, are, as Johnſon juſtly ſuppoſes, remains of the ſame practice *. It would not be eaſy to conjecture what hath miſled ſome writers ſo far as to make them adopt the uncouth term *methoughts*, in contempt alike of uſage and of analogy, and even without any colourable pretext that I can think of, for *thoughts* is no part of the verb at all.

I SHALL now conſider another ſuſpected idiom in Engliſh, which is the indefinite uſe ſometimes made of the pronoun *it*, when applied in the ſeveral ways following: firſt, to perſons as well as to things, ſecondly, to the firſt perſon and the ſecond, as well as to the third, and thirdly, to a plural as well as to a ſingular. Concerning the ſecond application and the third, Dr. Johnſon ſays in his Dictionary, " This mode of ſpeech, " though uſed by good authors, and ſupported " by the *il y a* of the French, has yet an appear- " ance of barbariſm." Dr. Lowth doubts only

---

* The ſimilar uſe of imperſonal verbs, and the *il me ſemble* of the French, render this hypotheſis ſtill more probable.

of

of the third application. "The phrase," says he, " which occurs in the following examples, " though pretty common, and authorised by " custom, yet seems to be somewhat defective " in the same way." He had been specifying inaccuracies arising from disagreement in number. The examples alluded to are,

>'Tis *these* that early taint the female soul *.

>'Tis *they* that give the great Atrides' spoils;
>'Tis *they* that still renew Ulysses' toils †.

>―――― Who was't came by?
>'Tis *two* or *three*, my Lord, that bring you word,
>Macduff is fled to England ‡

AGAINST the first application, to persons as well as to things, neither of these critics seems to have any objection, and it must be owned, that they express themselves rather sceptically than dogmatically, about the other two. Yet, in my judgment, if one be censurable, they all are censurable, and if one be proper, they all are proper. The distinction of genders, especially with us, is as essential as the distinction of persons or that of numbers. I say, especially with us, because, though the circumstances be few wherein the gender can be marked, yet, in those few, our language, perhaps more than

---

* Pope. † Prior. ‡ Shakespeare.

any other tongue, follows the dictates of pure Nature. The masculine pronoun *he* it applies always to males, or at least to persons (God and angels, for example) who in respect of dignity are conceived as males, the feminine *she* to females, and unless where the style is figurative, the neuter *it* to things either not susceptible of sex, or in which the sex is unknown. Besides, if we have recourse to the Latin syntax, the genuine source of most of our grammatical scruples, we shall find there an equal repugnancy to all the applications above rehearsed †.

But, to clear up this matter as much as possible, I shall recur to some remarks of the last mentioned critic, concerning the significations and the uses of the neuter *it*. " The pronoun " *it*," he tells us, " is sometimes employed to " express, first, the subject of any inquiry or " discourse, secondly, the state or condition of " any thing or person, thirdly, the thing, what- " ever it be, that is the cause of any effect or " event, or any person considered merely as a " cause, without regard to proper personality." In illustration of the third use, he quotes these words,

---

† In Latin *id fuit ille* would be as gross a solecism, as *id fuit ego*, or *it fuit nos*.

You heard her say herself, it was not I——
'Twas I that killed her——[*].

The observations of this author concerning the neuter pronoun, are, as far as they go, unexceptionable. He ought to have added to the word *personality* in the third use, the words *gender or number*. The example which he hath given, shows that there is no more regard to *gender*, than to *personality*; and that there ought to be no more regard to *number*, than to either of the former, may be evinced from the considerations following.

When a personal pronoun must be used indefinitely, as in asking a question whereof the subject is unknown, there is a necessity of using one person for all the persons, one gender for all the genders, and one number for both numbers. Now in English, custom hath consigned to this indefinite use, the third person, the neuter gender, and the singular number. Accordingly, in asking a question, nobody censures this use of the pronoun, as in the interrogation, *Who is it?* Yet by the answer it may be found to be *I* or *he*, *one* or *many*. But whatever be the answer, if the

---

[*] Shakespeare

question be proper, it is proper to begin the answer by expressing the subject of inquiry in the same indefinite manner wherein it was expressed in the question. The words *it is* are consequently pertinent here, whatever be the words which ought to follow, whether *I* or *he, we* or *they**. Nay, this way of beginning the answer by the same indefinite expression of the subject that was used in the question, is the only method authorised in the language, for connecting these two together, and showing that what is asserted, is an answer to the question asked. And if there be nothing faulty in the expression, when it is an answer to a question actually proposed, there can be no fault in it, where no question is proposed. For every answer, that is not a bare assent or denial, ought, independently of the question, to contain a proposition grammatically enunciated; and every affirmation or negation ought to be so enunciated, as that it might be an answer to a question. Thus by a very simple sorites it can be proved, that if the pronoun *it* may be used indefinitely in one case, it may in every case. Nor is it possible to conceive even the shadow of a

* In this observation I find I have the concurrence of Dr. Priestley.

reason,

reason, why one number may not as well serve indefinitely for both numbers, as one person for all the persons, and one gender for all the genders.

THAT which hath made more writers scrupulous about the first of these applications than about the other two, is, I imagine, the appearance not of the pronoun, but of the substantive verb in the singular adjoined to some term in the plural. In order to avoid this supposed incongruity, the translators of the Bible have in one place stumbled on a very uncouth expression. " Search the scriptures, for in them ye think ye " have eternal life; and *they are they* which tes- " tify of me *." In the other applications they have not hesitated to use the indefinite pronoun *it*, as in this expression: " It is I, be not a- " fraid †." Yet the phrase *they are they* in the first quotation, adopted to prevent the incongruous adjunction of the verb in the singular, and the subsequent noun or pronoun in the plural, is, I suspect, no better English, than the phrase *I am I* would have been in the second, by which they might have prevented the adjunction not less incongruous of the third person of the verb

---

* John v. 39.   † Matt. xiv. 27.

to the first personal pronoun. If there be any difference in respect of congruity, the former is the less incongruous of the two. The latter never occurs, but in such passages as those above quoted, whereas nothing is commoner than to use the substantive verb as a copula to two nouns differing in number; in which case it generally agrees with the first. " His *meat was locusts* and " wild honey *," is a sentence which I believe nobody ever suspected to be ungrammatical. Now as every noun may be represented by a pronoun, what is grammatical in those, must, by parity of reason, be grammatical in these also. Had the question been put, " What was his " meat?" the answer had undoubtedly been proper, " It was locusts and wild honey." And this is another argument which in my apprehension is decisive.

But " this comes," as Dr. Lowth expresseth himself in a similar case, " of forcing the Eng- " lish under the rules of a foreign language, " with which it has little concern †. A convenient

---

* Matt. iii. 4

† The English hath little or no affinity in structure either to the Latin or to the Greek. It much more resembles the modern European languages, especially the French. Accordingly

we

nient mode of speech which custom hath established, and for which there is pretty frequent occasion, ought not to be hastily given up, especially when the language doth not furnish us with another equally simple and easy to supply its place. I should not have entered so minutely into the defence of a practice sufficiently authorised by use, but in order, if possible, to satisfy those critics, who though both ingenious and acute, are apt to be rather more scrupulous on the article of language, than the nature of the subject will admit. In every tongue there are real anomalies which have obtained the sanction of custom; for this at most hath been reckoned only dubious. There are particularly some in our own, which have never, as far as I know, been excepted against by any writer, and which,

we find in it an idiom very similar to that which hath been considered above. I do not mean the *il y a*, because the *a* is part of an active verb, and the words that follow in the sentence, are its regimen, consequently no agreement in person and number is required. But the idiom to which I allude is the *il est*, as used in the following sentence, " *Il est des animaux* qui " *semblent reduits au* toucher, *il en est qui semblent* participer " a notre intelligence." Contemplation de la nature par Bounet. I am too zealous an advocate for English independency, to look on this argument as conclusive. But I think it more than a sufficient counterpoise to all that can be pleaded on the other side from the syntax of the learned languages

never-

nevertheless, it is much more difficult to reconcile to the syntactic order, than that which I have been now defending. An example of this is the use of the indefinite article, which is naturally singular, before adjectives expressive of number, and joined with substantives in the plural. Such are the phrases following, *a few persons, a great many men, a hundred* or *a thousand ships*.

THERE is another point, on which, as both the practice of writers, and the judgment of critics, seem to be divided, it may not be improper to make a few remarks. It is the way of using the infinitive after a verb in the preterit. Some will have it that the verb governed ought to be in the past, as well as the verb governing; and others that the infinitive ought to be in what is called the present, but what is in fact indefinite in regard to time. I do not think that on either side the different cases have been distinguished with sufficient accuracy. A very little attention will, I hope, enable us to unravel the difficulty entirely.

LET us begin with the simplest case, the infinitive after the present of the indicative. When
the

the infinitive is expressive of what is conceived to be either future in regard to the verb in the present, or contemporary, the infinitive ought to be in the present. Thus, " I intend *to write* to " my father to-morrow." " He seems *to be* a " man of letters." In the first example the verb *to write*, expresses what is future in respect of the verb *intend*. In the second the verb *to be* expresses what is equally present with the verb *seems*. About the propriety of such expressions there is no doubt. Again, if the infinitive after the verb in the present, be intended to express what must have been antecedent to that which is expressed by the governing verb, the infinitive must be in the preterperfect, even though the other verb be in the present. Thus, " From " his conversation he appears *to have studied* " Homer with great care and judgment." To use the present in this case, and say, " He ap- " pears *to study* Homer"——would overturn the sense.

The same rule must be followed when the governing verb is in the preterit, for let it be observed, that it is the tense of the governing verb only that marks the absolute time; the tense of the verb

verb governed marks solely its relative time with respect to the other. Thus I should say, "I always intended *to write* to my father, though I have not yet done it." "He seemed *to be* a man of letters." "From a conversation I once had with him, he appeared *to have studied* Homer with great care and judgment." Propriety plainly requires that in the two first Instances the infinitive should be in the present tense, and in the third instance, in the preterit.

PRIESTLEY has not expressed himself on this subject with precision. *I found him better than I expected to find him,* is the only proper analogical expression. *Expected to have found him,* is irreconcilable alike to grammar and to sense. Indeed all verbs expressive of hope, desire, intention, or command, must invariably be followed by the present and not the perfect of the infinitive. Every body would perceive an error in this expression: " It is long since I commanded him to have done it." Yet *expected to have found* is no better. It is as clear that the *finding* must be posterior to the expectation, as that the *obedience* must be posterior to the command. But though the anonymous remarker formerly quoted ed is in the right as to the particular expressions criticised by him, he decides too generally, and seems to have imagined that in no case ought the preterperfect of the infinitive, to follow the preterit of the indicative. If this was his opinion, he was egregiously mistaken. It is however agreed on both sides, that, in order to express the past with the defective verb *ought*, we must use the perfect of the infinitive, and say for example, " he ought to *have done* it;" this in that verb being the only possible way of distinguishing the past from the present.

There is only one other observation of Dr. Lowth, on which, before I conclude this article, I must beg leave to offer some remarks. "Phrases
" like the following, though very common, are
" improper: Much depends upon the *rule's be-*
" *ing observed*; and error will be the consequence
" of *its being neglected*. For here is a noun and
" a pronoun representing it, each in the pos-
" sessive case, that is, under government of ano-
" ther noun, but without other noun to govern
" it: for *being observed*, and *being neglected*, are
" not nouns: nor can you supply the place of
" the possessive case by the preposition *of* before
" the

"the noun or pronoun *." For my part, notwithstanding what is here very speciously urged, I am not satisfied that there is any fault in the phrases censured. They appear to me to be perfectly in the idiom of our tongue, and such as on some occasions could not easily be avoided, unless by recurring to circumlocution, an expedient which invariably tends to enervate the expression. But let us examine the matter more nearly.

This author admits that the active participle may be employed as a noun, and has given some excellent directions regarding the manner in which it ought to be construed, that the proper distinction may be preserved between the noun and the gerund. Phrases like these therefore he would have admitted as unexceptionable, " Much " depends upon *their observing* of the rule, and " error will be the consequence of *their neglecting* " of it." Now, though I allow both the modes of expression to be good, I think the first simpler and better than the second. Let us consider whether the former be liable to any objections, which do not equally affect the latter.

* Introduction, &c. Sentences, Note on the 6th Phrase.

One principal objection to the first is, "You cannot supply the place of the possessive case by the preposition *of* before the noun or pronoun." Right; but before you draw any conclusion from this circumstance, try whether it will not equally affect both expressions; for if it does, both are on this account to be rejected, or neither. In the first, the sentence will be made to run thus, "Much depends upon *the being observed of* the rule, and error will be the consequence of *the being neglected of* it." Very bad without question. In the second, thus, "Much depends upon *the observing of them* of the rule, and error will be the consequence of *the neglecting of them* of it." Still worse. But it may be thought that as, in the last example, the participial noun gets a double regimen, this occasions all the impropriety and confusion. I shall therefore make the experiment on a more simple sentence. "Much will depend on *your pupil's composing*, but more on *his reading* frequently." Would it be English to say, "Much will depend on *the composing of your pupil*, but more on *the reading of him* frequently."—No certainly. If this argument then prove any thing, it proves too much, and consequently can be no criterion.

The only other objection mentioned is, that "*being observed* and *being neglected*, are not nouns." It is acknowledged that in the common acceptation of the word, they are not nouns, but passive participles; neither is the active participle commonly a noun, neither is the infinitive of the verb active or passive, a noun. Yet the genius of the tongue permits that all these may be construed as nouns in certain occurrences. The infinitive in particular is employed substantively when it is made either the nominative or the regimen of a verb. Now in this way not the infinitive only, but along with it all the words in construction are understood as one compound noun, as in the examples following: "*To love God and our neighbour* is a duty incumbent on us all," and "The gospel strongly inculcates on us this important lesson, *to love God and our neighbour*." But in no other situation can such clauses supply the place of nouns. They are never used in construction with other nouns followed by a preposition. The quotation brought from Spenser is, I suspect, a mere Grecism, which was not in his time more than it is at present conformable to the English idiom. *For* is the only preposition that seems

ever

ever to have been conftrued with fuch claufes, after another verb. And even this ufage is now totally laid afide.

I AM of opinion, therefore, upon the whole, that as the idiom in queftion is analogical, fupported by good ufe, and fometimes very expedient, it ought not to be entirely repudiated.

THE END OF THE FIRST VOLUME.

ERRATA.

Page 16, line 15, after is, read as.
— 19, Note, for l, read e.
— 34, l. 7, for part, only, read part only,
— 37, Note, l. 4, for qu'on, read qu'en.
— 38, Note, l. 5, for Orem, read O rem.
— 40, Note, l. 6, for lati, read laté
— 52, l. 14, for oppofite, read appofite.
— 60, l. 10, for humorous, read humours.
— 73, Note, l. 11, for right, read rights
———————— l. 12, for friendships, read friendship.
— 86, Note, read δραματοποιησας in one word.
— 89, l. 13, for hath, read have.
— 112, Note, l. 11, for of belief, read or belief.
— 160, l. 2, for this, read their.
— 188, Note, l. 19, for υμειας, read υγειας.
— 231, Note, l. 29, for oration, read orations.
— 252, l. 16 and 17, for teach patience, read teach, patient.
— 335, l. 2 and 3, for fictious, read fictions.
— 343, l. 22, for be entrue, read been true.
— 367, l. 18, from the beginning of the Chap. for preceded, read proceeded.
— 411, Note, for Book I. Chap XI. read Book II. Chap. I. Sect. III.
— 414, l. 22, for clarifies, read clarifier.
— 419, l. 5 from the foot, for portie, read portic.
— 422, l. 17, for derivations, read derivatives.
— 426, l. 6, for pariffology, read periffology.
— 461, l. 10, dele [,] after people.
— 486, l. 29, for participle, read participial.

CPSIA information can be obtained
at www.ICGtesting.com
Printed in the USA
LVHW100235070721
692073LV00016B/227

9 781140 894230